To Lala...

An w...

E. P. Thompson and

E. P. Thompson and English radicalism

Edited by
ROGER FIELDHOUSE *and* RICHARD TAYLOR

Manchester University Press

Published by Manchester University Press
Altrincham Street, Manchester M1 7JA, UK
www.manchesteruniversitypress.co.uk

British Library Cataloguing-in-Publication Data is available

Library of Congress Cataloging-in-Publication Data is available

ISBN 978 0 7190 9748 5 *paperback*

First published by Manchester University Press in hardback 2013

This paperback edition first published 2015

Printed by Lightning Source

Contents

Contents

Notes on contributors

Roger Fieldhouse is Emeritus Professor at the University of Exeter. After studying history at the University of Reading he was appointed tutor-organiser for the Workers' Educational Association in North Yorkshire in 1964. Six years later he transferred to the Extramural Department at the University of Leeds, where he was a lecturer and later senior lecturer and obtained his Ph.D. in 1984. In 1986 he was appointed Professor of Adult Education and Director of Continuing Education at the University of Exeter, retiring in 1999. He was awarded a Leverhulme Emeritus Fellowship in 2000–1. He has written extensively about both history and adult education, including numerous contributions to books and articles in journals, and ten books and monographs including *A History of Richmond and Swaledale* (1978), *Adult Education and the Cold War* (1985), *Optimism and Joyful Irreverence: the Sixties Culture and its Influence on British University Adult Education and the WEA* (1993), *A History of Modern British Adult Education* (with associates, 1996) and *Anti-Apartheid: A History of the Movement in Britain* (2005).

David Goodway taught sociology, history and Victorian studies to mainly adult students from 1969 until the University of Leeds closed its School of Continuing Education in 2005. He was then, in 2006–7, Helen Cam Visiting Fellow in History at Girton College, Cambridge. For twenty years he has written principally on anarchism and libertarian socialism, publishing collections of the writings of Alex Comfort, Herbert Read, 'Maurice Brinton' (the pseudonym of Christopher Pallis) and Nicolas Walter and of the correspondence between John Cowper Powys and Emma Goldman, as well as *Talking Anarchy* (with Colin Ward, 2003) and *Anarchist Seeds Beneath the*

Snow: Left-Libertarian Thought and British Writers from William Morris to Colin Ward (2006). But his first book was *London Chartism 1838–1848* (1982). He is currently working on a selection of George Julian Harney's late journalism.

Theodore Koditschek is Professor of History at the University of Missouri, Columbia, USA. He is the author of the prizewinning *Class Formation and Urban Industrial Society: Bradford 1750–1850* (2008) and *Liberalism, Imperialism and the Historical Imagination: Nineteenth Century Visions of a Greater Britain* (2011). He is currently working on three projects: a broad analysis of the relationship between capitalism and imperialism from the sixteenth through to the nineteenth centuries; a monograph on race and society in the late Victorian British Empire; and a history of social history.

Michael Newman is Emeritus Professor at London Metropolitan University, where he was a Professor of Politics while also holding a Jean Monnet Personal Chair in European Studies. He is currently teaching at the London Centre of New York University. His main works on the Left are *Socialism and European Unity* (1983), *John Strachey* (1989), *Harold Laski – A Political Biography* (1993), *Ralph Miliband and the Politics of the New Left* (2002) and *Socialism – A Very Short Introduction* (2005). He has also written about Europe and wider issues of peace and conflict, including *Democracy, Sovereignty and the European Union* (1996) and *Humanitarian Intervention: Confronting the Contradictions* (2009).

Bryan D. Palmer is a Canadian social historian, editor of *Labour/ Le Travail* and the author or editor of sixteen books including *E. P. Thompson: Objections and Oppositions* (1994). He completed his Ph.D. at the State University of New York, Binghamton, USA in 1977 and has taught in the USA, Brazil and China as well as Canada. He is currently the Canada Research Chair in the Canadian Studies Department at Trent University, Peterborough, Ontario, Canada. Forthcoming books include an account of the Minneapolis Teamsters' strike of 1934, volumes on James P. Cannon and dissident communism in the USA and, with Gaetan Heroux, a history of capitalist crisis and the Toronto dispossessed 1830–2000. A Fellow of the Royal Society of Canada, Palmer has received the A. B. Corey Prize and the Wallace K. Ferguson Prize for his writing.

Nina Power is Senior Lecturer in Philosophy at the University of Roehampton and also teaches Critical Writing in Art and Design at the Royal College of Art, London. She has written widely on European philosophy and politics and is a founding member of Defend the Right to Protest, a campaign group set up after the UK student protests of 2010 which seeks to campaign against police brutality, against the criminalisation of protesters and against the erosion of public rights.

Kate Soper is Emerita Professor of Philosophy at London Metropolitan University and a Visiting Humanities Professor at Brighton University. She worked as a journalist and translator before becoming a full-time academic. She has published widely on environmental philosophy, the aesthetics of nature, the theory of needs and consumption and cultural theory. Her more recent writings include *What is Nature? Culture, Politics and the Non-Human* (1995); *To Relish the Sublime: Culture and Self-Realisation in Postmodern Times* (with Martin Ryle, 2002); *Citizenship and Consumption* (co-editor, 2007) and *The Politics and Pleasures of Consuming Differently* (co-editor, 2008). She has been a member of the editorial collectives of *Radical Philosophy* and the *New Left Review* and a regular columnist for the US journal *Capitalism, Nature, Socialism*. During the 1980s, she was very active in her local peace movement, and a member of the Coordinating Committee and a chairperson of European Nuclear Disarmament.

Luke Spencer is a retired Senior Fellow of the University of Leeds, where he was a full-time extramural tutor from 1969 to 1999. His research interests have been mainly in twentieth-century British and American literature. He has written widely on the relationship between politics and imaginative writing and on individual writers from John Berryman and Tony Harrison to E. L. Doctorow and Adrienne Rich.

Richard Taylor was Professor and Director of Continuing Education at the University of Cambridge from 2004 to 2009. He is now Emeritus Professorial Fellow at Wolfson College, Cambridge. He was previously at the University of Leeds, where he had been Professor of Continuing Education and Head of Department, and subsequently Dean of the Faculty of Business, Law, Education and Social Sciences. Until recently he was Chair of the Board of Trustees of the Workers' Educational Association and was previously Chair of the National Institute of Adult Continuing Education and Secretary of the Universities Association for Lifelong Learning. In addition to over one hundred journal articles and book chapters, he has written, co-written or edited 13 books including *Campaigns for Peace: British Peace Movements in the Twentieth Century* (edited with Nigel Young, 1988), *Against the Bomb: The British Peace Movement 1958–1965* (1988), *For a Radical Higher Education: After Postmodernism* (with Jean Barr and Tom Steele, 2002) and *British Labour and Higher Education 1945 to 2000: Ideology, Policy and Practice* (with Tom Steele, 2011).

Preface

Fifty years ago, in 1963, Edward Thompson's *The Making of the English Working Class* was published. It was a remarkable book that contributed significantly to a sea-change in the way history was studied and written not only in Britain but in many countries. Instead of history being seen through the eyes of kings, courtiers, aristocrats and politicians, it began to be viewed from below, from the standpoint of the common people. This historiographical shift did not go unchallenged – there was, and still is, a concerted effort by elitist and conservative historians and social commentators to retain their control of the historical viewpoint. Nevertheless, 'history from below' has become an essential element in our study of the past and our understanding of how society has become what it is. In his obituary of Thompson in the *Independent* (30 August 1993), Professor Eric Hobsbawm opined that *The Making of the English Working Class* was 'almost certainly the most influential single book of history in the Anglo-Saxon radical Sixties and Seventies'.

This collection of essays, by people who knew Thompson or taught in the same University of Leeds department as him, or were much influenced by him in their own work, commemorates the fiftieth anniversary of the publication of his hugely influential book. In addition to his work as an historian Thompson was a notable and passionate political polemicist, peace campaigner and activist. He saw all his public activity as complementary parts of a unified whole, and in this book we attempt to review critically all the facets of Thompson's work and to bring these to the attention of a new generation of students and scholars, and all those who are concerned with radical, egalitarian change to make the world a better place.

Acknowledgements

We are very grateful to: the late Dorothy Thompson for her advice in 2010 when we were planning this book; Wade Matthews for making available to us his unpublished research findings on 'E. P. Thompson in the Provinces' and Thompson's letters 1956–60; Tom Steele for making his notes and photocopied documents available to us and for his most helpful advice; Tom Caldwell and Bernard Jennings for their recollections of Thompson in the University of Leeds Extramural Department in the 1950s and early 1960s; the late Dorothy Greenald for information, encouragement and assistance relating to the making of 'The Making'; John Gillis for reading and commenting on the draft of chapter 4; Mary Kaldor for her recollections of Thompson's role in END; Joanne Fitton for her helpful guidance in the archives at Leeds University; Tony Simpson of the Bertrand Russell Peace Foundation for his help and advice and for access to END papers in the BRPF archive; the staff at the Modern Records Centre at the University of Warwick for access to the James Hinton papers, at the Special Collections at the University of Bradford for access to the Ted Edwards (END) papers, and at the Hull University archive for access to the John Saville papers; and especially to the staff at Manchester University Press for all their help in the production of this book.

We are also grateful to Kate Thompson for permission to reproduce in the appendix extracts from the preface to *The Making of the English Working Class*, *Warwick University Ltd.* (pp. 153–4), and part 1 of 'The Peculiarities of the English' (*The Poverty of Theory*, pp. 35–8), and also lines from 'The Place Called Choice' (in *Collected Poems*); and to the following publishers for permission to quote from their publications: Bloomsbury (E. P. Thompson, *The Sykaos Papers*); Cambridge University Press (E. P. Thompson, *Witness Against the Beast: William Blake and the Moral Law*); Lawrence & Wishart (E. P. Thompson, *William Morris*, 1955, and M. Kenny, T*he First New Left*); Merlin Press (E. P. Thompson, *William Morris*, 1977, *The Poverty of Theory*, *The Heavy Dancers* and *Customs in Common* and D. Thompson, *The Romantics: England in a Revolutionary Age*); The New Press (excerpt from E. P. Thompson, *Customs in Common*); Polity Press (K. Soper, 'Socialist Humanism', in H. J. Kaye and K. McClelland (eds), *E. P. Thompson: Critical Perspectives*); and Verso (B. Palmer, *E. P. Thompson: Objections and Oppositions*).

List of abbreviations

ABCA	Army Bureau of Current Affairs
BCP	British Communist Party
BRPF	Bertrand Russell Peace Foundation
CND	Campaign for Nuclear Disarmament
CP	Communist Party
CPGB	Communist Party of Great Britain
CPSU	Communist Party of the Soviet Union
END	European Nuclear Disarmament
ILP	Independent Labour Party
INF	Intermediate-Range Nuclear Forces Treaty
JTCC	Joint Tutorial Classes Committee
LUA	Leeds University Archive
MARHO	Mid-Atlantic Radical Historians' Organisation
NATO	North Atlantic Treaty Organisation
NIACE	National Institute of Adult Continuing Education
NLB	New Left Books
NLR	*New Left Review*
NR	*New Reasoner*
ULR	*Universities and Left Review*
USSR	Union of Soviet Socialist Republics
WEA	Workers' Educational Association

1

E. P. Thompson: a short introduction

Roger Fieldhouse, Theodore Koditschek
and Richard Taylor

Romantic polymath

Edward Thompson was a passionate and romantic polymath whose range of intellectual and political achievements was remarkable. Diverse though his activities and writings were, spanning literature, history, fiction and poetry, biography, adult education, socialist and libertarian politics, and not least peace-movement activism, they had a unity and coherence.

This study aims to explore in some detail various aspects of his intellectual and political work, and its legacy to later generations of radical thinkers and activists in Britain and internationally. It will be apparent that this is *not* a biography: that challenging task cannot yet be attempted for several reasons, not least that the Thompson archive of personal papers and correspondence has been embargoed for fifty years from his death. (As he himself wrote, in relation to the University of Warwick conflicts (see below): 'One of the difficulties in writing "contemporary history" is that, until the files have been opened, the actual thoughts and motives of the actors may be difficult to determine.'[1]) What we hope to have achieved here is rather some original, critical and rigorous, though generally sympathetic, analyses of various aspects of Thompson's work by a range of scholars from relevant disciplinary backgrounds (and also from a variety of radical political viewpoints) .Our approach is supportive but critical. Edward Thompson had faults and weaknesses (as do we all). With hindsight, it can be seen, for example, as David Goodway has argued, that 'Thompson's great blind spot was his sentimental loyalty to pre-1956 Communism.'[2] This explains, *inter alia*, his irrational aversion to George Orwell.[3] Nor was he always an easy colleague to work with, as some of us can testify from personal experience. None of this detracts, however, from our collective admiration and respect for Thompson's intellect, commitment and passionate humanity. In summary, then, our approach is not hagiographic but it *is* supportive.

The title of our book deliberately links Thompson and 'English radicalism': and it is in this, we believe, that the key lies to the unity in his work, referred to earlier. 'Radicalism', like many 'political' words, has complicated and contentious definitions.[4] In this context we use it to refer to that particular English tradition, dating approximately from the seventeenth-century Civil War (with traces back to the fourteenth-century Peasants' Revolt), which emphasises freedom, equality and democracy, within the framework of the law. Thompson himself, in *The Making of the English Working Class*, lays great emphasis upon such components of 'The Liberty Tree'[5] as freedom under the law, freedom from arbitrary arrest and from absolutist government (especially monarchy), trial by jury, habeas corpus and the whole spectrum of individual rights.[6] In *The Making of the English Working Class* there are repeated references to, and proclaimed identity with, the dominant figures of the English radical canon: amongst others, Cobbett, Paine and Owen. When asked which thinkers were his chief theoretical forebears, or inspirations, Thompson cited 'Vico, Marx, Blake and Morris; the latter two showing how English I am'.[7] And Thompson was indeed a quintessentially English radical. Although he was by nature and belief an internationalist (and had an especial interest in Indian culture and politics), his reference point and his idiosyncratic Romanticism were both rooted in his Englishness. (This was not, it should be noted, synonymous with 'Britishness'. Thompson was always careful to point out, for example in the Preface to *The Making of the English Working Class*, that the histories, cultures and politics of the other component parts of the UK were separate and different from those that characterised England.)

Informed by this tradition, part radical liberal and individualist, part socialist and oppositional, Thompson's key conceptual assertion was of the importance of *human agency* in the study of history and the development of radical politics. As Perry Anderson has written in his perceptive, major study of Thompson's theoretical position, '(t)he pivot of Thompson's construction … is the notion of agency', side by side with his unbending emphasis upon the importance of empirical enquiry in the study of history.[8] Similarly, in the same vein, David Goodway has argued persuasively that Thompson's ideological perspective can be identified through the oft-cited dichotomy between 'Necessity' and 'Desire'. 'Necessity' focuses upon economic determinism, the course of the productive forces and the relations of production in society. Thompson, by contrast, emphasises 'Desire' defined as 'morality, conscience, human will and, what became Thompson's defining term, "agency"'.[9]

In Marx's famous formulation that 'Men make their own history, but they do not make it just as they please; they do not make it under circumstances chosen by themselves, but under circumstances directly encountered, given and transmitted from the past', Thompson's emphasis is consistently upon the first, 'agency' clause. And this characterises not only his historical method but also his political and peace-movement activities, and indeed his life as a whole.

In this context, we should also note that Thompson, though not a central figure in the development of cultural studies in Britain, did make an important intellectual contribution to its formation. Two of the three 'classic' texts of cultural studies were written in Yorkshire in the late 1950s and early 1960s in the milieu of the Workers' Educational Association (WEA) and university adult education: Thompson's *The Making of the English Working Class* (1963) and Richard Hoggart's *The Uses of Literacy* (1957). Raymond Williams's *Culture and Society* (1958) was produced from similar circumstances at Oxford. All three works emphasised the role of cultural activity in the making of the working class and the shaping of class relations. This emphasis differed significantly from orthodox Marxist accounts in signalling the area of conscious agency rather than rigid material determinism. Moreover, they all resolutely refused to be bound by conventional academic divisions of knowledge. The concern of all three with the complexity of social relations and their flexible reworking of Marxist and socialist approaches is the crucible for the radical interdisciplinary approach of cultural studies. As previously noted, Thompson's historical analysis in particular focused upon the importance of consciousness and human agency: in effect, history with a more cultural and humanistic orientation.[10] This complemented the work of literary and cultural theorists, such as Raymond Williams and Stuart Hall, and found articulation, for example, through 'History Workshop', in which Thompson participated fully, and often polemically and acerbically for many years.

Another important aspect of Thompson's work, reflecting his literary background and interests (see chapter 5), is that his writing was always rich, erudite and engaging. He was also a master of the political polemic: kindness itself to students, more junior colleagues and political allies in both academic and political contexts, he could be merciless and withering in his criticisms of those he believed to be mistaken (or worse). Some brief examples of his writing are reproduced in the appendix at the end of the book as illustrations of his inimitable style.

Early years, 1924–48

Thompson was born in Oxford on 3 February 1924.[11] His childhood and adolescence were greatly influenced by his father, Edward John Thompson, whom he later described as 'a very tough liberal',[12] and by the political, intellectual and cultural atmosphere of his home in Boar's Hill, the house his parents built and moved into in 1925, a few miles south-west of Oxford. Thompson senior had worked as a Methodist missionary and teacher in India before and after the First World War. During this time he began his study of Indian society that made him a respected authority on the subject, enabling him to obtain a part-time lecturing post in Bengali at Oriel College, Oxford on his return to England in 1923. He was elected an Honorary Fellow of Oriel in 1925 and appointed Oxford Leverhulme research fellow in 1934 and then research fellow in Indian history from 1936 to 1946. He published numerous books about India. He had gradually become disillusioned with both Methodism and Britain's imperialist role in India, although he retained a grudging respect for some aspects of colonial rule and therefore became an ambivalent, though active, advocate of Indian independence. Despite his reservations, the Thompsons received many visits from writers, scholars and political activists from India, including both Gandhi and Nehru.

The other major personal influence on Edward Thompson as he was growing up was his elder brother, Frank, whom he greatly respected, admired and held in awe.[13] Frank became committed to active left-wing politics while studying at pre-war Oxford and eventually joined the Communist Party (CP), either because in the late 1930s that seemed the most dynamic way of actively promoting anti-fascist and left-wing causes or because he was persuaded to join by Iris Murdoch. Whichever was the stronger influence he was never a doctrinaire, orthodox Communist but rather a utopian, romantic idealist, too much a rebel to conform to Party discipline.[14] In reality, although they differed fundamentally on some issues, both father and elder son remained in many ways ideologically radical liberals until their deaths.

It was in this household, alive with political and cosmopolitan ideals, that Edward Thompson grew up, where 'the power of rhetorical persuasion and poetic imagination was not so much extolled as lived'.[15] Despite living in the shadow of his elder brother, regarded as the 'duffer' of the family, and constantly criticised, particularly by his mother, Thompson remembered his Oxford home as 'supportive, liberal, anti-imperialist, quick with ideas and poetry and international visitors'.[16] This atmosphere helped to formulate his lifelong poetic aspirations, his commitment to the principles and causes of freedom, and his 'refusal to compromise when integrity, truth and justice were at stake'.[17] As he acknowledged many years later, he also rather more sceptically 'grew up expecting governments to be mendacious and imperialist, and expecting that one's stance ought to be hostile to government'.[18]

Despite his father's lapsed faith, Methodism was another significant, if largely negative, influence in Thompson's upbringing, reinforced by being sent to his father's old Wesleyan school, Kingswood, on the outskirts of Bath, where he received a puritanical, moralistic Methodist education that he later reacted strongly against. In 1941, at the age of 17, he gained a minor scholarship to Corpus Christi College, Cambridge to study history, although interestingly (in the light of his post-war choice of university employment – see chapter 2), not before he contemplated applying to an 'unfashionable' Scottish university.[19] He quickly became involved in left-wing politics at Cambridge and was elected president of the University Socialist Club. In 1942 he joined the CP which, after Hitler's invasion of the Soviet Union, had 'converted' to a broad anti-fascist, popular-front political stance. Like many wartime students, Thompson's studies were interrupted by his being called up for military service, which he spent largely in North Africa and as a tank-troop commander in Italy. He seldom referred to his wartime experiences in later life but did recall the depressing irrationality of war tempered by the camaraderie amongst soldiers. During his time in Italy he, like his elder brother, had some practical experience in adult education, teaching Army Bureau of Current Affairs (ABCA) courses to the troops.[20]

For the rest of his life Thompson maintained the beliefs he adopted in these early years between 1936 and 1946. He tellingly referred to this period as the 'decade of heroes' when 'authentic liberalism (the choices of the autonomous individual) and perhaps also of Romanticism (the rebellion of spirit against the rules of fact)' flourished.[21]

After the war Thompson returned to Cambridge to complete his degree, reading mainly history and literature, obtaining first-class honours in the Part I History Tripos and being elected to a college Foundation Scholarship. He renewed his membership of the CP, which he had allowed to lapse during the war, and also at this time met Dorothy Sale (*née* Towers), his future wife, with whom he shared academic and political interests. He stayed on at Cambridge for a while, not to complete the History Tripos Part II but to read widely and undertake largely undirected research in English literature and social history. During this period he undertook some part-time teaching for the WEA Eastern District.[22]

In 1947 Thompson and his mother retraced his brother's fatal wartime odyssey through Bulgaria, seeking to discover what Frank had achieved and why he had died.[23] Frank had enlisted in the army at the beginning of the war, spending most of the time in secret intelligence units in Egypt and North Africa. At the beginning of 1944 he was parachuted into the Balkans, where he joined a small British liaison group attempting to strengthen the Yugoslav and Bulgarian partisans. In May he and a signalman, together with around 180 partisans, crossed from the relative safety of Serbia into Bulgaria. With hindsight, their ill thought-out and under-supported mission, struggling directionless through the snow, constantly harassed by the Bulgarian army, can be seen as doomed from the start. After two weeks Frank was captured, brutally interrogated, probably tortured, and then executed by firing squad.[24]

The trauma of his elder brother's death stayed with Thompson throughout his life.[25] He was convinced that Frank could have been rescued if it had not been for the early onset of the Cold War in the Balkans. In his painstaking reconstruction of what he believed (but could not prove) had happened, he claimed that the British abandoned the partisans and Frank's mission as a consequence of Churchill's agreement with the USSR to save Greece for the West after the war by allowing Bulgaria to fall under Soviet control. The Russians were equally unsupportive because they wanted the Red Army to be the sole agent of the anti-fascist victory. A signal was given to the Bulgarian government that it was acceptable to execute a British officer in uniform. 'Somebody winked.'[26]

Later that summer he and Dorothy joined the British Youth Brigade in helping a team of peasants, workers, soldiers and students to construct a 150–mile railway in Yugoslavia. This proved to be a permanently influential experience in shaping his understanding of the importance of popular collective struggle.[27]

Teacher, writer and political activist, 1948–70

When he and Dorothy returned to England towards the end of 1947 they were determined not to drift into conventional academia. Instead, they decided to live in the north of England and saw adult education as an obvious career choice. In March 1948 Thompson applied for a post of staff tutor in adult education at the University of Leeds and was appointed to start the following August. For the next seventeen years he taught mainly evening classes in literature and history, mostly in the industrial towns of the West Riding, but occasionally further afield in the more northerly parts of the Leeds extramural empire at Harrogate, Northallerton and Middlesbrough.[28]

A writer who came to occupy an increasingly central position in Thompson's syllabuses was William Morris. He later said that Morris 'claimed him': he was seized by him. He used Morris as a means of making literature significant to the lives of his working-class students. But Morris also became the subject of the first of Thompson's major publications. It started out as a short article attempting to rescue Morris's socialist ideas from the many studies that had effectively airbrushed them out of his writing, concentrating exclusively on his contribution to the Arts and Crafts movement. *William Morris: Romantic to Revolutionary* grew into a tome of over eight hundred pages by the time it was published in 1955, establishing or re-establishing Morris as

> the first creative artist of major stature in the history of the world to take his stand, consciously and without the shadow of a compromise, with the revolutionary working class: to participate in the day-to-day work of building the Socialist movement: to put his brain and his genius at the disposal of the struggle.[29]

As Thompson explained in the foreword to the revised edition published in 1977, he wrote the book

> in an embattled mood, from a position of strong political commitment, addressing an audience in the adult education movement and in the political movements of the Left rather than a more academic public.[30]

7

In 1950 Thompson registered to take a Ph.D. degree at Leeds, probably at the instigation of his head of department, S. G. Raybould, who was keen that all the department's academic staff should obtain doctorates as part of his strategy to gain full academic status for his infant department. Thompson's proposed subject was 'Working-class adult education 1840–1860, with special reference to the West Riding', which he abandoned a year later for 'The background and origins of the formation of the Independent Labour Party in Yorkshire and its development between 1880 and 1900'.[31] However, Thompson never completed his Ph.D., which he most likely regarded as an unwarranted academic straitjacket or simply one demand too many on his time. For not only was he busy preparing for four or five classes per week and researching and writing his book on Morris: this, he later estimated, occupied only half his time. The other half was devoted to his political work, particularly in the peace movement. He became chair of the Halifax Peace Committee, Secretary of the Yorkshire Federation of Peace Organisations and editor of a regional peace journal. He was also a member of the Yorkshire District Committee of the CP. He remained a Party member partly because of his sentimental nostalgia for his 'decade of heroes' and loyalty to his wartime and Yugoslav experiences, but by this time William Morris was leading him intellectually towards a broader, more liberal interpretation of Marxism.[32] (For Thompson's involvement in the early peace movement, see chapter 9.)

The 'strong political commitment' that had encouraged Thompson to write the Morris book, and his already qualified support for the British Communist Party (BCP), were shattered in 1956 by Khrushchev's revelations about Stalin at the Twentieth Congress of the Communist Party of the Soviet Union and the Soviet Union's invasion of Hungary later that year. The politics of the post-war period were utterly transformed by these events and by Britain's disastrous Suez escapade and the war that followed. Over a quarter of the BCP's membership, including Thompson, left the Party because of the events in Hungary and the BCP's refusal to criticise the Soviet Union's actions. This experience remained a watershed year for Thompson. He and fellow historian John Saville, whilst still members of the CP, began producing a duplicated publication initially entitled *The Reasoner*, attacking the Party's stance.[33] Subsequently, on their resignation from the Party, this became *The New Reasoner* and was, in effect, the beginning of the New Left (see chapter 8).

At the same time that he was heavily involved in New Left activities Thompson was, of course, still teaching four or five evening classes a week for about two-thirds of each year. The research and preparation for these classes contributed significantly to the publication in 1963 of *The Making of the English Working Class* (see chapters 3 and 4). As noted in the preface, it was as much its 'history from below' approach as the historical content of the book that quickly won it general acclaim as a tour de force. In his recommendation of Thompson for a readership the following year Professor Asa Briggs commented that 'there is a strong argument for thinking this is the best piece of social history since the Hammonds,'[34] but he added that it was 'shot through with the Marxist humanism which provides Mr. Thompson with his working philosophy. It is not a book, therefore, for those who like their history to be scrupulously fair and balanced.'[35] For this reason the reaction was not uniformly enthusiastic. Its sometimes polemical analysis drew criticism from Whig historians and others who concentrated attention on what they saw as its ideological bias. Professor Ashworth, whilst also supporting Thompson's nomination for a readership, confessed that he found some of the book's largest conclusions unconvincing and some of Thompson's 'controversial writing rather distasteful and marked by an arrogance which its content often does little to justify', and that 'in the occasional passages where he is particularly contemptuous of other scholars he seldom has more evidence in his favour than they have'.[36]

A more recent criticism of *The Making of the English Working Class* is that it suffers from gender blindness, as noted by numerous feminist historians since the 1980s. In *Gender and the Politics of History*, published in 1988, Joan Wallach Scott argues that '[d]espite their presence, women are marginal in the book', allotted 'a subordinate status ... in the emerging radical movement', their role (in Thompson's own words) 'confined to giving moral support to the men'. '[O]ne is struck not by the absence of women in the narrative but by the awkward way in which they figure there.'[37] She suggests that Thompson perceived class as a masculine gendered construct in antithesis to female domesticity, expressiveness and irrationality, and that his book is written in a language that confirms rather than challenges the masculine representation of class. Moreover, he ignored the evidence in the sources he used of the significant roles of women in the labour force.[38] More recently, Mary Davis, in the introduction to her *Class and Gender in British Labour History*, argues that Thompson failed to provide any 'substantial examination of the female half of the English working class' and that this resulted in a failure to recognise the part played by women in the 'making' of the working class.[39] Like Scott, Davis goes on to show that many of the primary sources used by Thompson contain plenty of evidence of the significant role played by women, and that therefore he had no excuse. Thanks to the work of Scott, Davis, Anna Clark, Sonia Rose, Barbara Taylor and several others, we now have a fairly good understanding of how *The Making of the English Working Class* would look with women and gender issues included. This would require some modification in Thompson's argument, since it is clear that male workers' efforts to improve their bargaining position in relation to capital often entailed marginalising women, excluding them wherever possible from the better-paid and better-organised trades.[40]

These are valid criticisms, but it is arguable that there were mitigating circumstances. Scott recognised that these issues did not 'become troubling' until they were 'posed by the feminist movement of the late 1960s and early 1970s (well after the publication of Thompson's book)' and that 'Thompson's text ... was not written within the new context created by feminist politics'.[41] There has indeed been a huge evolution in gender analysis and language during the half-century since *The Making of the English Working Class* was written. Much of Thompson's 'blindness', as perceived from the twenty-first century, can be accounted for by the almost universal use of masculine language in the 1960s that would be unthinkable on the Left today. The fact that this was common practice in the mid-twentieth century does not make it acceptable or justifiable, but it does make it more understandable. There is, in fact, some evidence in Thompson's life and work to rebut the accusation of gender blindness, as noted by Michael Newman in chapter 8. In apparent contradiction to the accusation, Anna Davin, one of Thompson's later postgraduate students at Warwick, recollected that he stood out as being particularly aware of women's part in history.[42] Catherine Hall has suggested, echoing Scott, that 'feminist history has been powerfully influenced by Thompsonian social history' and that his rescue of the common people from oblivion inspired the subsequent 'feminist commitment to recover the forgotten sex'.[43]

Even before the enthusiastic reception of *The Making of the English Working Class* Thompson was contemplating resigning from the university and trying to live by writing. He recognised that this was a hazardous step to take with a family to support, and therefore explored the possibility of 'liquidating' (cashing in) his pension in order to raise enough capital to provide a year or two's livelihood before other returns began to come in.[44] For whatever reason, this did not happen. Possibly to persuade Thompson to stay at Leeds, Raybould recommended him for a senior lectureship in January 1962, which was confirmed later that year. A similar manoeuvre occurred two years later when Raybould recommended Thompson for a readership, probably in an attempt to dissuade him from accepting an equivalent post at the University of Warwick. Thompson was promoted to Reader at Leeds but he nevertheless accepted the post of Reader in Social History and Director of the Centre for the Study of Social History at Warwick, to commence in October 1965.[45]

During his time at Warwick teaching postgraduate students, Thompson was drawn more into mainstream academia. His research moved back into the eighteenth century, laying down the basis for much of his later writing whilst also upsetting 'the gentlemanly balance of English eighteenth century studies where deference to the grace and goodwill of lordly rule had long been accepted', thereby redefining the historiography of eighteenth-century England[46] (see chapter 4).

From the mid-1960s, then, Thompson's professional life occupied a larger amount of his time and energies. This was certainly one of the reasons for his relative withdrawal from activist politics, but this was also due to his strong disagreements with the emerging 'new Marxism' within the New Left (see chapter 8). Thompson was, by the early 1970s, optimistic about the prospects for a revitalised Left, and was clearly seeking a rapprochement with Anderson and the other leading members of the new New Left. However, several events later in the decade, in particular the authoritarian crisis in India – always a touchstone for Thompson, as noted above – and domestically the rise of neoliberal politics represented by Margaret Thatcher, induced a much darker mood. Crucially, in this context, Thompson also reacted with increasing vehemence against the influence of Marxist structuralist theorising. This culminated in his memorable polemical attack on Althusser in *The Poverty of Theory* (see chapter 7). This dispute eventually came to a head in the well-known confrontational debate at the History Workshop conference in Oxford in December 1979 between Thompson and Stuart Hall (and Richard Johnson).[47] This angry and bitter argument was the last occasion on which Thompson publicly debated Marxist ideas and theories, and from then on he ceased in any full sense to be 'a Marxist'. (In common with most other ex-CP intellectuals of 1956, he also had a deep antipathy to Trotskyism and to its 1970s offshoot, the neo-Trotskyist student movement.)

However, this is not to say he undertook *no* political activity during the decade between the late 1960s and the late 1970s. In 1968 he contributed, with Raymond Williams and Stuart Hall, to *The May Day Manifesto*.[48] Two years later, in 1970, Thompson gave active support to the student sit-in at Warwick following the discovery of files containing information about students' political activities in the university Registry. He helped the protesters to disseminate evidence not only of how the university kept a record of students' political activities but also of the dominant role of capitalist industry within the university. This critique developed into a book, *Warwick University Ltd*, which disputed the prevailing ethos of society which assumed that 'the summation of social good may be achieved by one thing only: the greater stability of the on-going industrial system'.[49] Thompson's attempts to circumnavigate polemical absolutes and steer a sophisticated path between the university management and its corporate backers on the one hand, and the Trotskyist and Maoist far-left critics of the sit-in on the other,[50] was reminiscent of the radical liberalism of his father, positioned between the imperialists and the Indian independence movements half a century earlier. Throughout the 1970s Thompson also wrote and campaigned about a series of what Wade Matthews refers to as 'humane restraints' in British society, including the National Health Service, the 'rule of law', the jury system and the right to strike.[51] The sit-in at Warwick was not the reason for Thompson's resignation in 1970, although it probably hastened his decision. In fact, he had made several previous attempts to resign. Never a good administrator, manager or 'committee man', he had quickly become impatient with how administrative and teaching responsibilities interfered with his writing, and contemptuous of what seemed to him the pomposity and self-importance of the academic body compared with his previous seventeen years' experience of extramural teaching.[52]

Writer and peace campaigner, 1970–93

During the last two decades of his life Thompson wrote many articles and most of his major books (listed in the bibliography). He also once again became very active in the peace movement, in particular taking a leading role in the newly formed, continent-wide European Nuclear Disarmament (END) movement: the most intense political campaign of his life (see chapter 9). 'END was Thompson's way of breaking back into politics in order to stop politics from ending the world.'[53] Between 1980 and 1985 his time was almost completely given over to END, seriously impeding his historical work and almost certainly causing or contributing to the ill health that led to his early death.[54] After 1985 he returned to the historical research and writing that had been neglected during the years devoted to the peace movement, as far as his health would allow.

Thompson was, as Sheila Rowbotham recalled at the time of his death in 1993, 'one of the great thinkers of our time'. She met him when she was 19,

> and loved and respected him for his sense of fun, his kindness, patience and intellectual courage. Those pale blue-green eyes and the hand through the shock of grey hair are unforgettable. So, too, is the snort of irreverent laughter ... With all his might, he struggled to keep open the common footpaths of radical inquiry. Even in moments of despair, he persistently pitted himself against seemingly invincible forces.[55]

Above all he epitomised a phrase written a few years before his birth by Rosa Luxemburg in *The Russian Revolution*: 'Freedom is always the freedom to think otherwise' – undogmatically, against the grain, on the other side of the dominant.[56]

Thompson's relevance today

How does Thompson, the historian, stand up in relation to the scholarship of our time? In some ways he was remarkably prescient. Given his own emphasis on the historical role of culture and agency, it is somewhat ironic that the most fundamental confirmation of his basic approach has come from research in economic history. At the time Thompson wrote, most economic historians were fixated on the industrial revolution: a rapid take-off of economic growth rates that was deemed, almost mechanically, to bring other aspects of modernisation in its wake. In this context, Thompson's effort to decentre the industrialisation, to look beyond the rise of the factory, and to understand capitalist class formation as a *longue durée* process, all went against the conventional grain. Since the early 1970s, however, economic historians have arrived at something close to Thompson's view. Industrialisation is now seen as being spread over a longer period, and the very notion of an industrial revolution has been questioned. During the first half of the nineteenth century, economic growth is now thought to have proceeded more slowly than was once envisioned, while the early eighteenth century is regarded as more robust than was formerly believed.[57]

Hand in hand with this new chronology of economic development has come a new concept, 'proto-industrialisation', that is deemed to mark the transition between the pre-industrial and industrial eras. Thompson himself expressed reservations about this neologism, but he acknowledged that it was more precise than much of the older terminology. In fact Thompson's *Making* makes a good deal more sense if we understand it as playing out in a proto-industrial context. Here, the factory is seen as spreading unevenly. Some traditional manufacturing centres were prospering at the expense of others, while certain forms of handicraft manufacture were expanding, only to be closed down a few decades later by the final triumph of the factory. These features of Thompson's story need no longer be considered as anomalies. Rather, they were logical pathways through which the complex and protracted structures of capitalist development gradually emerged. Understanding proto-industrialisation as a transitional, *longue durée* process also enables us to avoid the sterile debate over whether Thompson's politically mobilised artisans were reactionary radicals or modern proletarians. It enables us to see that these conventional categories are simply too rigid to capture what was actually going on.[58]

Yet, not all aspects of Thompson's approach to class formation have entirely stood the test of time. The most glaring deficiency is Thompson's almost total neglect of the middle class, both in *The Making of the English Working Class*, and in his subsequent analyses of the eighteenth-century patrician/plebeian polarity. Thompson justified this neglect by claiming that the middle class lacked an independent class-consciousness, and was usually content to hide behind the hegemony of an already capitalistic landed elite. This is patently inadequate for making sense of politics and class relations in the era of nineteenth-century bourgeois liberalism, and it is problematic even in the more overtly aristocratic eighteenth century. Recent studies of the eighteenth-century middle class have shown just how far its pioneering activities in market expansion, urban institution-building, domesticity and consumerism worked to create a new middle-class culture.

Moreover, this culture was finding many adherents among prosperous workers and forward-looking aristocrats. Adding the middle class to the Thompson narrative, however, raises a host of new problems and questions: it suggests that class relations are not always about conflict, but sometimes also about consensus. Moreover, it demonstrates that even the conflicts are complicated, and cannot be understood in terms of simple, dualistic class polarities.[59]

In other respects, recent scholarship has called into question aspects of Thompson's account of working-class formation. His partial neglect of gender, for example, has been noted above. Similar arguments have also been made with regard to the 'Englishness' of Thompson's working class. Given the centrality of the 'free-born Englishman' to Thompson's argument, it is difficult to see where workers of other nationalities fit in. 'What about the working classes – for instance the Indian one – whose heritages do not include such liberal baggage?' wondered the labour historian Dipesh Chakrabarty.[60] Here too, it seems clear that the exclusionary practices of English workers need to be given more attention than they received in any of Thompson's writings. Efforts to exclude the Irish, for example, were a consistent policy of many nineteenth-century trade unions, although it is also possible to find other instances when organisers understood that the only hope for successful organisation lay in mobilising both English and Irish, side by side. The opposition to slavery, articulated by many working-class groups – some of whom gave extensive support to the abolitionist cause – demonstrates that it will not do simply to write off Thompson's workers as racists, any more than they can be dismissed as misogynists, *tout court*. Clearly, one task for the coming generation will be to find the right balance between the evidence of exclusionary and inclusionary behaviour that was exhibited by English working-class communities in general and, in particular, by the industrial and political organisations of male artisans.[61]

If Thompson himself did not address these matters as fully as he might have, it was perhaps because academic history was only one of his commitments. Whilst his central academic and intellectual contribution lay undoubtedly in his historical research and writing, Thompson was active and influential throughout his adult life in political writing and campaigning. His values, and his fundamental belief in the 'common people' and the cause of radical democracy, permeated not only his academic work but also his political writing and activism. The contexts differed markedly over the turbulent period on the Left from the 1940s to the 1990s, but there was a consistency to Thompson's approach.

Kate Soper, in chapter 6, discusses Thompson's concept of socialist humanism and argues that it retains a resonance and distinctiveness for the twenty-first century. This concept both derived from and was a defining characteristic of the early New Left after 1956. Thompson was one of the most influential and original thinkers in the New Left of this period. The formulation and practice of a socialist politics that was neither social democratic and conformist in the Labour Party mould, nor communist in the authoritarian tradition of communist parties within the orbit of the Soviet Union, was one of the pivotal moments in the development of socialism in the modern, Western, context.

This had both practical, political aspects and innovative theoretical foundations. In both spheres, Thompson's work and thinking were central. As Michael Newman argues in chapter 8, Thompson engaged with Ralph Miliband and others on the New Left in discussion and analysis of the appropriate strategy for a truly democratic socialism. Thompson consistently placed emphasis upon the importance of popular social movements, and the centrality of co-operative, collective protest and creating alternative social institutions, structures and cultures. Whilst, he argued, most gains for the cause of socialism had been achieved through direct action, this did not preclude working also within the political system: 'the context will dictate to the politicians, and not the reverse. And socialists must make the context.'[62] Thompson saw the traditional dichotomy between reform and revolution (and similarly between base and superstructure) as anachronistic and unhelpful. (See chapters 6 and 8.) His emphasis was consistently upon human agency and popular mobilisation. In the 1950s and early 1960s this found its main articulation through the Campaign for Nuclear Disarmament (CND) and the mass protests against nuclear weapons, the North Atlantic Treaty Organization (NATO) and the whole 'warfare state' complex. (See chapter 9.)

The same theme was pursued in a different context in his period of relative political quietism from the mid-1960s to the late 1970s (see chapter 8), when he wrote and campaigned against the explicit attacks by Margaret Thatcher and her allies upon what he saw as the core cultural and institutional freedoms of the people: the jury system, habeas corpus, the democratic rights of trade unionists, and the freedom of the press and the media in general.[63]

In the 1980s Thompson, in his campaign for END and his accompanying demands for democratic freedoms in Eastern as well as Western Europe and a new European politics, gained a high public profile: for the first time, Thompson's particular perspective of socialist humanism was widely debated outside the confines of both the Left and the progressive academic journals. (See chapter 9.) His powerful personality, passion and charisma inspired a new generation of radicals.

Running through all these passionate political campaigns were three central themes: Thompson's belief in popular, democratic movements; his advocacy of a libertarian (though not anarchistic) human agency perspective as the central aspect of political activism; and a Romantic vision of the continuing struggle of the common people for a better world.

Thompson was not a political theorist, still less a philosopher or economist. His many interventions into theoretical debates – from 'The Peculiarities of the English' to *The Poverty of Theory* – were always incisive and written with elegance and wit. But, as Michael Newman and Kate Soper argue, he did not achieve, nor indeed attempt, an overall synthesis; his theoretical contributions were somewhat piecemeal; and his political vision is open to a number of criticisms. (See chapters 6, 7, 8 and 9.) However, the political interventions he made and the influence he had were not only relevant and important at the time but have continuing resonance. The politics, the moral passion and the historical vision, rearticulated in different form in our own time, underlie the presently inchoate movements of opposition to the dysfunctional and immoral capitalism of the twenty-first century.

Notes

1 E. P. Thompson, 'Highly Confidential: A Personal Comment by the Editor', in E. P. Thompson (ed.), *Warwick University Ltd* (Harmondsworth: Penguin, 1970), p. 147.

2 D. Goodway, *Anarchist Seeds Beneath the Snow: Left-Libertarian Thought and British Writers from William Morris to Colin Ward* (Liverpool: Liverpool University Press, 2006), p. 285.

3 See in particular Thompson's polemical essay in E. P. Thompson (ed.), *Out of Apathy* (London: New Left Books, 1960), reprinted in E. P. Thompson, *The Poverty of Theory and Other Essays* (London: Merlin Press, 1978).

4 R. Williams, *Keywords: A Vocabulary of Culture and Society* (London: Fontana, 1976), pp. 209–11.

5 'The Liberty Tree' is the title of Part One of Thompson's *The Making of the English Working Class* (rev. edn, Harmondsworth: Pelican, 1968), pp. 19–206.

6 *Ibid.*, pp. 86–7.

7 M. Merrill, 'An Interview with E. P. Thompson', in Mid-Atlantic Radical Historians' Organisation (MARHO), *Visions of History* (Manchester: Manchester University Press, 1983).

8 P. Anderson, *Arguments within English Marxism* (London: New Left Books and Verso, 1980), pp. 17–18.

9 Goodway, *Anarchist Seeds Beneath the Snow*, p. 276.

10 T. Steele, *The Emergence of Cultural Studies, 1945–1965: Cultural Politics, Adult Education and the English Question* (London: Lawrence & Wishart, 1997), ch. 7.

11 The following biographical section is based largely on B. Palmer, *E. P. Thompson: Objections and Oppositions* (London: Verso, 1994); H. J. Kaye, 'Towards a Biography of E. P. Thompson', *Socialist History*, 8 (1995); M. Lago, *India's Prisoner: A Biography of Edward John Thompson 1886–1946* (Columbia: University of Missouri Press, 2001); S. Hamilton, *The Crisis of Theory: E. P. Thompson, the New Left and Post-war British Politics* (Manchester: Manchester University Press, 2011), pp. 2–51; P. J. Conradi, *A Very English Hero: The Making of Frank Thompson* (London: Bloomsbury, 2012); W. Matthews, 'E. P. Thompson in the Provinces', in *The New Left, National Identity and the Break-up of Britain* (Leiden and Boston: Brill, 2013).

12 Merrill, 'An Interview with E. P. Thompson', p. 11.

13 E. P. Thompson, *Beyond the Frontier: The Politics of a Failed Mission* (London: Merlin Press, 1997), pp. 49–51 (this booklet is a reconstruction by Thompson's widow, Dorothy, from his lecture notes after his death, of three lectures given by Thompson at Stanford University in 1981); Conradi, *A Very English Hero*, p. 359.

14 Thompson, *Beyond the Frontier*, pp. 56–64; Conradi, *A Very English Hero*, pp. 117–18, 122–4, 246, 359; F. Wilson, 'A Man in Love with Easeful Death', review of *A Very English Hero*, *Observer Review* (29 July 2012), p. 35.

15 Palmer, *E. P. Thompson*, p. 25.

16 Conradi, *A Very English Hero*, pp. 68–71; Thompson, *Beyond the Frontier*, p. 47.

17 Palmer, *E. P. Thompson*, p. 27.

18 Merrill, 'An Interview with E. P. Thompson', p. 11.

19 Conradi, *A Very English Hero*, pp. 72–5, 173–4; Leeds University Archive (LUA) Departmental Records: Adult Education and Extramural Studies: Supplementary Papers: Thompson's application to University Registrar, 18 March 1948; H. J. P. Lee's reference for Thompson to Leeds University Registrar, 14 April 1948.

20 Palmer, *E. P. Thompson*, pp. 45–6; E. P. Thompson, 'The Liberation of Perugia', in *The Heavy Dancers* (London: Merlin Press, 1985), pp. 183–202; LUA, Adult Education and Extramural Studies: Supplementary Papers: Thompson's application, 18 March 1948; Conradi, *A Very English Hero*, pp. 246–9; R. Fieldhouse, *A History of Modern British Adult Education* (Leicester: National Institute of Adult Continuing Education (NIACE), 1996), pp. 55–7.

21 E. P. Thompson, *The Poverty of Theory* (London: Merlin Press, 1978), p. 264; Matthews, 'E. P. Thompson in the Provinces'.

22 LUA, Adult Education and Extramural Studies: Supplementary Papers: Thompson's application, 18 March 1948; H. J. P. Lee's reference, 14 April 1948; F. M. Jacques to J. Roach (Registrar), 14 April 1948 and to S. G. Raybould, 17 March 1948.

23 E. P. and T. J. Thompson, *There is a Spirit in Europe: A Memoir of Frank Thompson* (London: Victor Gollancz, 1947).

24 Thompson, *Beyond the Frontier*, pp. 41, 84–6; Conradi, *A Very English Hero*, pp. 291–324, 355, 366, 369. Conradi raises the question (without resolving it) as to whether Frank made the 'reckless decision' to undertake the suicidal mission into Bulgaria as a 'peevish reprisal' at the news of his dear friend, Iris Murdoch's, lost virginity. *Ibid.*, pp. 258–9, 310–14, 360. He also argues that some of the heroic mythology that has been attributed to this mission (including Thompson's description of Frank's execution in *Beyond the Frontier*) originated in the propaganda-motivated backstory invented for Frank after the war with the help of false evidence by the new Bulgarian communist regime to contribute towards creating a 'heroic ancestry' for the regime. *Ibid.*, pp. 339–41.

25 D. Thompson, 'Introduction', in Thompson, *Beyond the Frontier*, p. 5.

26 Thompson, *Beyond the Frontier*, pp. 87–98. Conradi, in *A Very English Hero*, pp. 355–7, challenges Thompson's analysis of the Machiavellian role played by Britain and the USSR. The partial evidence (much having been lost, destroyed or fabricated) leaves a choice between 'cock-up' and conspiracy.

27 E. P. Thompson, *The Railway: An Adventure in Construction* (London: British-Yugoslav Association, 1948); H. J. Kaye, *The British Marxist Historians* (Cambridge: Polity Press, 1984), p. 169.

28 LUA, Adult Education and Extramural Studies: Supplementary Papers: Thompson's application, 18 March 1948; Registrar to Thompson, 28 May 1948; S. G. Raybould papers, Joint Tutorial Classes Committee (JTCC) minutes, 5 July 1948.

29 Palmer, *E. P. Thompson*, pp. 58–9; Merrill, 'An Interview with E. P. Thompson', p. 12; E. P. Thompson, *William Morris: Romantic to Revolutionary* (London, Lawrence & Wishart, 1955), p. 841 (rev. edn London: Merlin Press, 1977, reprinted 1996), p. 727.

30 *Ibid.*, p. ix.
31 LUA, Adult Education and Extramural Studies: Supplementary Papers: Registrar to Thompson, 17 October 1950 and Professor Chapman to Registrar, 6 July 1951.
32 Merrill, 'An Interview with E. P. Thompson', p. 12; Palmer, *E. P. Thompson*, pp. 56–7.
33 F. Beckett, *Enemy Within: The Rise and Fall of the British Communist Party* (London: John Murray, 1995), pp. 124–40; Matthews, 'E. P. Thompson in the Provinces'.
34 J. L. and B. Hammond, *The Village Labourer* (London: Longman, 1911).
35 LUA, Adult Education and Extramural Studies: Supplementary Papers: Briggs to the Vice-Chancellor, 30 June 1964.
36 *Ibid.*, Ashworth to the Vice-Chancellor, 1 September 1964.
37 J. W. Scott, *Gender and the Politics of History* (New York: Columbia University Press, 1988), pp. 71–3.
38 *Ibid.*, pp. 74, 79–83.
39 M. Davis (ed.), *Class and Gender in British Labour History* (London: Merlin Press, 2011), pp. 4–5.
40 Scott, *Gender and the Politics of History*; Davis, *Class and Gender in British Labour History*; C. Hall, 'The Tale of Samuel and Jemima: Gender and Working-class Culture in Nineteenth-century England', in H. J. Kaye and K. McClelland (eds), *E. P. Thompson: Critical Perspectives* (Cambridge: Polity Press, 1990); A. Clark, *The Struggle for the Breeches: Gender and the Making of the British Working Class* (Berkeley: University of California Press, 1995); B. Taylor, *Eve and the New Jerusalem: Socialism and Feminism in the Nineteenth Century* (New York: Pantheon, 1983); S. Rose, *Limited Livelihoods: Class and Gender in Nineteenth-Century England* (Berkeley: University of California Press, 1992).
41 Scott, *Gender and the Politics of History*, p. 71.
42 Palmer, *E. P. Thompson*, p. 100.
43 Hall, 'The Tale of Samuel and Jemima', pp. 81–2.
44 LUA, Adult Education and Extramural Studies: Supplementary Papers: Thompson to Mr. Williamson (the Bursar), 16 June (year not stated, (?)1961).
45 *Ibid.*, Raybould to Registrar, 26 January 1962, 5 May 1964 and 10 July 1964; Thompson's CV, May 1964; Raybould to Thompson, 20 July 1964; Registrar to Thompson, 19 March 1965; LUA, S. G. Raybould Papers, JTCC minutes, 2 November 1964; Palmer, *E. P. Thompson*, p. 100.
46 *Ibid.*, pp. 100–6. See chapter 4 for a detailed account of Thompson's deconstruction of earlier eighteenth-century British social history.
47 Hamilton, *The Crisis of Theory*, Ch. 5, 'The Road to St. Paul's', pp. 155–79, esp. 175–9.

48 R. Williams (ed.), *The May Day Manifesto* (rev. edn Harmondsworth: Penguin, 1968).

49 E. P. Thompson (ed.), *Warwick University Ltd* (Harmondsworth: Penguin, 1970), pp. 31–41, 162.

50 *Ibid.*, pp. 146–64.

51 Matthews, 'E. P. Thompson in the Provinces'; E. P. Thompson, *Writing By Candlelight* (London: Merlin Press, 1980), *passim*. Most of the essays in this collection had been first published in various periodicals from the early to mid-1970s.

52 Thompson, *Warwick University Ltd*, pp. 157, 153–4; Palmer, *E. P. Thompson*, pp. 108, 113. See the Appendix for Thompson's eloquent description of 'the species *Academicus Superciliosus*'.

53 Matthews, 'E. P. Thompson in the Provinces'.

54 *Ibid.*; A. Rattenbury, 'Convenient Death of a Hero', *London Review of Books* (8 May 1997).

55 S. Rowbotham, 'E. P. Thompson: A Life of Radical Dissent', *New Statesman and Society* (3 September 1993), pp. 14–15.

56 J. Rose, 'What More Could We Want of Ourselves?', *London Review of Books* (16 June 2011).

57 N. F. R. Crafts, *British Economic Growth during the Industrial Revolution* (Oxford: Oxford University Press, 1985); C. H. Lee, *The British Economy since 1700: A Macroeconomic Perspective* (Cambridge: Cambridge University Press, 1986).

58 F. Mendels, 'Proto-Industrialization: The First Phase of the Industrialization Process', *Journal of Economic History*, 32:1 (1972), pp. 241–61; P. Kreidte, H. Medick and J. Schlumbohm, *Industrialization Before Industrialization: Rural Industry in the Genesis of Capitalism* (Cambridge: Cambridge University Press, 1981).

59 P. Earle, *The Making of the English Middle Class: Business, Society and Family Life in London, 1660-1730* (Berkeley: University of California Press, 1989); M. Hunt, *The Middling Sort: Commerce, Gender and Family in England: 1680-1780* (Berkeley: University of California Press, 1996); J. Smail, *The Origins of Middle-Class Culture: Halifax, Yorkshire, 1660-1780* (Ithaca, NY: Cornell University Press, 1994); N. McKendrick, J. Brewer and J. H. Plumb, *The Birth of A Consumer Society: The Commercialization of Eighteenth Century England* (Bloomington: Indiana University Press, 1982); L. Weatherill, *Consumer Behaviour and Material Culture in Britain: 1660-1760* (2nd edn London: Routledge, 1996); B. Cowan, *The Social Life of Coffee: The Emergence of the British Coffeehouse* (New Haven, CT: Yale University Press, 2005).

60 D. Chakrabarty, *Rethinking Working Class History: Bengal, 1890-1940* (Princeton, NJ: Princeton University Press, 1989), p. 222.

61 For an early attempt at this see P. Linebaugh and M. Rediker, *The Many-Headed Hydra: Sailors, Slaves, Commoners and the Hidden History of the Revolutionary Atlantic* (Boston: Beacon, 2000).

62 E. P. Thompson, 'Revolution', *New Left Review*, 1:3 (May/June 1960), p. 8.

63 See, e.g., Thompson, *Writing By Candlelight*.

Part I

Adult education, history and literature

2

Thompson: the adult educator

Roger Fieldhouse

Post-war adult education

Immediately after the Second World War there were great expectations that British society could be changed fundamentally for the better. The evil of fascism had been exhaustively defeated, the fear of communism was temporarily forgotten in the euphoria of victory, and there was widespread belief in the possibility of a pluralist world. The war-weary population and the returning troops voted overwhelmingly for a Labour government and looked forward to a fairer, more egalitarian society, the implementation of the Beveridge Report, and the creation of a Welfare State. For a brief period the pre-war and wartime broad popular front unity flourished as progressives of all tendencies worked together for the new, better society – challenging the old, discredited conservative hegemony. In this optimistic atmosphere many left-wing intellectuals returning from the war regarded adult education as an ideal agency for promoting the anticipated radical reforms by preparing people for greater democratic participation in society. Many found posts in the WEA and the rapidly expanding university extramural departments.[1]

Thompson did not immediately follow this route, although he did teach two part-time courses in English social history and some single lectures for the WEA whilst finishing his degree at Cambridge.[2] As we saw in chapter 1, he spent much of 1947 retracing his brother's wartime steps in Bulgaria and helping to build a railway in Yugoslavia. When he did get round to applying for an adult education job the brief post-war Popular Front was turning into a Cold War nightmare. This greatly reduced the adult education job opportunities for a member of the Communist Party. Thompson eschewed the most obvious choice of the Oxford Extramural Delegacy, the fastest-growing adult education department in the country which, under the direction of Thomas Hodgkin, was happily recruiting left-wing and communist staff.[3] Instead he chose to move north in search of a more enticing social and political milieu. This may have been, as Scott Hamilton suggests, a pilgrimage to establish closer contact with British working-class and radical traditions and authentic English socialism. It was also something of a repetition of his initial inclination to apply to a Scottish university rather than Oxbridge in 1941. (See chapter 1.)[4] Whatever his exact motives, in March 1948 he applied for a post of staff tutor in adult education in the new Department of Extramural Studies at the University of Leeds. In his application he claimed to have long been interested in adult education and that his recent work with the WEA had been undertaken in the hope that he might later be able to do some full-time work of this nature. He offered to teach classes in history, political science, international relations and English literature. He admitted he had no qualification to teach the last but expressed enthusiasm and a willingness to prepare to take on work in this field.[5]

Despite the dubious conduct of two of his referees who, between them, informed the University Registrar and his putative head of department that he was a member of the Communist Party, Thompson was appointed a probationary staff tutor in the Leeds Extramural Department, starting in August 1948 at a salary of £425 a year.[6] Frank Jacques, the WEA Eastern District Secretary, felt obliged to tell Thomson he had informed Sidney Raybould, the head of department at Leeds, about his Party membership. Thompson was remarkably sanguine about it, although he did ask Jacques whether on principle he 'would take the same precaution with a member of the Conservative Party?'[7]

Thompson recalled years later, 'I went into adult education because it seemed to me to be an area in which I would learn something about industrial England and teach people who would teach me.'[8] Surprisingly, considering his admission in his application for the post, Thompson taught exclusively literature classes for the first three years at Leeds. This may have reflected his stated enthusiasm for the subject or the greater demand for literature from the WEA branches in the West Riding where he taught, but it may also have had a more ideological reason (see below). Later, the ratio of literature to history fluctuated.[9]

The University of Leeds Extramural Department

What kind of department did Thompson find himself in when he arrived in Yorkshire towards the end of the summer of 1948? Raybould had been appointed as the first head of the new Extramural Department two years previously. He was steeped in the particular traditions of the WEA Yorkshire North District, having worked part- and full-time for the District between 1929 and his university appointment in 1946. As John Harrison noted, his formidable mentor during that time was George Thompson, the highly revered District Secretary and leading light of

> a whole generation of working men who devoted their time and energy to the WEA in Yorkshire. Socialism was the new evangelical movement from which they derived their peculiar strength and inner direction. From this secular puritanism the workers' educational movement derived its main dynamic.[10]

The other major influence on Raybould's adult education thinking (although not his politics) was R. H. Tawney, who played such a dominant role in the tutorial class movement for many years and was President of the WEA from 1928 to 1945.[11] Raybould inherited from these two both a strong belief in the progressive social purpose of adult education which would advance both knowledge of, and desire for, a more democratic and just society; and also the particular role of the WEA as provider of university adult education for the working class. He carried these beliefs into the new department, emphasising the importance of recruiting working-class or educationally deprived students into the three-year university tutorial classes. He saw it as the WEA's responsibility to find and deliver the students to the tutorial classes, preferably via its shorter preparatory classes. Once enrolled in a university class, students were expected to submit to a set of stringent regulations intended to ensure that they were engaging in an educational experience of genuine university standard. Raybould could be quite ruthless in his attempts to maintain and enforce these basic principles.[12]

His other major concern was to secure full academic status for the new department and its staff. He was very conscious that extramural staff did not enjoy the same funding or salaries as other university academics and were not even known by the same title of 'lecturer' but were designated as 'staff tutors'. Over the next few years he took various steps to eliminate these disadvantages by bringing the department's appointment and promotional procedures and salaries into line with 'intramural' departments. To ensure that his academic staff had sufficient time to acquire and maintain their academic credentials they were relieved (at least theoretically) of responsibilities for organising classes which were to be undertaken by the WEA or the department's administrative staff. Raybould also strongly encouraged staff to register for a doctorate to further enhance their academic standing. He particularly promoted research into adult education as a 'distinctive field of study' to establish the department's own research identity. (This explains Thompson's reluctant registration in 1950 for a Ph.D. on 'adult education 1840–60 with special reference to the West Riding', which he abandoned the following year – see chapters 1 and 3.) In the early 1950s Raybould established three lectureships in adult education – the first such posts in any English university. In 1953 he persuaded the university to institute a chair in adult education to which he was appointed in October of that year. In order to protect the reputation of the department's teaching it was decided to phase out the use of part-time tutors, relying instead predominantly on the department's own full-time staff or lecturers drawn from other departments of the university. This was intended to ensure that only tutors 'possessing both the academic equipment and the opportunities for study and preparation' would be employed.[13]

His aim to attain and maintain a university standard of adult education also drove Raybould to advocate that university extramural departments should avoid rushing headlong into the expansionist period after the Second World War by attempting to do everything themselves. He consistently argued that the universities should concentrate on the one sector of adult education that they were uniquely qualified to undertake – liberal adult education of university standard – leaving other forms of adult education to other bodies better equipped to provide them, particularly the WEA and the local education authorities.[14]

One of the major differences between an extramural department and other university departments was that it was centred outside the university. Staff mostly worked at home, dotted around the extramural area. In the case of Leeds it was a very extensive area covering not only the densely populated West Riding but also the huge but sparsely populated North Riding, stretching as far north as Middlesbrough. Thompson lived in Halifax, fifteen miles from Leeds, and taught mainly in the industrial towns of the West Riding. Departmental meetings were infrequent and, when they ended, everyone went off home to get on with their work. There was relatively little collegiality. In this 'comparative isolation tutors had to sustain pressures that a more closely-knit community would have helped to diffuse'.[15] Discussions about adult education policy more frequently took place not in the department but in the very active Tutors' Association meetings, often 'quite rigorously'. However, Thompson rarely if ever attended these meetings, although he was a regular attender at the Department's Academic Advisory Committee (effectively a staff meeting).[16]

By the time Thompson joined the Leeds Department the beginnings of the Cold War were undermining the utopian dreams and social-purpose objectives of the post-war adult education world. Divisions and differences were beginning to be felt between 'acceptable' social democratic reformers and the more left-wing socialists and Marxists who were suspected of aiding and abetting the communist 'enemy'.[17] '[A]dult education had always had to exist within certain ideological parameters ... [b]ut the cold war was imposing a much narrower definition of acceptability, a much stricter consensus.'[18] Over the next few years the prejudices against committed left-wingers became more intense. Hodgkin and Raybould engaged in a public and private debate about the extent of the threat in late 1950 and early 1951. Hodgkin stated that he was more gloomy than Raybould 'about the present tendency for all who are, or thought to be, Marxists (*not* simply members of the C.P.) to be *prima facie* suspect'. He went on to suggest that they, as heads of adult education departments, were being pushed

> in an undesirable and dangerous direction – so that – instead of its being taken for granted that a tutor's political and religious beliefs and associations (and even affiliations) are a personal matter which, provided he does his job properly, are no concern of anyone but himself – it is tending to be taken for granted that such matters are relevant and should be enquired into.[19]

'I agree with everything you say in your letter,' Raybould replied a week later, 'though I still think that the C.P. Member is a special case.'[20] He drew the line at dismissing staff because they were communists but he did feel it was justifiable to ask applicants for posts whether they were members of certain religious or political organisations. In *principle* he believed there was justification in refusing employment to anyone who was 'committed to particular opinions ... which prevent him from entering into free examination of them with his students'.[21] In *practice* Raybould was more pragmatic, but he had quite clearly hardened his attitude to communists since appointing Thompson less than three years previously, knowing him to be a member of the Communist Party. He undoubtedly had some misgivings about Thompson as an openly avowed communist, but whether there is evidence that he restricted him or discriminated against him is debatable.[22] However, Raybould did encourage Thompson to teach literature rather than history, a much more potentially political subject[23] (resulting in his teaching only literature during his first three years in the department, as previously noted). It is also very surprising that Thompson never taught on the trade-union day-release classes that were developed in the department in the 1950s. Although Thompson apparently did not believe that Raybould discriminated against him personally, he did on one occasion protest that Raybould's public assertion that communists were 'a threat to professional standards' and 'likely to abuse their position' was not only wrong but improper. 'Such assertions,' he wrote privately to Raybould –

> especially when made before the student body – are likely to undermine the confidence of classes and branches in Communist tutors, and make their work extremely hard going … .When one had voluntarily tied one's hands, one does not like to get clouted.[24]

This does suggest that Thompson did feel somewhat aggrieved at the treatment he received from his head of department because he was a communist.

Thompson's adult education 'social purpose'

Raybould's notion of the social purpose of adult education derived from his long immersion in the 'Great Tradition' of the WEA and the tutorial class movement before the war, his political ideas drawn from the right of the Labour Party, and his strong commitment to an idealised concept of 'university standards', sometimes confused with 'objectivity'. Thompson's, of course, came from a very different, Marxist, stable. It is not surprising that his understanding of the social purpose of adult education (like other Marxists who had been drawn to adult education after the war) was rather more radical than that of his head of department, who interpreted it as helping people to understand *and want* 'unpleasant economic policies, like, for example, wage freezing or labour redeployment', and securing 'the voluntary accept-ance, by those affected, of the necessary measures' to resolve these economic problems.[25] Conversely, Thompson declared on more than one occasion that his aim was to make socialists, create revolutionaries and transform society. In his first year Thompson taught poetry at Batley 'within the context of developing industrial capitalism' and two years later he taught 'Literature and Democracy' – a literary version of the Communist Party's *British Road to Socialism* – at Shepley. At Bingley that same year he chose texts for the class to study that were 'calculated to arouse insistent social, political and religious discussion and questioning', but the following year he complained that 'there is too little rebellion' in the Bingley class, who were too content to be *taught!*[26] However, this revolutionary fervour had a less frightening connotation then, despite the Cold War, than it does in the more terror-conscious twenty-first century. One of Thompson's colleagues, Roy Shaw, who certainly did not share his political views, recalled that when Thompson breezily declared at a meeting in Raybould's room that his aim was to create revolutionaries, '[t]here was no shock-horror in anyone's reaction, rather admiration tinged with amusement'.[27]

Nevertheless, sooner or later these different political agendas were destined to collide, as they did in a series of 'Adult Education Papers' launched by Raybould within the department in January 1950 to provide an opportunity for staff to exchange views on aspects of adult education. Within the department there was already an ongoing debate about how best to make certain that its provision was reaching 'genuine university standards', and several of the contributions in the first three volumes of papers referred to this issue.[28] In July 1950 Thompson pitched a heavyweight brick into the debate, ostensibly a riposte to three named colleagues but in reality aimed at several of the fundamental tenets of 'Raybouldism'.[29] He began by demonstrating in some detail the misleading or erroneous use of various terms, including 'objectivity', 'moderation', 'tolerance', 'calmness', 'equitable' and 'wise'. These, he suggested, were all being subsumed into a concept of 'university standards' and were employed to sanction a theory of adult education hostile to the healthy development of working-class adult education. This fostered an attitude not only to students' learning but to their activity and involvement in society which, if 'adopted as the *aim* of education, would constitute a form of indoctrination, and would be directly opposed to the concept of "education for social purpose"'.[30] This brought Thompson to 'the crux of the matter':

To prescribe an attitude of calmness, or moderation, or tolerance towards a society or social problems is to pre-judge that this attitude is an appropriate one. The exponents of this theory of 'objectivity' are not only agreeing to make available facts about society to their students, but are also claiming to dictate the student's [sic] response, and therefore, behaviour in relation to these facts.[31]

The tutor's scholarship was assumed to be more valid than the student's experience, Thompson argued, and therefore students who joined a class because they were seeking ways of combating class injustice, or because of a feeling of compassion for their fellow workers, were taught to change their attitudes of indignation or compassion to one of tolerance. This identification of objectivity and tolerance as the decisive aims of adult education – as the end of education itself – rather than an essential discipline of study, fostered a particular attitude to facts and experience indistinguishable from 'the fostering of a particular view of history or current problems'.[32] The belittling of the validity of the student's experience and the prescription of an attitude (usually of 'tolerance' or some associated response) to situations which might well demand an attitude of militancy or indignation was a typical form of class indoctrination, fulfilling the wishes of the ruling class that the working class should be tolerant in the face of injustice or exploitation.[33]

However, Thompson did not abandon the Enlightenment values of tolerance and rationality. He readily recognised that objectivity and tolerance were generally desirable dispositions, but they were *by-products*, not *aims* of education; nor were they appropriate in all situations. There were other equally valuable by-products – responsiveness to others, sensitivity, democratic association – and other desirable or appropriate dispositions or attitudes – compassionate, militant, generous or spontaneous. 'Our tolerant attitude must take place in a complex of other attitudes, and the situation … should determine which attitude is appropriate.'[34] Thompson regarded objectivity as a form of intellectual discipline of the highest importance, but as a discipline of study, not an end in itself. It developed students' rational processes and was therefore inseparable from serious study. But he could not resist qualifying this judgement by noting that as a communist he was aware that in some classes little attempt was made to give a fair presentation of unpopular, minority views outside the prevailing orthodoxies.[35]

Towards the end of his paper Thompson returned to the standards debate, contrasting, perhaps a little nostalgically, what he regarded as the fallacious standards advocated by Raybould and his supporters with the spirit of the early tutorial class movement:

> Just as we believe that truth emerges from the dialectics of discussion, the clash of opinion, and the pooling of experience: so we can find a deeper social dialectic in the heart of the tutorial class movement. It was precisely this dialectic which made the tutorial class movement a thing so unique and so full of possibilities: the testing of academic scholarship by the action and experience of a social class too long neglected: the interplay and conflict of abstract, passive, contemplative experience and concrete, active, productive experience. It is this dialectic which both recent practice (as analysed by Mr. Raybould in 'W.E.A. – the Next Phase') and current theory (against which, I fear, Mr. Raybould himself is not proof), are conspiring to destroy.[36]

Thompson suggested that the failure to attract large numbers of working-class students to tutorial classes in the industrial West Riding could be a consequence of what was being offered:

> Can it be that as tutors we have given the impression that we welcome them into our classes only on our own terms, asking them to leave their suspicion outside the class-room door: instead of welcoming them in, suspicions and all, yes, even welcoming the suspicion as a rich ingredient of the class.[37]

The university, with its tutorial class rules and regulations, was alienating potential working-class students and WEA volunteers alike. The danger was that 'the dynamic of "social purpose" will be replaced by the dynamic of "providing recruits for university tutorial classes for aims prescribed by the university at all costs!"'[38]

Thompson concluded his paper by suggesting some changes to the department's practices. First, abandon the term 'university standards' with all its emotive associations, then work out a new education theory and methods without reference to university conditions. Instead, they should reflect adult education values and objectives whilst remaining committed to serious study. The department should open itself up to frank criticism by the WEA and students and foster self-criticism by tutors. A sense of service to the student movement should be restored, whilst the desire to intervene if WEA branch demands or suggestions seem mistaken should be restrained. The branches should be encouraged to formulate their own education policies with guidance from the WEA District. He exhorted his colleagues to 'remember that while we may know more than [the students] about satisfactions, they will know more than us about needs. Above all, let us re-learn humility towards our students' because it was an impertinence to suppose that academic experience was more valid than students' life experience.[39] Thompson ended by recommending the 'true illumination' that fell on Jude (in Hardy's *Jude the Obscure*) as he passed a stonemason's yard in Christminster: 'that here in the stone yard was a centre of effort as worthy as that dignified by the name of scholarly study within the noblest of the colleges'.

There is little evidence of Thompson taking an overtly active political role in the department after his 1950 polemic, although his constant struggle against the inflexible 'university standards', as revealed in his annual class reports (see below), is clear evidence of his continuing battle within the department for a more democratic and student-friendly form of adult education.

Against 'university standards'

The department's regulations, intended to ensure that the desired standard of university education was reached in the tutorial classes, required students to commit themselves to regular attendance over a three-year period and to undertake prescribed reading and written work. After a short introductory period the registration of new students was not normally permitted. Thompson's criticism in his 1950 paper of these regulations, which he regarded as (unintentionally) elitist because they favoured middle-class and well-educated students, had very little impact. Indeed, the time allowed for permitted registrations was controversially reduced from twelve to six weeks in the late 1950s.[40] But he did not give up the struggle. At the end of each academic year the tutors wrote reports on their classes that included a record of how many students had 'qualified' by meeting the regulatory requirements. Thompson's reports contain much railing against the inflexibility and unsuitability of the regulations.[41]

At Cleckheaton in 1951–52 he reported that 'on the register, the class appears a sad failure'. He explained that this was largely due to students' political activities during the general election in October and other commitments, and suggested that a lively WEA class must expect this kind of difficulty. '[A] case can be made out for a certain laxity in the interpretation of regulations in order to take into account the[se] calls on their time and energy.' A couple of years later he admitted that five or six of the students at Batley did not fulfil the stipulated requirements, but nevertheless argued that they should not be excluded from the third year because they contributed vigorously to discussions, all the other students liked to see them and they had no ill effect on the class. '[T]he most admirable regulations of the most enlightened administrators must bend before the facts of life in Batley', he pleaded, with tongue in cheek. A year previously he suggested that with a solid class at Bingley which was well settled to a pattern of work which no 'outsider' would dare to alter, there were actual advantages to admitting some added students in the second and third years provided they agreed to the same commitments as the existing students. And *apropos* his Leeds class in 1959–60 Thompson proposed that students should be allowed to join a class after the sixth meeting at the tutor's discretion, and provided they fulfilled the obligations during the remainder of the first year they should be formally admitted for the second and third years.[42]

A bigger problem was the widespread student reluctance to undertake the required reading and written work. Thompson appears to have arrived in Leeds with a somewhat optimistic notion of what to expect from tutorial-class students, probably gleaned from reading about the 'Great Tradition' of adult education or perhaps from talking to some of the pre-war generation of tutors. He was not totally disappointed. He eulogised that the students in his 1952–53 Batley class, through independent reading and a willingness to use original sources, 'began to show signs of becoming what I had once dreamed a tutorial class in industrial Yorkshire could be like – but which I had never before begun to experience.'[43] But more frequently he was up against stiff resistance. In his first year Thompson found that 'knitting and tea interval set the tone of the evening' at Ossett, where there was a vocal demand for entertainment, students were 'little prepared to enter into the effort of study' and few attempted any background reading. That same year at Batley there was a very poor response to written work from half the students, although others responded well. Despite the high proportion of teachers in the class there was a tendency for the students to listen over-respectfully and passively. At Shepley in his first year Thompson tried, with the enthusiasm of a novice, 'to introduce the students to some serious poetry but met with so little response that he found he was losing weight'. The students did read, or attempted to read, the set novels and most did some written work, but only with 'painstaking effort'. The following year at Shepley written work was of small quantity and regarded as an irksome obligation rather than an element of study. When Thompson embarked on a literature tutorial class in Harrogate in 1959 the recruitment was excellent. but there was little experience of sustained study. He met with vocal opposition to the required written work and three-year commitment. Only eleven of the original twenty-eight students met the attendance and written work requirements, although this remnant did become a first-rate class and a pleasure to teach. In his report for the 1963–64 class at Morley, as with many of his reports, Thompson stressed the 'obligatory' nature of the written work, which was often 'little more than a performance of duty'.[44] He had little answer to this resistance to the department's requirements. But despite his obvious disappointment about the standard of some of the students' input, he was always ready to recognise good work and effort and more inclined to seek ways of keeping the students in the class rather than excluding them because they failed to satisfy some regulation. And, as we shall see in the next section, he tried hard to overcome the reluctance to embark on reading and written work by varying his teaching methods. In his report for his second-year history class at Batley in 1953–54 he argued that discussion papers prepared for presentation at the class should serve in lieu of written work. 'Indeed, with a good class this would seem to be one of the best ways of solving the written work problem in social history', because it represented elementary research, as opposed to an essay regurgitating the tutor's lecture or a textbook.[45]

Thompson also felt some allowance should be made for the age of the students and their social class or educational background. At a first-year literature class in Batley in 1956–57 there was an unexpected influx of young people who proved to be poor attenders because of competing interests and engagements and who tended not to do even a minimum amount of reading or written work. But Thompson argued that it would be wrong to simply exclude them. 'I think it is important to the adult education movement that we should not give up at the first failure', he wrote in his report. He advocated that they should be permitted to return for the second year. However, unfortunately by the third year most of the young students failed to stay the course because of a higher than normal casualty rate through 'natural causes' such as illness, removals and marriage.[46]

On a number of occasions Thompson argued that working-class students should be treated more leniently when it came to deciding whether they should be excluded for failing to satisfy the regulations. At his first-year class at Shepley in 1948–49 he claimed that the class might well be performing a more worthwhile function than another class of a far higher standard. 'Even if the going is hard and the results unspectacular this sort of class *must* be kept alive' to provide working-class students in this small industrial community 'an opportunity to gain acquaintance with the major works of literature under qualified guidance', he pleaded. He added the provocative suggestion that closing the class might mean the abandonment of working-class education in favour of the much easier task of encouraging a middle-class intellectual elite. When his class at Hemsworth a decade later caused considerable administrative problems, Thompson stated that it was 'important … that a branch of this quality, with a good tutorial record, should be kept alive in the heart of the Yorkshire coalfield'. And a few more years on he opposed the exclusion of all the non-qualifiers in his Leeds history class because this would have cut out more than half the manual workers and tip the balance of the class towards civil servants, teachers and a bank manager. 'Surely therapy rather than surgery is to be recommended', he suggested.[47]

With no specified entry qualifications and with the enshrined aim of recruiting working-class or educationally-deprived adults, it was inevitable that many tutorial class students would embark on their studies at a level well below that of a typical university undergraduate. The tutorial class mantra was that over a three-year period it was possible to raise this level, albeit in a limited field of study, to 'university standard'. There was indeed some validity in this theory, at least regarding the keen, committed students, but the practical question was *how* this was to be achieved. Thompson's answer was that instead of trying to raise his students' learning experience to 'university standard' by the surgical implementation of regulations that he considered inappropriate, he would therapeutically adapt his teaching methods to suit his students' needs.

Thompson as teacher

Thompson is best known for what he wrote and for his political activities rather than for his teaching. But for the seventeen years he was at Leeds his teaching had first call on his time and attention. Not long after his death his widow, Dorothy Thompson, explained that 'Edward did most of his historical research for his classes and only began to write it up when he was directly commissioned to do a book … . [W]riting was always second to teaching at that stage, except writing poetry.'[48]

Thompson was 24 and quite inexperienced when he began his extramural teaching, although he had given some lectures in the army and taught one or two short WEA courses while at Cambridge after the war, as previously noted. As was common at that time, there was no training other than some random words of advice. It is not surprising that he felt insecure and frequently blamed himself for early failures. At Shepley in his first year he regretted his 'inexperience in working out a satisfactory technique for studying the novel' (D. H. Lawrence's *Sons and Lovers*). At Todmorden he felt his second-year history class (1952–53) had been a failure, for which he blamed the fact that he 'did not take stock earlier in the year, and realise the degree of my own demoralisation', whilst two years later he lamented that his teaching at Middlesbrough had 'tended to be a bit dim'.[49] One of his early shortcomings was cramming too much into his syllabuses and then trying to cover everything. He soon realised his mistake. '[B]oth tutor and students began to find this cross-country rather heavy going', he noted at Batley in 1951–52,[50] but this did not stop him doing much the same many times again. However, Thompson's greatest frustration was his perceived inability to generate enough class discussion and critical argument. He returned to this time and time again in his class reports. Mulling it over with Dorothy, they decided that her greater success in stimulating her students 'to wade in and criticise and also to volunteer their own judgements' was because she was a woman, younger than most of the class and not very authoritative, whereas 'he was impressive as a speaker … so that discussion in his classes was much more inhibited'. He was very envious.[51] However, his later class reports were less self-critical.[52]

The young Thompson need not have felt so unconfident, according to Bill Baker, who was Raybould's right-hand man in the department's early years. In January 1949, four months into Thompson's first teaching year, Baker visited his Cleckheaton class, expecting to find Thompson ill at ease because of his 'lack of knowledge of the character of WEA classes'. But when Thompson sprang a play-reading on the class unexpectedly, 'he justified the experiment by a very good performance'. He gave 'just the right kind of judicious introduction on background and comments on the text'. Baker was impressed by the way the class participated with freedom and abandon. The chairman of the WEA branch also enthused about Thompson's performance.[53] In November Baker visited another of Thompson's classes, at Bingley. He reported that

> In many respects this was one of the most satisfactory classes that I have ever visited. Thompson's work was quite first-class, both in his introduction of the subject (Dickens's 'Hard Times') and in stimulating the discussion. His technique, perfectly adapted to the needs of this particular class, showed a remarkable advance on last year, when I heard him at Cleckheaton. It was really all very good indeed ... . [The students] all took an active part in discussion, they all knew the text.[54]

It is clear from his discussion with Dorothy that Thompson was anxious to encourage his students to participate in class discussion, but equally clear from Baker's reports that he was achieving this right from the beginning of his teaching career. At the end of his first year at Cleckheaton Thompson confirmed Baker's assessment, reporting that the class had worked 'as a group combining various talents and pooling differing knowledge and experience for a common end'. But he felt less satisfied with the participation at his Batley class that year, although by the end of the year there was an improvement. However, the following year at Batley there were still too many non-participants 'silent in discussion'. Thompson put this down partly to too many social and educational divisions between the students, but also to tradition.[55]

By 'tradition' Thompson was almost certainly referring to adult education's 'Great Tradition' of the earlier twentieth century, which extolled the virtues of the one-hour lecture followed by an hour of questions and discussion. This model was beginning to fall out of favour by the time Thompson began teaching, but even ten years later Professor Robert Peers, doyen of the extramural world, noted that 'the lecture is still the method most commonly used in adult education to-day [1958] .... An hour's lecture followed by an hour of somewhat desultory discussion tends too frequently to be the standard pattern.'[56] It was still the prevailing methodology in the 1950s, according to Professor Bernard Jennings, who was a colleague of Thompson's at Leeds.[57] The students in Thompson's class at Shepley in 1948–49 liked to have an hour's lecture 'followed by diffuse discussion on any subject under the sun'. Thompson tried to escape from this formula. In his syllabus for his Keighley class in 1953–54 he stated that his aim was *not* to give a one-hour lecture but rather to engage in co-operative

39

study and discussion. Students' unwillingness to become actively involved sometimes forced Thompson reluctantly to revert to the 'solid straight from the shoulder lecture',[58] but he constantly sought ways to encourage students to participate by drawing on their experience, as advocated in his 'Against University Standards' paper.

Therefore, although he regarded his second-year class at Shepley (1949–50) as in many ways unsuccessful, he was pleased about how the mainly working-class students were ready to correct him when they felt themselves to be more expert. Similarly at Todmorden (1951–52) he praised the fluent and relevant discussion based on a great variety of experience. At Cleckheaton that year he introduced a 'reminiscence book' for students to record reminiscences collected from old people in the locality. Unfortunately there is no mention of this experiment in the class report for the following year and an attempt to replicate it at Todmorden completely failed. But some years later the use of a tape recorder for the same purpose at Keighley was a partial success. He was more successful at a new class at Batley in 1952–53, where he persuaded students to draw on evidence from their grandparents of evasions of the factory acts regarding child employment at the local mills in the 1860s and 1870s. The following year a number of student presentations to the class led to extremely vigorous discussion which mostly occupied a whole evening. Sometimes this discussion was swamped by local reminiscences but, as Thompson observed, 'we cannot have our cake and eat it. If we want academic tidiness we will not have the variety of experience.' In the final year at Batley Thompson felt he was more chairman than tutor and the members of the class were 'excellent colleagues' rather than 'orthodox students'. At Northallerton in 1954–55 and Hemsworth in 1956–57 Thompson persuaded the students to present introductions to contemporary documents to the class, but at Halifax he was disappointed that students were unwilling to undertake some research into local records and the history of the local industries.[59]

In his pursuit of participation Thompson (like many adult education tutors) even paid attention to the pedagogic suitability of the furniture, complaining that the formal lecture room where his Leeds class met in 1959–60, with the tutor separated by furnishings and lighting from the students, inhibited discussion. He pleaded for a more suitable room in the department with a round table, similar to the ideal reading room at the public library where he held his class in Morley, with its large oval table.[60]

The corollary of Thompson's encouraging students to participate by contributing their personal experiences was his equal emphasis on the tutor's responsibility to take these contributions seriously and, indeed, to learn from them. Throughout his time in adult education his class reports clearly reflect this. In his first year, at Cleckheaton, he believed that he had learnt as much as he had imparted, whilst at his 1961–62 Harrogate class he reported that 'there were few class meetings in which the tutor did not find himself being taught'. In the preface to *The Making of the English Working Class* he acknowledged that he had 'learned a great deal from members of my tutorial classes, with whom I have discussed many of the themes treated' in the book. Two years after he had left Leeds Thompson returned to give a Mansbridge Memorial Lecture in which he advocated education that combined the life experience of the student with the teacher's formal learning:

> It is commonly argued – perhaps more so a few years ago than it is now – that liberal adult education offers a relationship between the teacher and the taught which is in certain respects educationally unique …
> [I]n liberal adult education, no tutor is likely to last out a session – and no class is likely to stay the course with him – if he is under the misapprehension that the role of the class is passive. What is different about the adult student is the experience which he brings to the relationship. This experience modifies, sometime subtly and sometimes more radically, the entire educational process.

He concluded his lecture by reminding his audience 'that universities engage in adult education not only to teach but also to learn'.[61] This emphasis in his teaching on the validity of the students' experience not only echoed his rejection, in his 'Against University Standards' paper, of the traditional top-down, liberal–paternalistic mode of university adult education, but also mirrored his extensive use of sources reflecting the range of working-class life in his 'bottom-up' historical writing and equally his stress in his political writing on the importance of human experience as a vital agency in historical development. Thompson's adult teaching was one more manifestation of his empirical method.

In his literature classes Thompson experimented from the very beginning with a variety of teaching methods in an attempt to catch students' attention and enthusiasm, with mixed success, as he frequently admitted in his class reports. These included comparative exercises and close analysis of poems and other texts, play-readings and 'seminar techniques' requiring students to write extended reviews of texts or prepare papers as introductions to critical discussion. He found these last were a more acceptable form of written work than normal essays.[62] Overall, Thompson's classes

> typically alternated between close textual study and synoptic sweeps around those nineteenth-century and early twentieth-century texts that were already becoming canonical in adult education, ... Apart from some classes in Elizabethan literature, his courses were devoted, on the whole, to the study of poetry and fiction ... although most classes studied a Shakespeare play, usually as an introduction to literary study.[63]

There was another advantage to teaching Shakespeare, as Thompson discovered at Morley in 1961–62, where there was

> a tendency to hang social or even local gossip on some literary peg and run away into irrelevances in discussion ... a class of this kind responds best to Shakespeare; the distance stimulates application, the in-bred respect keeps philistinism at bay, and it is difficult to graft onto Falstaff a discussion on the Morley local elections.[64]

With his history classes Thompson decided early on that exclusive use of secondary sources was unsatisfactory, so he distributed duplicated documents and encouraged analysis of original sources. This proved a popular and successful alternative form of written work, for example a paper on the trades council and Independent Labour Party (ILP) in Dewsbury and Batley in the period 1890–1900, prepared from minute books and local papers, and a 'most exciting and informative talk' on local government in Batley in 1906–14 by a blind student who was the first ILP councillor in Batley in 1906. However, as previously noted, attempts to involve students in historical research were not always successful. Similarly, experiments in choosing topics for students to study according to their individual interests met with mixed responses. As with his literature classes, Thompson on occasion adopted a seminar method with students preparing introductions to particular topics, although again this sometimes ran into difficulties. Some students were diffident about 'performing' in class, whilst others found insufficient time to prepare properly.[65]

Thompson was always willing to experiment and looking for new ways to stimulate his students. In 1950–51 he organised a weekend school at Grantley Hall (the North Riding Local Education Authority [LEA] residential centre) on the poet W. H. Auden for his Cleckheaton and Batley classes. The students 'benefited enormously from a brief, highly concentrated and fairly high-level bout of study'.[66] Not the least benefit was their being exposed to different teachers, a notion he returned to a decade later, suggesting that it was a hazard of three-year tutorial classes that students and tutor got sick of each other's prejudices and stock arguments. He suggested that 'more thought should go into planning ways in which the class can be relieved of the monotonous diet of one tutor's teaching style and emphasis'.[67]

In recommending him for a senior lectureship in 1962 Raybould wrote, 'Thompson is an exceptionally good teacher',[68] which by Raybouldian standards was high praise indeed. Students, colleagues and other observers have paid many tributes and used many adjectives to describe Thompson's adult teaching: intellectual, inspirational, stimulating, compelling, challenging, sympathetic, empathetic, enthusiastic, articulate, humorous, unpredictable, energetic, humble, critical (often at great length) and adaptive to students' educational levels, needs and interests: all contributing to a genuine, two-way interaction between the tutor and the students.[69] It is as advocate, innovator and practitioner of a 'bottom-up' approach to adult education, always valuing his students' contributions and enthusiastic to learn from their experiences, that Thompson as teacher should be remembered.

Time to move on

Thompson had contemplated resigning from the Leeds department and trying to live by writing from the early 1960s probably because he had grown tired of the considerable organisational and administrative burdens as well as the teaching and research that was expected of university extramural staff (as many of us who have been in much the same situation can vouch for). Some years previously Thompson had admitted to Raybould that when he first joined the department he had 'an over-rosy picture of the organisational strength and initiative of WEA branches', but later became disillusioned by their organisational and recruiting weaknesses as well as their frequent lack of enthusiasm for the tutorial class ideal.[70] In 1954 he found it difficult to restrain himself when the Halifax branch offered him little practical help, so that he had to keep the register and the book box, make WEA announcements, collect subscriptions and fees and try to keep in touch with absent students, which was 'both distracting and embarrassing'.[71] Nevertheless he stayed the course for a few more years but in 1965, despite having been promoted to Reader at Leeds, he applied for and accepted a post as Reader and Director of the new Centre for the Study of Social History at the University of Warwick. (See chapter 1.) After seventeen years teaching extramural students in Yorkshire he ceased to be, at least formally, an adult educator.[72]

Notes

1 R. Fieldhouse, *Adult Education and the Cold War* (Leeds: University of Leeds, 1985), p. 1; R. Fieldhouse, *A History of Modern British Adult Education* (Leicester: National Institute of Adult Continuing Education (NIACE), 1996), pp. 180–2, 212.

2 Leeds University Archive (LUA), Adult Education and Extramural Studies: Supplementary Papers: Thompson's application, 18 March 1948; F. M. Jacques to J. Roach (Registrar), 14 April 1948.

3 Fieldhouse, *Adult Education and the Cold War*, pp. 29–54; Thomas Hodgkin, interview with the author, 16–17 November 1979.

4 S. Hamilton, *The Crisis of Theory: E. P. Thompson, the New Left and Post-war British Politics* (Manchester: Manchester University Press, 2011), pp. 51, 234; P. J. Conradi, *A Very English Hero: The Making of Frank Thompson* (London: Bloomsbury, 2012), p. 173.

5 LUA, Adult Education and Extramural Studies: Supplementary Papers: Thompson's application, 18 March 1948. P. J. Conradi, in *A Very English Hero*, pp. 358, 401, echoing a blog from Hamilton, claims that Thompson did not think of himself as an historian until the late 1950s, but this is contradicted not only by Thompson's history degree but also by the wording of his application to Leeds in 1948.

6 *Ibid.*, H. J. P. Lee to Registrar, 14 April 1948; F. M. Jacques to S. G. Raybould, 17 April 1948; Registrar to Thompson, 28 May 1948; S. G. Raybould Papers, Box 34, Joint Tutorial Classes Committee (JTCC) minutes, 5 July 1948.

7 *Ibid.*, Supplementary Papers, Jacques to Thompson, 23 April 1948; Thompson to Jacques, 28 April 1948.

8 M. Merrill, 'An Interview with E. P. Thompson', in MARHO, *Visions of History* (Manchester: Manchester University Press, 1983), p. 12.

9 D. Goodway, 'E. P. Thompson and the Making of *The Making of the English Working Class*', in R. Taylor (ed.), *Beyond the Walls* (Leeds: University of Leeds, 1996), p. 133; A. Croft, 'Walthamstow, Little Gidding and Middlesbrough: Edward Thompson, Adult Education and Literature', *Socialist History*, 8 (1995), p. 24.

10 J. F. C. Harrison, *Learning and Living 1790–1960* (London: Routledge & Kegan Paul, 1961), pp. 292, 299, 342–3; R. Fieldhouse, 'Sidney Raybould,

Fred Sedgwick and the Early Department', in Taylor (ed.), *Beyond the Walls*, pp. 3–4.

11 R. Fieldhouse, 'A Collective Political Biography of Four Influential British Adult Educators', in M. Friedenthal-Hasse (ed.), *Personality and Biography in the History of Adult Education*, 2 (Frankfurt: Peter Lang, 1998), pp. 847–65, esp. 851, 855–6; R. Taylor and T. Steele, *British Labour and Higher Education 1945–2000* (London: Continuum, 2011), especially chs 1 and 3.

12 Fieldhouse, 'Sidney Raybould, Fred Sedgwick and the Early Department', pp. 10–17.

13 *Ibid.*, pp.17–18; S. G. Raybould, 'Research in Adult Education', *Adult Education*, 23 (1950), pp. 16–22; Leeds Extramural Department *Annual Report*, 1955–56, pp. 10–11.

14 S. G. Raybould, *The English Universities and Adult Education* (London: Workers' Educational Association (WEA), 1951); Fieldhouse, *A History of Modern British Adult Education*, p. 212; Fieldhouse, 'Sidney Raybould, Fred Sedgwick and the Early Department', pp. 18–19.

15 P. Searby, 'Edward Thompson as a Teacher', in J. Rule and R. Malcolmson (eds), *Protest and Survival* (London: Merlin Press, 1993), p. 2.

16 Tom Caldwell, letters to author, 10 August 2010 and 4 March 2012 and interview, 12 September 2010; LUA, Departmental Records: Adult Education, Box 7, Academic Advisory Committee minutes.

17 Fieldhouse, *Adult Education and the Cold War, passim*.

18 *Ibid.*, p. 7.

19 LUA, Adult Education and Extramural Studies: Raybould Papers, Box 36, Hodgkin to Raybould, 21 December 1950.

20 *Ibid.*, Raybould to Hodgkin, 28 December.

21 *Ibid.*, S. G. Raybould, unpublished paper 'Academic Freedom and Propaganda', n.d.

22 Searby, 'Edward Thompson as a Teacher', p. 3, n. 5; R. Shaw, 'Recalling Raybould's Department', in Taylor (ed.), *Beyond the Walls*, p. 37; T. Caldwell, letter to author, 10 August 2010.

23 T. Caldwell, interview with author, 12 September 2010.

24 Thompson to Raybould, 10 August (?1949), quoted in Fieldhouse, *Adult Education and the Cold War*, p. 18.

25 R. Fieldhouse, 'The problem of objectivity, social purpose and ideological commitment in English university adult education', in R. Taylor, K. Rockhill and R. Fieldhouse, *University Adult Education in England and the USA* (London: Croom Helm, 1985), p. 35; LUA, Raybould Papers, Box 36, unpublished papers by S. G. Raybould, 'Adult Education and Democracy', 'Objectivity and Toleration' and 'Academic Freedom and Propaganda' (1949–50).

26 B. Palmer, *E. P. Thompson: Objections and Oppositions* (London: Verso, 1994), p. 65; Searby, 'Edward Thompson as a Teacher', p. 10; Croft, 'Waltham-

stow, Little Gidding and Middlesbrough', p. 38; LUA, Departmental Records: Adult Education, Box 47 and Supplementary Papers, Thompson's class reports for Batley 1948–49, Shepley 1950–51, Bingley 1950–51 and 1951–52.

27 R. Shaw, 'Recalling Raybould's Department', in Taylor (ed.), *Beyond the Walls*, p. 37.

28 Searby, 'Edward Thompson as a Teacher', p. 5; LUA, Department of Extramural Studies, unpublished 'Adult Education Papers', 1, 1–3 (1950).

29 *Ibid.*, vol. 1, 4, pp. 16–39, E. P. Thompson, 'Against "University" Standards' (1950).

30 *Ibid.*, p. 24.

31 *Ibid.*, pp. 24–5.

32 *Ibid.*, p. 26.

33 *Ibid.*, pp. 31–2; Croft, 'Walthamstow, Little Gidding and Middlesbrough', p. 36.

34 Thompson, 'Against "University" Standards', p. 27.

35 *Ibid.*, pp. 27–9.

36 *Ibid.*, pp. 35–6.

37 *Ibid.*, p. 36.

38 *Ibid.*, p. 37.

39 *Ibid.*, p. 38. The strength of Thompson's legacy to the Leeds Department is illustrated by this author's comment in 1985 (in Fieldhouse, *Adult Education and the Cold War*, p. 2) that '[t]he class is treated more as a mutual exploration of the subject than a one-way transmission of a body of knowledge from "expert" lecturer to ignorant students'.

40 LUA, Adult Education and Extramural Studies, Box 47 and Supplementary Papers. These reports will subsequently be referred to as 'class reports' followed by the location and date.

41 *Ibid.*, Departmental Records: Adult Education, Supplementary Papers, Leeds class report, 1959–60.

42 *Ibid.*, class reports, Cleckheaton 1951–52, Bingley 1952–53, Batley 1953–54, Leeds 1959–60.

43 *Ibid.*, Batley 1952–53.

44 *Ibid.*, Ossett and Batley 1948–49, Shepley 1948–49 and 1949–50, Harrogate 1959–60, Morley 1963–64; Searby, 'Edward Thompson as a Teacher', pp. 15–16.

45 LUA class reports, Batley 1953–54.

46 *Ibid.*, Batley 1956–57 and 1958–59.

47 *Ibid.*, Shepley 1948–49, Hemsworth 1958–59, Leeds 1963–64.

48 LUA, Departmental Records: Adult Education Supplementary Papers, Dorothy Thompson to Andy Croft, 3 July 1995.

49 LUA class reports, Shepley 1948–49, Todmorden 1952–53, Middlesbrough 1954–55.

50 LUA class reports, Batley 1951–52; A.Croft, 'Walthamstow, Little Gidding and Middlesbrough', in Taylor (ed.), *Beyond the Walls*, pp. 145–6.

51 *Ibid.*, pp. 152–3, 156 n. 5.

52 *Ibid.*, p. 153.

53 LUA, Departmental Records: Adult Education Supplementary Papers, W. P. Baker to Raybould, 19 January 1949.

54 *Ibid.*, W. P. Baker, class inspection report, Bingley, first year English literature, E. Thompson, 26 November 1949.

55 LUA class reports, Cleckheaton and Batley 1948–49, Batley 1949–50.

56 R. Peers, *Adult Education: A Comparative Study* (London: Routledge & Kegan Paul, 1958), p. 227.

57 B. Jennings, letter to the author, 10 August 2010.

58 LUA class reports, Shepley 1948–49, Batley 1957–58; Keighley syllabus, 1953–54.

59 LUA class reports, Shepley 1949–50, Todmorden and Cleckheaton 1951–52, 1952–53, Batley 1952–53, 1953–54, 1954–55, Northallerton 1954–55, Hemsworth and Halifax 1956–57.

60 *Ibid.*, Leeds and Morley 1959–60.

61 *Ibid.*, Cleckheaton 1948–49, Harrogate 1961–62; E. P. Thompson, *The Making of the English Working Class* (rev. edn Harmondsworth: Pelican, 1968), p. 14; E. P. Thompson, *Education and Experience* (Leeds: Leeds University, 1968), pp. 1, 23.

62 LUA class reports, Ossett and Batley 1948–49, Cleckheaton 1948–49, 1949–50, 1950–51, Batley 1956–57.

63 Croft, 'Walthamstow, Little Gidding and Middlesbrough', p. 144.

64 LUA class reports, Morley 1961–62.

65 *Ibid.*, Cleckheaton 1951–52, Todmorden 1952–53, Batley 1952–53, 1954–55, Keighley 1953–54, Halifax 1954–55, Leeds 1959–60, 1961–62.

66 *Ibid.*, Cleckheaton 1950–51.

67 *Ibid.*, Leeds 1961–62.

68 LUA, Departmental Records: Adult Education Supplementary Papers, Raybould to Registrar, 26 January 1962.

69 Goodway, 'E. P. Thompson and the Making of *The Making of the English Working Class*', p. 141; Searby, 'Edward Thompson as a Teacher', pp. 10–14; B. Palmer, *E. P. Thompson: Objections and Oppositions* (London: Verso, 1994), pp. 67–8.

70 LUA, Departmental Records: Adult Education Supplementary Papers, Thompson to Raybould, 3 February ?1954.

71 LUA, Departmental Records: Adult Education, Box 47, Thompson's Halifax class report, 1954–55.

72 Thompson did teach one or two WEA classes later, while living at Worcester. I am indebted to David Goodway for this information.

3

The making of *The Making*

David Goodway

> I have also learned a great deal from members of my tutorial classes,
> with whom I have discussed many of the themes treated here.[1]

So Edward Thompson acknowledges in the preface to *The Making of
the English Working Class*; and this chapter examines primarily the
way in which this great book grew out of his day-to-day work at the
University of Leeds. As noted in chapter 2, he had been appointed
in 1948, at the age of 24, as a staff tutor in the then Department of
Extramural Studies. He lived in Halifax, the major town of the Calder
Valley, and worked for the department until he left for the University
of Warwick and its Centre for the Study of Social History in 1965,
two years after the publication of *The Making of the English Working
Class*. Yet concerned with the genesis – the making – of *The Making
of the English Working Class*, the chapter necessarily considers how
William Morris came to 'seize' Thompson, enabling him to revise his
Marxism radically, formulate his mature political philosophy and
thereby proceed to the fundamental, organising innovation of *The
Making of the English Working Class*, as well as outlining his intense
political activism from the late 1940s through to the early 1960s.[2]

Thompson had gone up to Corpus Christi College, Cambridge, in
1941, but his time there was interrupted by three years' service as a
tank commander in North Africa and Italy. On his return he took a
first in Part I of the History Tripos and this, under wartime regulations, allowed him a degree. He remained at Cambridge, however,
for another year (1946–47) of independent study in English literature
and social history, mainly Elizabethan.

When he applied for the post of staff tutor at Leeds he offered to
lecture not only in history but also in English literature, of which he
wrote:

I have no qualifications to lecture in this subject. However ... it has long been my chief interest, both in my attempts as a practising writer and as a field of study.[3]

It has to be stressed that at this time – and indeed for much of the 1950s – Thompson saw himself principally as a poet, a *Collected Poems* being eventually published in 1999. This goes far to account for his superlative style, as he is – although it has been little acknowledged – one of the great English prose writers. (See the appendix.) He seems to be one of those, like Henry David Thoreau and his Cambridge near-contemporary, Alex Comfort, 'whose best poetry is found in their prose – who can't stop playing with words'.[4] On being appointed at Leeds he married Dorothy Sale (*née* Towers) who, as Dorothy Thompson, was also to become a respected historian, particularly of Chartism. Their agreement was that Dorothy should look after their children until they were old enough for her to take a full-time job, at which point Edward would resign his academic position and become a full-time writer.[5] (In the event, this is exactly what happened, yet in the unanticipated circumstances of his having become a professional historian, who quit Warwick, which he designated a 'business university', in great disgust in 1970.[6] He never held another permanent post and Dorothy, now a lecturer at the University of Birmingham, became the main breadwinner.)

For his first three years at Leeds all his classes were in literature. Then, in 1951–52, he taught two history as well as two literature classes. The proportion of history to literature fluctuated over the following ten years (four history to one literature in 1954–55, for example). Yet in each of the three years 1959–62, the period when he was writing *The Making of the English Working Class*, he taught three literature classes and only one in history.[7]

During his early years in Yorkshire Thompson was not only active in the Communist Party of Great Britain (CPGB) – as Eric Hobsbawm remarks, he was 'politically important enough' to be elected to the Yorkshire District Committee – but was also deeply involved in the peace movement: he was chair of the Halifax Peace Committee, secretary of the Federation of West Yorkshire Peace Organisations, and editor of the monthly *Yorkshire Voice of Peace*. 'This', he remembered, 'probably occupied half my time and professional teaching the other half.'[8]

The Department of Extramural Studies for which Thompson was teaching professionally was new. It had been set up in 1946 with ten staff tutors and the formidable adult educator, S. G. (Sidney) Raybould, as its head. By 1950 the number of academic staff had leapt to thirty-four with appointments such as Thompson's. Raybould insisted on a policy of 'assimilation' of conditions of service, and this he had implemented by 1953: with parity of status, salaries and titles between full-time extramural staff and their internal colleagues. The department was renamed the Department of Adult Education and Extramural Studies (1952); a chair of Adult Education was instituted, with Raybould as the first occupant (1953); and the post of staff tutor disappeared, all academic staff becoming lecturers without organisational responsibilities.[9]

There must therefore have been significant pressure on Thompson to devote some of his time to research; and in June 1950 he was proposing to write a Ph.D. thesis on 'The Influence of the Chartist Movement upon Adult Education in the Nineteenth Century', which was approved as 'Working-class Adult Education, 1840–60, with special reference to the West Riding', with the start later delayed until 'the beginning of session 1951–2'.[10] (See chapter 2.) But by December 1950, having 'read one or two books *so* dreadful and ideological about Morris that I thought I *must* answer these', he was 'more or less committed to do a short booklet on William Morris for Lawrence and Wishart as soon after Easter as I can'.[11] The book which enraged Thompson was Lloyd Eric Grey's *William Morris: Prophet of England's New Order* (1949), originally published in the USA in 1940 under, bizarrely, an entirely different name and title, and which he dissected in a lengthy article which appeared in *Arena* in the spring of 1951 (when it was said to have been written 'nearly a year ago').[12] Morris was far from a novel subject for a member of the CPGB, which viewed him as the outstanding intellectual exemplar of British communism. Robin Page Arnot, in particular, had written his *William Morris: A Vindication* to mark the centenary, in 1934, of Morris's birth.[13] Thompson's Ph.D. subject was correspondingly changed to 'The Background and Origins of the Formation of the Independent Labour Party in Yorkshire and its Development between 1880 and 1900', with Professor Guy Chapman of the Department of History still as supervisor (but this was ultimately abandoned, without a word of it produced, at the end of 1953).[14]

The 'short booklet' developed, of course, into the magisterial 908-page *William Morris: Romantic to Revolutionary*, which appeared in 1955. Early the following year he told an appreciative reader that he had not been 'under much pressure to cut it'. Maurice Cornforth, his publisher, he said, 'may have been, but he was extremely gentle in passing it on to me'. Yet even so soon after completion he acknowledged some self-indulgence: 'I am sure now that I *ought* to have cut it in the socialist section by about 100 pages.'[15] Thompson's *William Morris* is one of the most important books ever written about Morris. Crucially, it reclaimed Morris for a socialism which is revolutionary, Marxist and highly original.

At this point it would have been natural for Thompson to have continued working on late nineteenth-century labour history, even moving into the early twentieth century; and indeed to some extent this is exactly what he did. The fine essay, 'Homage to Tom Maguire', devoted to the Socialist Leaguer who had appeared in *William Morris*, was written for the Festschrift for G. D. H. Cole, which in 1960 became his memorial volume.[16] It was also intended that Thompson should bring to publication the second volume of *Tom Mann and His Times*, covering the years 1890–1900 (including the formation and first years of the ILP). He had been recruited, along with Christopher Hill (who was to bring in A. L. Morton) and John Saville, during the winter of 1954–55 to assist the ailing Dona Torr in completing the first two volumes (out of a projected four). Torr was the 'Communist scholar' to whom Thompson expressed deep indebtedness in the foreword to *William Morris* of January 1955:

> From the conception of this book until its completion, [she] has given me her encouragement, her friendship, and her criticism. She has repeatedly laid aside her own work in order to answer enquiries or to read drafts of my material, until I have felt that parts of the book were less my own than a collaboration in which her guiding ideas have the main part.[17]

Thompson completed two chapters of *Tom Mann and His Times*, on 1890–92, which were to open the second volume. After Torr's death in late 1956 he remained 'committed to the Dona'; but in March(?) 1957 the CP publisher, Lawrence and Wishart, withdrew from him 'the "commission"' since, in the words of her companion, Walter Holmes, 'judging by what I have learned, a public conflict between you and the Party is hardly to be avoided'.[18] This reads very oddly, given the dramatic events that had already taken place in 1956 with the crisis in the CPGB. The two finished chapters eventually appeared in 1962 as the *Our History* pamphlet, *Tom Mann and His Times, 1890–92*, albeit maliciously 'massacred' by Joan Simon.[19]

In the turmoil following the Twentieth Congress of the Communist Party of the Soviet Union in February 1956 and the publication of Khrushchev's 'secret letter' in the West, Thompson and John Saville, a lecturer at the University of Hull, had co-edited the *Reasoner*, a mimeographed discussion journal, the first unauthorised publication ever to have been circulated within the CPGB since its foundation in 1920. The masthead carried a quotation from Marx: 'To leave error unrefuted is to encourage intellectual immorality.' After three issues and the outbreak of the Hungarian revolution the two men resigned from the Party – along with around 7,000 other people.[20] In 1957 Thompson and Saville began to bring out the *New Reasoner* (*NR*), with an editorial board that was to include Ken Alexander, Michael Barratt Brown, Mervyn Jones, Doris Lessing, Ralph Miliband, Peter Worsley and Randall Swingler (an editor of *Left Review* in the 1930s, significantly older than the others and a particular friend of Thompson's). Several months before the first issue of the *NR*, the *Universities and Left Review* (*ULR*) had begun publication in Oxford, edited by four recent graduates, Stuart Hall, Gabriel Pearson, Ralph (later Raphael) Samuel and Charles Taylor. When the *ULR*, by then relocated to London, constructed its editorial board, among its members were Alasdair MacIntyre, Alan Lovell and Michael Barratt Brown (the formal link between the two journals). After ten issues of the *NR* and seven of the *ULR*, they merged in 1960 to become the *New Left Review* (*NLR*), the composite board of which was also to bring in Denis Butt, Lawrence Daly, Paul Hogarth, John Rex, Dorothy Thompson and Raymond Williams.[21]

The coming together of the British New Left was exactly concurrent with, although with entirely unrelated origins, the mobilisation of the nuclear disarmament movement, to which its members and journals gave vigorous support. The unilateralist campaign had begun to mobilise with the British government's announcement in 1957 that it was to develop the hydrogen bomb. The Emergency Committee for Direct Action Against Nuclear War was immediately set up to support Harold Steele in his attempt to enter the testing area in the Pacific. At the end of 1957 the Emergency Committee became the Direct Action Committee Against Nuclear War (DAC), which launched a series of small non-violent and illegal actions at missile bases and against the deployment of Polaris submarines on Holy Loch in Scotland, as well as an industrial campaign to halt the production of nuclear weapons. The following year saw the beginning of a mass legal agitation for unilateral nuclear disarmament with the foundation of the CND, with its annual marches between the Atomic Weapons Research Establishment at Aldermaston in Berkshire and Trafalgar Square, London, initially from London to Aldermaston, but from Easter 1959 starting at Aldermaston and ending in London. With a strong presence in the working-class movement, CND's preoccupation was with the Labour Party adopting unilateral nuclear disarmament as party policy. This was actually achieved at Labour's annual conference at Scarborough in 1960, only to be overturned the following year.[22]

Besides making a key organisational contribution to the formation of the British New Left – of which also, in its early years, he was undoubtedly the principal theoretician – Thompson flung himself into the nuclear disarmament movement. In the preface to the 1980 edition of *The Making of the English Working Class* he commented that 'looking back, I am puzzled to know when and how the book got itself written, since in 1959–62 I was also heavily engaged in the work of the first New Left, the Campaign for Nuclear Disarmament, and so on'. As he complained to Samuel in December 1961:

> I have also SIX CLASSES, plus additional teaching for hospital administrators (NINE classes this week) plus being on four Department Committees, plus three children who keep having Guy Fawkes and birthdays, plus a miraculous growth of YCND [Youth CND] and CND in Halifax this past two months – which after so many dead years we can't just ignore (from nought to 150 for YCND in two months!) – plus the correspondence of Chairing a Board [of *New Left Review*] you may have heard of. My only affinity to Marx is that I get boils on my neck.[23]

There was also conflict within the New Left: between the old guard around Thompson and the next generation. In June 1960 he had actually briefly resigned completely from the Board; eventually, in April 1963, a second New Left took control of the *NLR*, with Perry Anderson as editor. For Thompson it was a coup, yet Anderson considered there had been 'an abdication'.[24]

When R. W. Harris wanted 'a textbook on the British labour movement, 1832 to 1945' for 'The Men and Ideas Series', intended for sixth-formers and university students, and which he was editing for Victor Gollancz, he approached John Saville. Saville declined, but recommended Thompson. Thompson suggested 1790 as the starting date; and because, as he afterwards admitted, 'I was hard up', in August 1959 a contract was signed for 'a book on "Working-Class Politics, 1790–1921", to be "approximately 60,000 words in length"'.[25]

As early as November 1953 Thompson had planned

As soon as my Morris is through the press ... to start work on a short history of the people of the West Riding (social and industrial) from about 1750 to the present day: this would take anything up to 10 years to complete, but it is something we need very much indeed in our tutorial class work, as a kind of companion volume to Cole & Postgate's 'Common People'.

In December 1955 he intended to apply for a Leverhulme Research Award in order to write this book, but over Christmas he mislaid the papers and missed the closing date; and his application twelve months later was unsuccessful. By then he was envisaging a study that was 'mainly nineteenth century' and was 'not a comprehensive work of detailed scholarship'. His Leverhulme Fellowship did not materialise until 1962–63 – at the very *end* of the writing of *The Making of the English Working Class*. But the outcome of the aborted and failed applications of the mid-1950s was a teaching programme reduced to half in the two years 1957–59, to allow him to 'devote extra time to research on aspects of the social and political history of the West Riding'.[26] The two projects, the social and industrial history of the West Riding and the textbook for Gollancz, were to fuse and emerged, radically transformed, as *The Making of the English Working Class*. The result is probably the most influential historical work to have been published in English since the Second World War.[27]

The key section of *William Morris: Romantic to Revolutionary* for my argument – and for Thompson's intellectual and political development – is the fourth and final part: 'Necessity and Desire'; and within it, especially, the sub-section, 'Desire and Necessity', with these central terms significantly reversed. 'Necessity' is Marxist economic determinism, the course of the productive forces and the relations of production in society. 'Desire', in contrast, is morality, conscience, human will and, what became for Thompson the defining term, 'agency'.[28] (See chapter 1.) Operating in tandem, 'desire' and 'necessity' together constitute 'moral realism'. This is the quality upon which Thompson identifies Morris's 'claim to greatness' being founded.[29]

Thompson quotes Morris distinguishing between 'the two great forces which rule the world, Necessity and Morality': 'if we give it all up into the hands of necessity, Society will explode volcanically with such a crash as the world has not yet witnessed'; and, again, from 'The Society of the Future':

I am not going into argument on the matter of free will and predestination; I am only going to assert that if individual men are the creatures of their surrounding conditions, as indeed I think they are, it must be the business of man as a social animal ... to make the surroundings which make the individual man what he is. Man must and does create the conditions under which he lives.[30]

In a passage excised from the second edition of 1977, Thompson contends:

This unity, in the fight for Socialism, of necessity and desire ... is central to the thought of Marx and Engels. It is perhaps Morris's most important contribution to English culture to have brought his rich store of historical and artistic knowledge, and the passionate moral insight of a great artist, to the task of revealing the full meaning of this.[31]

Yet elsewhere in the book Thompson criticises Morris for being, in effect, too Marxist: 'Morris has not emphasised sufficiently the *ideological* role of art, its active agency in *changing* human beings and society as a whole, its agency in man's class-divided history'; and again: 'while this dialectical understanding of change, growth and decay, was everpresent in his writing, he saw man's economic and social development always as the master-process, and tended to suggest that the arts were passively dependent upon social change'.[32] Raymond Williams cited these two passages in *Culture and Society*, rightly commenting of the latter: 'It has normally been assumed that this was precisely what Marx taught, and the position that Marxists wished to defend ... Morris's "master-process" ... is surely Marx's "real foundation", which "determines consciousness".'[33]

Morris's insistence upon the central role of morality must have been influenced by – maybe even derived from – his collaborator, the heterodox Marxist, Ernest Belfort Bax, co-author with him of 'Socialism from the Root up', serialised in 23 articles in *Commonweal* between 1886 and 1888, and reprinted in 1893 as *Socialism: Its Growth and Outcome*. Bax, who had been partly educated in Germany and was an initiate of its philosophy, recast historical materialism by stressing the autonomy of other ideas also and of cultural factors in general, just as Thompson himself (despite a disparaging assessment of Bax) was eventually to do.[34]

Thompson was later to consider 'Morris, by 1955, had claimed me';[35] and we can see that he had already begun to revise classical Marxism in this volume, rather remarkably published by the CP's Lawrence and

Wishart. In what must have been his last interview he contended, too sweepingly: 'Apart from my first edition of *William Morris*, I haven't written any pious, orthodox Marxist history at all.'[36] He came to realise that 'Morris could (and did) take certain Marxist propositions as his point of departure, but used these as a springboard from which his imagination made a utopian leap'; and that 'Morris may be assimilated to Marxism only in the course of a process of self-criticism and re-ordering within Marxism itself'.[37] What this entailed, practically, was that: 'When, in 1956, my disagreements with orthodox Marxism became fully articulate, I fell back on modes of perception which I'd learned in those years of close company with Morris.'[38] In his editorials and articles in the *Reasoner*, the *NR* and the early *NLR*, Morris's name and example are continually invoked and the dialectical interaction between necessity and desire elaborated upon. Especially noteworthy articles are 'Socialist Humanism' (*NR*, 1, Summer 1957) and 'Agency and Choice' (*NR*, 5, Summer 1958).

The emphasis on agency is what I referred to at the outset as the organising innovation of *The Making of the English Working Class*, which is structured in part by the rejection of academic positivist social science but, fundamentally, by a critique of Marxist orthodoxy, 'which supposed that the working class was the more-or-less spontaneous generation of new productive forces and relations'.[39] *The Making of the English Working Class* opens famously:

> This book has a clumsy title, but it is one which meets its purpose. *Making*, because it is a study in an active process, which owes as much to agency as to conditioning. The working class did not rise like the sun at an appointed time. It was present at its own making.[40]

Thompson thus derived the foundation of his life's work – its 'key organising theme', as Perry Anderson has put it[41] – from his great predecessor, William Morris. His odyssey from Stalinism to libertarian communism had been virtually effected in terms of theory as early as 1955. For Thompson, 'the prevailing note of Morris's later actions and writings [is] the appeal to man's conscience as a vital agency of social change'.[42] Similarly, he believed that Morris discovered independently

> The understanding that ... the age-old contradiction between the unfolding possibilities of life and their negation by class oppression, between aspiration and reality, was at last ended; or, if not ended, at last transmuted into the contradiction between man's boundless desire and the necessary limitations imposed by his environment and nature.[43]

'The writing' of *The Making of the English Working Class*, Thompson explained in 1980,

> was only possible because some part of the research had already been laid down during the previous ten years in the course of my work as a tutor in extra-mural classes in the West Riding. Discussion in these classes, as well as practical political activity of several kinds, undoubtedly prompted me to see the problems of political consciousness and organization in certain ways.[44]

As noted in chapter 2, most of the courses Thompson taught were three-year tutorial classes, running for 24 weeks each year, from September to April. Each staff tutor took four or five classes each winter. Thompson generally taught only four evenings, but in two years (1953–54 and 1954–55) this rose to five.

Although the Leeds extramural area reached north as far as Teesside, Thompson's classes were overwhelmingly located in the old West Riding and principally in the textile region (roughly present-day West Yorkshire). So he had classes that lasted between one and four years in Ossett, Batley, Cleckheaton, Shepley (not Shipley, but 'a small industrial valley, south-west of Huddersfield'),[45] Bingley, Todmorden, Keighley, Leeds, Halifax and Morley. Outside, but still in the West Riding, were Hemsworth and Harrogate. To the north were Northallerton in the North Riding and, in Cleveland, Middlesbrough and, but only after *The Making of the English Working Class* had been written, Brotton.

Central to this activity were Batley, Cleckheaton and Halifax. A four-year literature class in Batley (1948–52) was followed by a three-year history class (1952–55); and after an interval of a year another three-year class in literature ran (1956–59). At Cleckheaton three years in literature (1948–51) were succeeded by two years in history (1951–53). Although he lived in Halifax Thompson did not teach in the town until 1954, when he began a three-year tutorial in history that lasted until 1957; and he had another three-year class there, from 1959 to 1962, in literature (and began a second literature class in 1963, the autumn that *The Making of the English Working Class* was published).

Thompson's history classes were on 'The Social and Industrial History of England'. The initial structure was: first year, 1780–1848; second year, 1848–1900; third year, 1900–50. When they were offered at Halifax and Northallerton in 1954–55, the opening date had been pushed back to 1750, although the first year was still to conclude in 1848. But the first year of a class in Keighley the preceding session had only reached 1832; and thereafter the period of the first year was fixed as 1750–1832 (and the second year as 1832–80, although the final year still came up the present day).

By the first repeat (Keighley 1953–4), the syllabus opened with the following preamble:

> This three-year course will deal with the life of the British people – their work, their leisure, their struggles for political freedom, industrial rights, and knowledge – from the eighteenth century to the present day. Special attention will be given to the social and industrial changes in the West Riding of Yorkshire, and to the growth of the working-class movement – trade unions, co-operatives, and political and educational societies: but the life of all classes in all parts of Britain will also be discussed. From time to time, aspects of the art, literature, and political and economic thought of each period will be discussed.
>
> It is not necessary to have any previous knowledge of history to join the class. Anyone with a serious interest in the subject will be able to keep up with the work, provided that he or she is ready to observe three conditions:
>
> (1) To attend regularly the 24 weekly meetings (between September and April) each year.
>
> (2) To read each week at least one chapter (and more if possible) of the books suggested by the Tutor.
>
> (3) To write, from time to time, comments or brief essays on aspects of the subject which interest them. In the first year, four such pieces of writing will be required. [In all later syllabuses this second requirement was dropped.]
>
> While allowance is made for the difficulties of members of the class (overtime, illness, other commitments, etc.), these conditions are laid down by a firm tradition in tutorial classes, in order to make sure that the work is really enjoyable and worth-while. The aim of the class is not to provide a series of lectures, followed by questions, but to engage in the co-operative study and discussion of problems which concern us all, and upon which every member of the class will have some special knowledge or viewpoint.[46]

The reading lists were unimpressive. Cole and Postgate's *The Common People* afforded the basic reading throughout – although described by Thompson in a class report as merely of 'some use to students wanting a sort of railway guide to events' – and was the text most frequently recommended for weekly preparation.[47]

The subject matter of the syllabuses was always more distinctive. By Leeds in 1959 – and the beginning of the writing of *The Making of the English Working Class* – the syllabus afforded a partial outline of the book completed more than three years later:

In the first year we will be engaged in the study of the period 1750 to 1832.

This course is designed to do the following things: (a) There will be general lectures on major trends and events in social, political and industrial history in Britain during these years; (b) There will be closer discussion of the dominant political and (to a less extent) religious ideas and controversies of the time, linked to selected texts; (c) There will be more detailed study of certain movements and events in the West Riding of Yorkshire, taking – where possible – examples from the Leeds region.

Any members of the class who can find time to do additional research into local history will be encouraged to bring their results into the general work of the class.

The course will probably develop along the following lines:

i. *Eighteenth-Century England*
The structure of English society in the second half of the eighteenth century. Population, and the revolution in agriculture. Religious controversy and the Wesleyan movement.
Special Yorkshire Topic: Religious controversy and Methodism in the West Riding.

ii. *French Revolution and English Reform*
The various sections of the people working for political reform. The impact of the French Revolution. Agitation for Reform, and repression.
Political Theory: Rousseau, *Social Contract*; Paine, *Rights of Man*; Burke, *Reflections upon the French Revolution*.
Special Yorkshire Topic: Rev. Christopher Wyvill and the Yorkshire Reformers of the 1780s; the Sheffield Corresponding

Society and the Leeds Constitutional Society of the 1790s.

iii. *The Industrial Revolution*
Population, agriculture and industry. Cotton and exports. Coal, iron and steam power.
Special Yorkshire Topic: Change in the Woollen and Worsted Industries.

iv. *Some Intellectual and Social Consequences of Industrialism*
Political Theory: Extracts from Adam Smith; Malthus; Bentham; Cobbett; Robert Owen; the Romantic Poets.
Special Yorkshire Topic: The Luddite Movement in West Yorkshire.

v. *England in the 1820s*
A general survey of social life after Peterloo. The struggle for the Reform Bill of 1832.
Yorkshire Topics:
(a) Early working conditions in Yorkshire mills and pits.
(b) The role of Baines and the *Leeds Mercury* in the struggle for the 1832 Reform Bill.

Who constituted the student body in these classes? The proportion of manual workers in tutorial classes was declining, while members of the lower middle class and teachers were much in evidence. The following table, derived from the departmental statistics, gives a breakdown of enrolments in Thompson's classes in 1954–55.

	Batley	*Halifax*	*Keighley*	*Northallerton*
Total in class	12	19	16	11
Manual workers	6	5	2	1
Non-manual workers	2	9	10	6
Teachers	1	1	1	–
Professional workers	1	–	–	–
Housewives	2	3	3	4

Since the only other occupational categories allowed are 'Not in paid work' and 'Unknown', 'Non-manual workers' must conflate working-class and middle-class jobs. This is borne out by Thompson's description of his students at Northallerton (where the North Riding County

Council offices were located) as 'largely made up of civil servants, housewives, retired persons (including two active in the Conservative Party) and "white-collar" workers'.[48] The 'retired persons' included a former grammar-school master and a doctor.[49]

More revealing than the statistical returns are Thompson's pen portraits of class membership (an assessment which would have delighted him, given his aversion to such tabularisation and what he and Dorothy dubbed 'Rudéfication'). So Batley in 1953 had 'two doctors, housewives, a textile worker, printer, painter, saw-mill manager, rag, wool, and waste merchant, post office engineer, clerical worker, and head teacher'.[50] Of Todmorden in 1951–52 he observed: 'The class members vary from a station-master with a degree in economics to two manual workers, and include an administrator in education who has been in his time a miner, a textile worker, and a schoolmaster.' At Leeds in 1959–60 the occupations were 'satisfactorily diverse, ranging from University Teacher to Crane Driver, Centre-lathe Turner to Typist ... Civil Servant, Teacher, Shop Assistant, Motor Engineer'.[51]

Despite the two Conservatives at Northallerton, most of the students seem to have been Labour supporters, many of these active party members, including councillors. There was a least one communist – one of the doctors at Batley, who was a Czech *émigré*. A good number were prominent in the peace movement of the early 1950s and then in CND and the New Left (Left Clubs were formed for the West Riding, meeting in Leeds, at Bradford, at Harrogate and on Teesside). Among these militants were Dorothy and Joe Greenald, to whom *The Making of the English Working Class* is dedicated. Students in the literature class at Cleckheaton in 1948–51, and then in the history class in 1951–53, they were expelled from the Labour Party for membership of the proscribed Federation of West Yorkshire Peace Organisations; they were very briefly in the CPGB (joining under Thompson's influence, they resigned with him six weeks later!); they were two of the six persons responsible for the administration of the *NR* (Joe Greenald was treasurer); and they became lifelong close friends of the Thompson family.[52]

Not all the activism – and experience – was contemporary. In the Batley history class one of the members, then 'in his late seventies', was 'the first ILP Councillor in Batley (1906)', and in 1954–55 he gave 'a most exciting and informative talk ... on the problems and controversies of local government in Batley between 1906 and

1914'. The following year he was invited to the Keighley class to give 'a reminiscent lecture ... which was tape-recorded'.[53] Also at Batley, and still within living memory, was the description by a significantly older man and fervent Gladstonian of 'his speech at the School Board election of 1877'.[54]

One or two of the class members were able to provide indirect, but personal, links to the period and subject matter of *The Making of the English Working Class*. At Cleckheaton the great-grandfather of a student had been named Feargus O'Connor (Ewart) after the Chartist leader.[55] At Batley in 1953 another 'revealed herself in the last evening to have been a lifelong collector of old songs and ballads'; and in his report Thompson quoted in full an example taken down 'fifteen to twenty years ago' from 'a blind workhouse inmate (who thought the song "Chartist")', but which he himself judged plausibly as 'an early (eighteenth century?) song – possibly sung at primitive trade-union ceremonies':

> Lo! here is fellowship!
> One faith to hold,
> One troth to seek,
> One wrong to wreake,
> And to dip in one dish faithfullische [*sic*]
> As lambkins of one fold,
> Either for other to suffer all thing,
> One song to sing, in sweet accord
> And maken melody.
> Lo! here is fellowship![56]

In ways such as these Thompson would have felt close to the years of the industrial revolution; and they would be reinforced by the semi-rural character and primitive technology of much of West Yorkshire (and which continue to survive in the early twenty-first century).[57] So of Morley in 1963–4 he was to comment, after the publication of *The Making of the English Working Class*:

> Within living memory ... it seems, miners have worked lying down in eighteen-inch seams, children have been in the mills at the age of nine, urine has been collected from pub urinals for scouring, while the brother of one of the students still uses teazles to raise the 'nap'. It is difficult to believe that the industrial revolution has yet occurred in Morley, and next year's syllabus (in the later 19th century) will seem like a tour through the space age.

But Thompson's students didn't contribute to his historical under-standing solely by reminiscence. They were also encouraged to engage in research of some kind. Of Batley in 1953 he enthused:

> In sum ... this class began to show signs of becoming what I had once dreamed a tutorial class in industrial Yorkshire could be like – but which I had never before begun to experience. Students have followed their own interests in their reading, and have not been afraid of original sources: a clerk working in local government has studied reports of the Poor Law Commissioners: a doctor prepared notes on the medical evidence in Dr Thackrah's study of Leeds (after saying he could not *possibly* find time for written work): a merchant did some detailed reading in Burnley's *History of Wool and Woolcombing* and in other nineteenth-century [treatises] on technical innovations in textile machinery: my copies of such books as Fielden's *Curse of the Factory System*, Bamford's *Life*, the trial of Hunt (after Peterloo), and Dodd's *Letters on the Factory System* have been eagerly read. At one time I loaned out some instal-ments of Wade's *Black Book*, and five students prepared interventions for class discussion from them, ranging from the abuses of the East India Company to the misgovernment of Charitable Institutions and the Expense of the Established Clergy. All were surprised at the interest of the documents, and the ease with which they could be read.[58]

Two students are acknowledged by name in the preface to *The Making of the English Working Class* among eleven people who 'have helped me at different points' (the others being Perry Anderson, Denis Butt, Richard Cobb, Henry Collins, Tim Enright, E. P. Hennock, Rex Russell, John Rex and Eric Sigsworth).[59] Both wrote essays, for direct entry to Cambridge, on key topics of reinterpretation in *The Making*.

Oliver Swift from Batley produced a 'very good paper', 'The Yorkshire Luddites of 1812', 'which introduced some new and inter-esting theories'.[60] Swift, in his concluding section, 'The Political Motives of the Luddites', took seriously the books of Frank Peel and the other local late Victorian writers, and attempted, sketchily, to situate Luddism in a context of English Jacobinism, suggesting, for example, that 'some croppers ... were Painites, or even members of the "United Englishmen"'.[61]

Derrick Crossley, a member of the 1948–51 literature class at Cleck-heaton (and also in a rival economic and social history class tutored by Thompson's colleague, Jack Prichard), was helped to produce an impres-sive essay on 'The Handloom Weavers in the Industrial Revolution: With Particular Reference to the West Riding of Yorkshire', which won him the Cambridge Extramural Scholarship in 1951. Crossley was, in Dorothy Thompson's judgement, one of the best students her husband ever had – at Leeds or Warwick – and indeed he was enlisted for the 'intense experience' of 'a week of research' in London with Thompson for *William Morris: Romantic to Revolutionary*. Born in 1925, the son of weavers, he himself was a laboratory assistant. For his work on the handloom weavers,

> Over a period of 3–4 months at the end of 1950 I made an effort that I have not equalled since. I was in weekly contact with Edward during that period by attending his class. How much of what I did was genuinely my own idea and how much came from his prompting I will never know. However, he was pleased with the result though he said it was but a beginning that I should continue later. Unfortunately, I was never in a position to do so, but that doesn't matter since Edward took over the best of it.[62]

Edward Thompson naturally made an indelible impact on his students:

> I was struck by his sheer enthusiasm, also a little bit awed by his undoubted intellect, which, combined with his humour, and his articulate and graphic method of expression, made his classes fascinating.

> The mixture of students, old, young, verbose, garrulous, set the stage for an evening – unpredictable – exciting, anything could happen.[63]

Derrick Crossley concluded:

> there is no doubt in my mind that Edward was exceptional. His sustained enthusiasm; his sharp eye for flannel, hypocrisy; his enormous energy; and his sympathetic (empathetic?) approach to the limited intellectual experience of his students – all these characteristics made it clear, despite his middle-class mannerisms, that he had a serious purpose and he was not patronising anyone.[64]

Edward Thompson's classes were not, then, a one-sided process, not just a flow from a tutor of outstanding gifts to his students. They consisted of a two-way interaction, which led him to conclude that 'the dynamic of the tutorial class movement has been derived ... from a fruitful conflict or interplay between the scholarship of the universities on the one hand, and the experience and social dynamic of the students on the other'. He believed that 'universities engage in adult education not only to teach but also to learn' – as he undoubtedly had himself.[65]

Notes

1 E. P. Thompson, *The Making of the English Working Class* (London: Victor Gollancz, 1963), p. 14.

2 M. Merrill, 'An Interview with E. P. Thompson', in MARHO, *Visions of History* (Manchester: Manchester University Press, 1983), p. 13.

3 Leeds University Archive (LUA), Adult Education and Extramural Studies: Supplementary Papers, Thompson to Registrar, application, 18 March 1948.

4 H. Drasdo, 'Alex Comfort's Art and Scope', *Anarchy*, 33 (November 1963), p. 355. E. P. Thompson, *Collected Poems* (Newcastle upon Tyne: Bloodaxe, 1999), was the first gathering, but included a booklet of 1983, *Infant and Emperor: Poems for Christmas*. For a rare discussion of Thompson's prose, see P. Anderson, 'Diary', *London Review of Books* (21 October 1993), reprinted in P. Anderson, *Spectrum* (London: Verso, 2005).

5 Information of the late Dorothy Thompson, to whom overall I am much indebted. For her autobiographical reflections, see D. Thompson, *Outsiders: Class, Gender, Nation* (London: Verso, 1993), 'Introduction', as well as the interview with S. Rowbotham, 'The Personal and the Political', *New Left Review*, 200 (July/August 1993).

6 See E. P. Thompson (ed.), *Warwick University Ltd* (Harmondsworth: Penguin, 1970).

7 A. Croft, 'Walthamstow, Little Gidding and Middlesbrough: Edward Thompson the Literature Tutor', *Socialist History*, 8 (1995) (a shorter version of which was published in R. Taylor (ed.), *Beyond the Walls: 50 Years of Adult and Continuing Education at the University of Leeds, 1946–1996* [Leeds: University of Leeds, 1996]), discusses Thompson as a teacher of literature.

8 E. J. Hobsbawm, 'The Historians' Group of the Communist Party', in M. Cornforth (ed.), *Rebels and Their Causes: Essays in Honour of A. L. Morton* (London: Lawrence & Wishart, 1978), p. 28; M. Bess, *Realism, Utopia and the Mushroom Cloud: Four Activist Intellectuals and Their Strategies for Peace, 1945–1989* (Chicago: University of Chicago Press, 1993), pp. 100–1; E. P. Thompson, 'Protest and Revise', *END Journal*, 37 (1989), pp. 36–7; Merrill, 'An Interview with E. P. Thompson', p. 13.

9 Department of Adult Education and Extramural Studies, University of Leeds, *Twenty-One Years of Adult Education, 1946–67*; S. G. Raybould, 'Leeds University Department of Adult Education and Extra-Mural Studies', *Tutors' Bulletin of Adult Education*, 85 (January 1952). See also J. F. C. Harrison, *Learning and Living, 1790–1960: A Study in the History of the English Adult Education Movement* (London: Routledge & Kegan Paul, 1961), pp. 341–4.

10 LUA, Department of History, Thompson file: letters from Thompson to G. Chapman, 11 June, 20 August 1950; G. Chapman to E. P. Thompson, 19 June 1950; G. Chapman to Registrar, 29 June 1950; Adult Education and

Extramural Studies: Supplementary Papers, letter from Registrar to E. P. Thompson, 17 October 1950.

11 Merrill, 'An Interview with E. P. Thompson', p. 13; LUA, Departmental Records: Adult Education, letter from E. P. Thompson to S. G. Raybould, 20 December [1950]. The emphases are Thompson's.

12 E. P. Thompson, 'The Murder of William Morris', *Arena* (April/May 1951). See also E. P. Thompson, 'William Morris and the Moral Issues To-Day', in *The American Threat to British Culture* (*Arena* special issue [1951]), and E. P. Thompson, *William Morris: Romantic to Revolutionary* (London: Lawrence & Wishart, 1955) [hereafter *WMRR* (1955)], pp. 741–6.

13 Cf. B. Schwartz, '"The People" in History: The Communist Party Historians' Group, 1946–56', in Centre for Contemporary Cultural Studies, *Making Histories: Studies in History-Writing and Politics* (London: Hutchinson, 1982), p. 77.

14 LUA, Department of History, Thompson file: letter from G. Chapman to Registrar, 6 July 1951; letter from E. P. Thompson to J. Le Patourel, 10 October [1953]; letters from E. P. Thompson to N. Gash, 29 November, 5 December 1953; letter from N. Gash to E. P. Thompson, 8 December 1953.

15 People's History Museum, Manchester: Communist Party Archive, Dona Torr Papers, CP/IND/TORR/01/03, letter from E. P. Thompson to J. Klugmann, 3 January [1956]. The emphasis is Thompson's.

16 A. Briggs and J. Saville (eds), *Essays in Labour History* (London: Macmillan, 1960). This essay is reprinted in E. P. Thompson, *Persons and Polemics* (London: Merlin Press, 1994).

17 Torr Papers, CP/IND/TORR/01/03; D. Torr, *Tom Mann and His Times: Volume One (1856–1890)* (London, Lawrence & Wishart, 1956); *WMRR* (1955), p. 8.

18 Personal papers of John Saville: letters from E. P. Thompson to J. Saville, n.d. [January (?) 1957], and to R. Swingler, K. Alexander and J. Saville, n.d. [March(?) 1957]; Torr Papers, CP/IND/TORR/01/03: letter from J. Klugmann to J. Gollan, 13 December 1956. (I am exceptionally grateful to the late John Saville for unrestricted access to his archive, now in the Brynmor Jones Library, University of Hull.)

19 [E. P. Thompson], 'Tom Mann and His Times, 1890–92', *Our History*, 26–7 (Summer/Autumn 1962); Communist Party Archive, CP/Cent/Cult/8/4.

20 N. Wood, *Communism and British Intellectuals* (London, Victor Gollancz, 1959), pp. 194 *et seq.*; J. Saville, 'The Twentieth Congress and the British Communist Party', in R. Miliband and J. Saville (eds), *The Socialist Register*, 1976; J. Saville, 'Edward Thompson, the Communist Party and 1956', in R. Miliband and L. Panitch (eds), *The Socialist Register*, 1994.

21 The best work on the New Left is Lin Chun, *The British New Left* (Edinburgh, Edinburgh University Press, 1993). There is also M. Kenny, *The First New*

Left: British Intellectuals after Stalin (London: Lawrence & Wishart, 1995).

22 R. Taylor, *Against the Bomb: The British Peace Movement, 1958–1965* (Oxford, Clarendon Press, 1988), is the major work on the first nuclear disarmament movement. See also chapter 9, *passim*.

23 E. P. Thompson, *The Making of the English Working Class* (Harmondsworth: Penguin, 3rd edn, 1980) [hereafter *MEWC* (1980)], p. 14; letter to R. Samuel, 1 December [1961] (now in the closed Thompson Papers, Bodleian Library, Oxford).

24 S. Hamilton, *The Crisis of Theory: E. P. Thompson, the New Left and Postwar British Politics* (Manchester and New York: Manchester University Press, 2011), pp. 96–105; P. Anderson, *Arguments within English Marxism* (London: Verso, 1980), pp. 135–6. For further discussion of Thompson's work in the early New Left, see chapter 8, *passim*.

25 J. Saville, *Memoirs from the Left* (London: Merlin Press, 2003), p. 119; Merrill, 'An Interview with E. P. Thompson', p. 14; *MEWC* (1980), p. 14.

26 LUA, Department of History, Thompson file: letter to N. Gash, 29 November 1953; LUA Departmental Records: Adult Education, letters to S. G. Raybould, 15 December 1955, 3 January [1956], 11 December [1956], 10 March [1957]; Department of Adult Education and Extramural Studies, University of Leeds, *Annual Report*, 1958–59.

27 Cf. E. J. Hobsbawm's splendid obituary of Thompson, *Independent*, 30 August 1993, reprinted in *Radical History Review*, 58 (Winter 1994). See also E. J. Hobsbawm, 'Edward Palmer Thompson, 1924–1993', *Proceedings of the British Academy*, XC (1996), pp. 527–8, 536–9.

28 *WMRR* (1955), p. 838.

29 *Ibid.*, p.828.

30 *Ibid.*, p. 838.

31 *Ibid.*, p. 837.

32 *Ibid.*, pp. 763, 770 (Thompson's emphases).

33 R. Williams, *Culture and Society, 1780–1950* (Harmondsworth: Penguin, 1961), p. 265.

34 R. Kinna, *William Morris: The Art of Socialism* (Cardiff: University of Wales Press, 2000), pp. 97–9, 110–12; E. Belfort Bax, *Reminiscences and Reflexions of a Mid and Late Victorian* (1918; New York: A. M. Kelley, 1967), pp. 46–8; E. P. Thompson, *William Morris: Romantic to Revolutionary* (London: Merlin Press, 2nd edn, 1977) [hereafter *WMRR* (1977)], pp. 372–5. See also M. Bevir, 'Ernest Belfort Bax: Marxist, Idealist, and Positivist', *Journal of the History of Ideas*, LIV (1993), esp. pp. 131–5.

35 *WMRR* (1977), p. 810.

36 'Edward Thompson, 1924–1993: Scholar and Activist' [edited transcript of BBC Radio Three interview, 20 May 1993], *Socialist History*, 6 (Autumn 1994), p. 29.

37 *WMRR* (1977), pp. 790, 802.

38 *Ibid.*, p. 810.

39 *MEWC* (1980), p. 14. See also Merrill, 'An Interview with E. P. Thompson', pp. 6–7; and 'Edward Thompson, 1924–1993', *Socialist History*.

40 *MEWC* (1963), p. 9.

41 Anderson, *Arguments*, pp. 159, 161–2.

42 *WMRR* (1955), p. 831. Gregor McLennan is dishonest in implying that this emphasis is new to the 1977 edition, where it merely reads 'the prevailing note of Morris's later actions and writings [is] the appeal to *the moral consciousness* as a vital agency of social change' (*WMRR* (1977), p. 721 (my italics)), although he is certainly right that the claim that 'Morris's moral criticism of society is … entirely compatible with dialectical materialism' (*WMRR* (1955), p. 832) is omitted from the second edition ('E. P. Thompson and the Discipline of Historical Context' in Centre for Contemporary Cultural Studies, *Making Histories*, p. 108).

43 *WMRR* (1955), p. 835.

44 *MEWC* (1980), p. 14.

45 LUA, Departmental Records: Adult Education, Box 47, Joint Tutorial Classes Committee Reports on Classes, Shepley, 1948–49.

46 This and Thompson's other syllabuses were preserved in the School of Continuing Education Archive now in LUA, Departmental Records, Adult Education and Extramural Studies, Supplementary Papers.

47 LUA, Departmental Records: Adult Education, Box 47 and Supplementary papers, Reports on Classes [hereafter RC] Cleckheaton, 1951/2. Thompson's class reports, often lengthy, were transcribed in the annual duplicated reports produced by his Department (a set of which is in the writer's possession).

48 RC, Northallerton, 1954/55.

49 *Ibid.*, 1956–57.

50 RC, Batley, 1952–53.

51 Ellipsis in the original.

52 I am especially grateful to the late Dorothy Greenald for this and other information, general assistance – and much encouragement. See D. Goodway, 'Dorothy Greenald', *Guardian*, 15 April 2002, for her obituary.

53 RC, Batley, 1954–55; Keighley, 1955–56.

54 RC, Batley, 1953–54.

55 Letter from Ann (Margaret Pyrah) to D. Greenald [3 September 1993] (in the present author's possession).

56 RC, Batley, 1952–53.

57 For the Calder Valley as it remained in the 1990s, see an admirable article by a local writer: G. Hughes, 'Withering Heights', *Observer Magazine*, 30 May 1993. From two decades earlier there is G. Hughes, *Millstone Grit* (London: Victor Gollancz, 1975).

58 RC, Batley, 1952–53. See also Batley, 1953–54; Hemsworth, 1956–57.

59 *MEWC* (1963), p. 14.

60 RC, Batley, 1953–54.

61 I am indebted to the late Oliver Swift for his memories and the loan of his essay. See E. P. Thompson, 'Introduction to the Fourth Edition', F. Peel, *The Risings of the Luddites, Chartists and Plug-Drawers* (London: Frank Cass, 1968).

62 Letters from D. Crossley to the author, 6 October, 6, 30 November 1993; LUA, Departmental Records: Adult Education, letter from E. P. Thompson to S. G. Raybould, 20 December [1950]; RC, Cleckheaton, 1950/51; *WMRR* (1955), p. 8. It was Jack Prichard who discovered among his papers a copy of Crossley's essay, which was then forwarded to its author, who had been unable to locate his own.

63 Letter from Iris Inesome to D. Greenald [August 1992]. This letter (now in the present author's possession) was written for the use of Peter Searby when he was researching his excellent contribution to 'Edward Thompson as a Teacher: Yorkshire and Warwick', in J. Rule and R. Malcolmson (eds), *Protest and Survival: The Historical Experience: Essays for E. P. Thompson* (London: Merlin Press, 1993), pp. 1–17.

64 Letter of 6 November 1993.

65 E. P. Thompson, 'Against University Standards: Comments upon the Reflections of Messrs Baxandall, Shaw, and McLeish', *Adult Education Papers* (University of Leeds), I, 4 (July 1950), p. 18; E. P. Thompson, *Education and Experience* (Leeds: Leeds University Press, 1968), p. 23.

4

The possibilities of theory: Thompson's Marxist history

Theodore Koditschek

As E. P. Thompson's historical writings recede ever further into their own past, his legacy seems difficult to assess. His books continue to be read by the dwindling tribe of British social historians, and he is remembered throughout the academic world as a progenitor of cultural studies, and as a founding father of 'history from below'. Yet his lifelong engagement with Marxism is often downplayed, even though, for many who came of age during the 1970s, it was Thompson's fusion of Marxism with social history that constituted the central attraction of his work.[1] In an age when Marxism has lost its lustre, it is hardly surprising that this attraction has faded but, in truth, Thompson himself bore a degree of responsibility for subsequent dismissals of the Marxist dimension in his work. For Thompson was a highly unorthodox Marxist, constantly at loggerheads with what he perceived as dogmatic official creeds. His rejection of Stalinism in 1956 was reprised during the 1960s through his polemic against Perry Anderson, and again, during the 1970s, in his even more furious polemic against Althusserian structuralism, which he depicted as some kind of Stalinism of the student left.[2]

That these thunderings ought not to be taken entirely at face value was tacitly acknowledged in a meditative moment when Thompson candidly admitted that 'it is only by facing into opposition that I am able to define my thought at all'.[3] Unfortunately, there is a price to be paid for such 'negative dialectics', and it is hardly surprising that a literal reading of these broadsides has convinced many that Thompson was never really much of a Marxist. This, in my view, is a mistake, since it obscures the degree to which his intellectual power (as well as his personal charisma) was bound up in his lifelong engagement with the politics of socialism and the theories of Marx. Indeed, if Thompson is worth rescuing from the condescension of posterity, it is surely not as some generic 'culturalist' or 'populist', but rather as the pioneer of a non-reductionist Marxist historical analysis that repudiated the dogmas of orthodox materialism in order to reconstitute theory through engagement with socialist practice and empirical research.

The making of working-class agency

Consider, for example, Thompson's famous Preface to *The Making of the English Working Class*. Fifty years on, this is often read in isolation from the lengthy volume it introduces, and is taken as a simple exhortation to recover the voice of the oppressed.[4] In its own time, however, when this document actually served as a preface, it signposted the way towards an unexplored continent of history that the scholarship of the day had scarcely opened up. Thompson's book would be grounded in Marxist theory, but it would remain open to the contingency of empirical evidence and the activity of human subjects. The author defiantly repudiated dogmatic Stalinism, but he rejected equally the consensus sociology and politics of the West. Class formation, he avowed, was a dynamic, interactive process that 'owes as much to agency as conditioning'. The productive relations of capitalism might well determine the class experience, but they afforded no formula for the 'class-consciousness', which handled these experiences 'in cultural terms'. 'Consciousness of class arises in the same way in different times and places, but never in *just* the same way.'[5]

Taken out of context (as it frequently is), this quote invites dismissal as a sophistical evasion. Yet Thompson pre-empts this reaction in his opening paragraph with the seemingly innocent observation that 'the English working class ... was present at its own making'. This simple point was historiographically ground-breaking because it opened the way for a new understanding of the proper relationship between structure and agency. Social structures could no longer be conceived as external abstractions, exogenous to the flow of *particular* events. Since they were constantly being made and remade by human agents, they had to be depicted in motion. 'If we stop history at a given point, then there are no classes, but simply a multitude of individuals. ... But if we watch these men over an adequate period of social change we observe patterns in their relationships, their ideas and their institutions.'[6]

This position was central to Thompson's approach both to history and to theory, and its consequences for his writings were profound. It meant that class formation in England (and presumably elsewhere) had to be apprehended as a singular drama, in which modes of production arose and operated in a distinctive political context, and the proletariat had some say in the way the performance played out. It meant that Thompson's stage would always be filled with people, and this dictated a tripartite organisation for his book. In Part I, they would first appear for an extended inventory of the cultural baggage they would carry with them into the maelstrom ahead. Part II would then put them through the traumas of early industrial capitalism, complicated by counter-revolution in the war against France. In Part III, they (or their children) would finally reappear as a self-conscious working class that was moulded by material structures and social experiences, but was also partly self-made. 'Class rather than classes', he insisted, because the experience of capitalism brought together a range of diverse trades and occupations, and gave them the chance to create a unified (if never uniform) response.[7]

Thompson's long lingering at the threshold of his story (Part I) was disconcerting to some of his early readers, who anticipated a quick horror-house tour of the 'dark satanic mills'. Thompson, however, was determined to take them back to the period just before the factory, since his goal was to show how his working-class subjects had acquired the cultural and psychological resources to survive industrialisation with their humanity intact. In particular, he spent a good hundred pages showing how they drew on the heritage of the 'freeborn Englishman'. This was a legacy bequeathed by their seventeenth-century ancestors, which authorised a series of more specific birthrights: equality before the law, trial by jury, habeas corpus and freedom of expression. Nurtured in a spiritual democracy inherited from Puritanism, these political and religious liberties were compounded in the minds of the people with expectations of economic protection: wage and price regulation, organisation of apprenticeship, and the right of the people to intervene (riot) when these expectations of elite paternalism were not met. Yet, the 'freeborn Englishman' was valuable precisely because it had been envisioned originally as a national rather than a narrowly class-based ideology. In Thompson's account, it was only the refining fires of the French Revolution (and consequent British counter-revolution) that hived off the bourgeois and petit-bourgeois adherents to this creed.

The crucial moment came with the appearance of Tom Paine's *Rights of Man*, which became the rallying point for skilled workers in their efforts to forge an artisanal consciousness that looked towards the revolutionary universalism of the future, while drawing its energy from the English liberties of the past.[8]

In Part II of Thompson's book, the 'freeborn Englishman' is finally put through the paces of proletarianisation. Yet, even here, the dark satanic mills do not entirely dominate the scene. To be sure, the rise of the new (mostly juvenile and female) factory workers is not neglected, but the big story is the decline and deskilling of male artisans. The northern handloom weavers are emblematic of this process, since they show how the rise of the factory and the degradation of crafts-manship were inextricably intertwined. Initially drawn to handloom weaving by the mechanisation of spinning, the men who rapidly populated this craft saw their trade destroyed a few decades later as they fell into competition with one another, and with the newly developed power looms. Yet Thompson shows that deskilling was a more general process, at work on a smaller scale throughout many occupations – tailoring, farming, shoemaking, coachmaking and others – where mechanisation was as yet inconsequential.[9]

More conventional Marxists, such as Perry Anderson, have complained that a full-dress account of the transformation of the mode of production is conspicuously missing from this part of Thompson's book. 'The advent of industrial capitalism in England is a dreadful backcloth to the book rather than a direct object of analysis in its own right.'[10] On a certain level, Anderson's complaint is justified, but it fails to appreciate the theoretical consistency of Thompson's belief that structures reveal themselves only through their impact on actual people. Hence, instead of a thorough reworking of the categories of Marx's *Capital*, Thompson gives us an innovative intervention into the standard-of-living debate. By focusing on the concrete circumstances of actual workers, he discountenances the quest for the average wage of the average earner with which quantitative historians had become obsessed. This average worker, he insists, was a mythical being. His/her 'wage' was a meaningless abstraction that diverted attention away from the realities of exploitation in the flesh. While some workers clearly benefited from market intensification, or mechanisation, the great majority found themselves subject to fines, speed-ups, periodic unemployment and loss of control over the labour process. Correspondingly, they experienced secondary poverty through the perils of

73

urban living – high rents, pollution, malnutrition and overcrowding, or injury, disability, disease and premature death.[11]

According to Thompson, working people were brought to acquiesce in these new conditions by 'the transforming power of the cross'. Particularly at moments of political or organisational defeat, when loss of control in life led to 'a chiliasm of despair', working people were drawn into Wesleyan Methodism's 'box-like, blackening chapels', which 'stood as great traps for the human psyche'. Yet even Methodism (when freed from its Wesleyan fetters) could be rejoined to the legacy of the freeborn Englishman, providing a new vehicle for working-class agency.[12] For industrialisation had enabled working people to create new community structures, such as trade unions, friendly societies and other institutions of mutuality that took root in the manufacturing villages that sprouted like mushrooms around the northern and Midland factory towns. Bringing men and women, English and Irish together, these novel institutions and practices afforded a framework for amplifying the response of beleaguered textile workers to encompass the emergent working-class community as a whole.[13]

Thompson's positing of this new working-class community enables him to rejoin his narrative in Part III of his book. With a deft hand, he shows how workers' steadily intensifying economic grievances were refracted through their sense of political entitlement, as the 'freeborn Englishman' was reworked to fit the circumstances of a capitalist (and also counter-revolutionary) epoch. Diverse trades experienced exploitation in seemingly divergent frameworks, and yet were gradually impelled towards a common response. Government repression distorted popular organisation and expression, leaving it hostage to bombastic demagogues or secret plots. Nevertheless, this interfusion of economic exploitation with state repression ensured that material grievances would always take a broadly *political* form.[14]

In his chapter on Luddism, Thompson hones this argument into a tour de force. The machine breakers, who erupted spontaneously in three disparate regions, were not anachronistic reactionaries who haplessly sought to inhibit the march of progress. They were forerunners of a communitarian political economy that did not so much reject technology as the distorted social relations which made it the bearer of misery to the masses, and profits to a few. Denied adequate redress of their grievances, Thompson allows that some of these workers turned to hopeless conspiracies that were easily penetrated by spies and provocateurs. Yet, during the 1820s, the working-class movement burst out into the open with a multitude of clubs, discussion groups, political associations and industry-wide unions, as collectivist visions for the reorganisation of industry were fused with political demands for democratic reform.[15]

In his final chapter, 'Class Consciousness', Thompson presents the case that the 1832 Reform Act, which uniquely disenfranchised the workers, brought his story of class-*making* to a satisfactory end. 'This collective self-consciousness', he concluded, was 'the great spiritual gain of the Industrial Revolution, against which the disruption of an older and in many ways more humanly comprehensible way of life must be set':

> True enough, one direction of the great agitations of artisans and outworkers, continued over fifty years, was to *resist* being turned into a proletariat. When they knew that this cause was lost, yet they reached out again, in the Thirties and Forties, and sought to achieve new and only imagined forms of social control.[16]

Advancing to the past

Among the first wave of labour historians influenced by Thompson, many turned to the mass movements of the 1830s and 1840s to show what his account of class formation had wrought.[17] Thompson himself, however, continued to be haunted by 'the loss of more humanly comprehensible ways of life' from the earlier period. His original insight that the English working class 'was present at its own making' reminded him that his most urgently unfinished business actually lay at the beginning of his book.[18] If the proletarian class-consciousness with which *The Making of the English Working Class* ended had been built out of cultural resources inherited from the pre-industrial past, from whence had this pre-industrial culture been drawn?

Thompson began to answer this question in a series of essays that he started in the immediate aftermath of his big book. First published was 'The Peculiarities of the English', a characteristic polemic, in which Thompson defined his own approach to early modern English society in opposition to the Marxist structuralism of Perry Anderson and Tom Nairn.[19] Where these authors depicted the evolution of British capitalism as delayed and deficient, Thompson insisted that it had been precocious, even premature. Two full centuries before the industrial revolution, a rural capitalism was already becoming rooted in the English countryside. So far from being atavistic feudal holdovers (as Anderson and Nairn had depicted them), England's gentry and aristocracy were pioneering market producers, whom he went so far as to label an 'agrarian bourgeoisie'. The competitive innovations introduced during this period 'involved not only rent-rolls, improvement and enclosures, but also far-reaching changes in marketing, milling, transport and in the merchandising of exports and imports'. The Revolutionary Settlement of 1688 'registers not some half-way house between "feudalism" and "capitalism" ... but an arrangement exquisitely adjusted to the equilibrium of social forces at that time'.[20]

The major gain that Thompson took away from his encounter with Anderson and Nairn was a new-found appreciation of Antonio Gramsci's theory of hegemony. Thompson had first encountered Gramsci's writings during the late 1950s; however, his acquaintance with them was initially sketchy. Certainly there is no visible trace of Gramscian influence on *The Making of the English Working Class*.[21] It was Thompson's anger at the way Anderson and Nairn were 'misusing' Gramscian concepts that gave him insight into how they might be applied constructively. Anderson and Nairn had been attracted to Gramsci's notion of a 'social equilibrium' because they envisioned it as some kind of retrogressive social stasis in which the British atavism had been permanently trapped. Thompson, of course, believed that this was nonsense, but he saw that in the century before the Industrial Revolution, the massive forces of capitalist development were accelerating in England, but were held back by the inertia of a still partly traditional society, whose pre-capitalist foundations remained present, if no longer robust.[22]

Thompson's initial application of Gramscian notions of hegemony can be seen in his second post-*Making* essay, 'Time, Work Discipline and Industrial Capitalism'.[23] This took up the problem of industrial discipline from the point where *The Making of the English Working Class*'s chapter on Methodism had left off. Wider ranging and more reflective than his earlier diatribe against Wesleyanism (which was represented as a kind of false consciousness), Thompson's new analysis depicted the transition to the time–work mentality of industrial capitalism as a more profound and protracted historical process of negotiation between dominant and subordinated classes. For pre-industrial peoples, who had worked for millennia according to the rhythms of the seasons and the sun, nothing seemed more unnatural and unpleasant than to adjust their labour to the artificial intervals of the clock. As a result, the transition was protracted and painful as – steadily and incrementally throughout the eighteenth century – a whole range of popular practices were whittled away and overthrown: fairs, festivals and village craft traditions, as well as drinking on the job. Before capitalism could dictate the pace in the workshop, working people had to be surrounded by bells, watches and clocks. Before mechanisation could drive the new factories, the reign of 'St Monday' had to be overthrown. Precisely because these transitions were not automatic, they became sites of contestation in Thompson's view. Since elites had few incentives to sweeten the pill of work speed-up, at the time, working people exerted their formidable powers of resistance throughout the eighteenth century.[24]

Here Thompson encountered a paradox: although eighteenth-century workers lacked many of the agitational tools enjoyed by their industrial successors – strikes, unions, newspapers, subscription funds and political associations – they possessed one resource of inestimable value – a still relatively intact traditional community. In these communities, where market values had penetrated only imperfectly, the imperatives of collective provision took precedence over the opportunities for private profit. In the popular culture of such villages, a 'moral economy' retained its vitality, and political economy had not yet been enthroned. To probe this moral economy, in all its anthropological depth, Thompson focused his third post-*Making* essay, 'The Moral Economy of the English Crowd in the Eighteenth Century', on a single type of event: the food riots which intermittently broke out when grain prices approached famine levels, and the subsistence of the poorest villagers was cast into doubt. These rioters, Thompson observed, were almost always close neighbours who lived and worked together, and whose 'attacks' generally followed a predetermined script. First, appeals would be made to local elites to invoke traditional regulatory powers and paternalist legislation to fix the price of food and to prevent its exportation. Only when these appeals to authority failed would the crowd act to seize the grain, 'sell' it to the needy at what they deemed a 'just price', and usually return the proceeds to the merchant or dealer.[25]

On one level, Thompson's 'Moral Economy' essay demonstrated that the market forces which would later fuel the Industrial Revolution were already at work through much of the eighteenth century. Yet, the popular expressions that he documented in this piece demonstrated that economic change was often resisted. This resistance, in turn, gave agrarian elites the opportunity to prove that they had not entirely abandoned the paternalism whose benefits they still claimed. This gave the scattered rioters who defended the moral economy a certain amount of power. Unlike their grandchildren in the age of Peterloo, they were too weak and separated from one another to pose any danger to the political regime at the national level. Yet, in their local communities, they could often force urban and rural elites into scenarios of *de facto* negotiation, in which a modicum of market regulation and communal protection would be retained, at least in the distributive realm of elementary consumption, if not in the productive, manufacturing sphere.

Thompson's analysis of the moral economy was taken up by a wide range of varied historians and social scientists, and the concept has been applied to many other times and places.[26] Thompson, however, was concerned to pursue, on a deeper level, the inquiry into eighteenth-century English social relations that 'The Moral Economy' had opened up. Clearly, the history of eighteenth-century English capitalism required more detailed study, not just as a prologue to the Industrial Revolution, but as a system in its own right. Yet, as he surveyed the existing historiography in the mid-1960s, the eighteenth century stood as a gaping hole of ignorance between two much better-understood centuries. Distinguished Marxists, such as Christopher Hill, C. B. Macpherson and other historians had written authoritatively about Britain during the revolutionary era of the seventeenth century. Their research into the lives of 'the industrious sort', the ideology of 'The Norman Yoke' and of 'possessive individualism', respectively, had provided Thompson with the benchmarks for Part I of his big book.[27]

But what about the period between 1688 and 1789? Even among mainstream social historians, the eighteenth century stood as a great blank. The only really innovative work had come from the pen of 'that inverted Marxist, Lewis Namier', and from his student, J. H. Plumb. Thompson was perfectly willing to acquiesce in Namier's picture of eighteenth-century politics, in which the ideological struggles of the earlier era had been supplanted by patronage and place-hunting, held together at the top by a narrow Whig oligarchy. But to read this *political* dominance as evidence of *social* stabilisation was to beg many questions from a reverted Marxist point of view. Nor could Thompson acquiesce in any of the other models of eighteenth-century stasis – Peter Laslett's 'One Class Society', or Harold Perkin's 'Open Aristocracy based on Property and Patronage' – that were being formulated at the time. These models utterly ignored the experience and agency of the common people, and failed to register their sub-political struggles with hegemonic elites.[28]

Before the mid-1960s, Thompson had regarded himself as much an activist as an historian. In 1965, however, his appointment as Director of the new Centre for Social History at the University of Warwick gave him fuller integration into the profession, and access to postgraduate students. The phenomenal impact of *The Making of the English Working Class* was bringing him fame and followers at the very moment when many students were becoming radicalised. Budding historians of the younger generation gravitated into Thompson's orbit, hoping to study with him, or at least participate indirectly in his programme of research. Thompson, for his part, began to see that his study of the eighteenth century could not be a single-authored book on the model of *The Making of the English Working Class*. Rather, it would have to be a collaborative effort, in which his students and junior colleagues would play important parts, each examining a different dimension of the eighteenth-century moral economy, in a unique locale.[29] Although Thompson resigned his academic post in 1970, he continued thereafter to collaborate with his students. By the mid-1970s they had divided the eighteenth-century field among themselves. However, the proliferation of books and monographs from the 'Thompson School' put its founding father in an unfamiliar role. While he continued to press on with his own empirical studies, Thompson found himself cast as an intellectual leader. As a result, his most important contribution during the 1970s was to craft a general model – based on the work of multiple researchers – that outlined the dynamics of eighteenth-century English society as a whole.

This model, I contend, was fundamentally Gramscian in character, and represented a significant departure from the argument of *The Making of the English Working Class*. Whatever we may make of the impact of Thompson's early reading of Gramsci (see note 21, above), the publication of *Selections from the Prison Notebooks*, in 1971, brought Gramscian concepts into wide circulation throughout the English-speaking world.[30] Among these concepts, none was more influential than Gramsci's dichotomisation of working peoples' struggles into two types: what he called 'wars of movement', when workers were able to create new forms of proletarian hegemony, and 'wars of position', when they were obliged to struggle within the terms constructed by bourgeois or some other pre-existing hegemony. While Gramsci himself introduced this terminology in the context of an analysis of twentieth-century Italian working-class struggles, other Marxists began to apply it to the circumstances of other times and places.

Thompson himself never used this specific terminology, although he acknowledged the general influence of Gramsci two years before his death. I believe we can go farther than this, however. Through a close reading of Thompson's major historical works of the 1970s, it is possible to see a systematic application of Marxist–Gramscian theory to forge a new understanding of eighteenth-century English society. The key insight that opened the way to this constructive breakthrough was the realisation that the story he had told in *The Making of the English Working Class* was akin to a Gramscian 'war of movement'. By contrast, eighteenth-century social relations between elites and people were akin to what Gramsci had termed a 'war of position'. This argument was sketched out in two seminal essays.[31]

Edward Thompson's eighteenth century

A casual glance at the title of the first of these essays, 'Patrician Society and Plebeian Culture', must have raised red flags in the minds of many readers who were familiar with Thompson's earlier historical work. To be sure, eighteenth-century Britons had their own penchant for this sort of neoclassical 'Roman' allusion, but was such a title really appropriate for a twentieth-century Marxist, who hoped to grasp the underlying logic of social organisation in Britain during the early capitalist age? The appearance of 'gentry' and 'labouring people' in the first sentence of the essay, as well as the reference to 'labour power' in the fourth, might have reassured such puzzled readers that the standard categories of Marxism were still in play. The mystery can now be finally resolved by a closer look at the title, in which 'patrician' and 'plebeian' are introduced as adjectives rather than as nouns. 'Patrician' is not meant to denote a class, but a certain style of aristocratic rule. It is a Roman style that accepts responsibility for the subsistence of the plebeians as the price for exacting their deference to patrician authority. What the title gives plebeians is also not a class, but a 'culture', one that makes legitimate demands on the paternalism of the rulers, but which cannot (unless it becomes something else) challenge the terms of rule. None of this indicates an abandonment of Marxism.

What we have here is rather a shift of genre, from a *narrative* of class formation to an *argument* about hegemony. It is a move from the 'who' to the 'how' of early capitalist domination; from the making of a class to the operation of hegemony. The neo-Gramscian character of this argument is further indicated by Thompson's claim that 'ruling-class control in the eighteenth century was located primarily in a cultural hegemony, and only secondarily in an expression of economic or physical (military) power'.[32]

This became even clearer, a few years later, in Thompson's second seminal article, 'Eighteenth Century Society: Class Struggle without Class'. Groping for a metaphor to articulate this proto-capitalist social order, he recalled an old school experiment in which the application of a current to iron filings on a magnetised plate distributed the filings along two oppositional 'fields of force':

> This is very much how I see eighteenth-century society, with, for many purposes, the crowd at one pole, the aristocracy and the gentry at the other, and until late in the century, the professional and merchant groups bound down by lines of magnetic dependency to the rulers, or on occasion hiding their faces in common action with the crowd ... The metaphor of a field of force can co-exist fruitfully with Marx's comment in the *Grundrisse*, that 'In all forms of society it is a determinate production, and its relations which assign every other production and its relations their rank and influence. It is a general illumination in which all other colours are plunged and which modifies their specific tonalities.'[33]

Such polarities, Thompson suggests, can be found in every pre- or proto-capitalist society, but they reached an extraordinary peak of intensity in eighteenth-century England, just before the urban industrial breakthrough: 'The gentry's hegemony may define the limits of the field of force within which the plebeian culture is free to act and grow but since this hegemony is secular rather than religious or magical it can do little to determine the character of this plebeian culture.' 'Innovation', on the other hand, 'is more evident at the top of society than below, but, since this innovation is not some normless and neuter technological/sociological process, but is the innovation of capitalist process, it is most often experienced by the plebs in the form of exploitation ... or the violent disruption of valued patterns of work and leisure.'[34] This antagonism could not be resolved within the eighteenth-century 'war of position'. It could only be held in an uneasy, ever-shifting balance within the terms of a contested hegemony:

The poor might be willing to award their deference to the gentry, but only for a price. The price was substantial. And the deference was often without the least illusion ... Seen in this way, the poor imposed upon the rich some of the duties and functions of paternalism just as much as deference was in turn imposed upon them. Both parties to the equation were constrained within a common field-of-force.[35]

Consider this last sentence in relation to the theoretical position that Thompson had staked out in his Preface to *The Making of the English Working Class*. There, he had refused to specify the structural limits on collective (or even individual) agency in the 'war of movement', which culminated in class formation. Yet now, in this eighteenth-century 'war of position', all parties are constrained by the magnetic power of the polar structures that constitute 'a common field of force'. The notion that structures must be apprehended in motion has been partly abandoned, supplanted by the fixed force of their magnetic polarity.

Certainly, as we read Thompson's 1974 and 1978 essays, it is striking just how far this self-professed enemy of Marxist structuralism is prepared to delineate the structures of production and distribution, which constrained all social groups within eighteenth-century English society. The eighteenth century, he avows, is 'the century which sees the erosion of half-free forms of labour, the decline of living-in, the final extinction of labour services and the advance of free, mobile wage labour'. During the course of this profound transformation, the gentry and the people alike hoped to obtain the best of both worlds. Wishing to abandon the responsibilities of paternalism in practice, the gentry still wanted to assert its prerogatives. 'They clung to the image of the labourer as an *un*free man, a "servant:" a servant in husbandry, the workshop, in the house.' They 'disclaimed their paternal responsibilities; but they did not cease, for many decades, to complain at the breach of the "great law of subordination," the diminution of deference'. A substantial part of the labour force, by contrast, 'actually became *more* free from discipline in their daily work, more free to choose between employers and between work and leisure, less situated in a position of dependence in their whole way of life, than they had been before or than they were to be in the first decades of the discipline of the factory and of the clock'. At the same time, they clung tenaciously to the perquisites and customary usages that brought them non-monetary benefits, or that might actually be translatable into monetary terms.[36]

We may recall that Thompson had traced the decline of these perquisites and usages in his earlier essay on the moral economy. From 1974 onwards, however, he used a different term, 'custom', to describe such worker expectations – a term that was more precise in identifying exactly those parts of the moral economy that eighteenth-century English workers hoped to preserve, often through quite novel methods, and in strikingly modern frames. Of course, the power of 'custom' resided precisely in its claim to deep antiquity; to the belief that it was something that had been practised since time immemorial, and that it was sanctioned with the authority of village prescription, or written law. In fact, as Thompson notes, in a culture that was still primarily oral, it was often difficult to trace the history of any particular practice with accuracy, and many of these 'customs' 'were of recent invention, and were in truth claims to new rights'.[37]

Custom, in other words, was a site of both contestation and negotiation. For agrarian and mercantile elites, the goal was to abrogate customs entirely or to translate them into monetised parcels of individual property. For the people (not yet really a class), the goal was to preserve the same customary usages or at least to retain their collective character. In contrast to the period of industrialisation, when customary modes of production were the main targets of attack, most eighteenth-century workers retained substantial control over their particular labour process. It was in the market that they were vulnerable, as the price of the goods that they made – and of those they consumed – fluctuated, sometimes wildly. Consequently, during this period, the capitalist attack on custom was felt most pervasively in the realm of consumption, where it was directed against usages such as after-harvest gleaning, commons pasturing, wood-gathering, forest access, grain-marketing, festivals and popular recreations. At the local level, throughout the South and Midlands, these practices were strenuously attacked by a wide range of agrarian capitalist initiatives, most notably enclosure, the abolition of feast days and the campaign for competitive markets for agricultural products.[38]

Yet, in resisting these barrages of privatisation, the plebs had some powerful weapons of their own. Parish wakes and other seasonal holidays had their own momentum, which was hard to suppress. Enclosure was often bitterly contested. Food riots could be suppressed *in extremis*, but there was a huge cost to bloody repression at the behest of local gentlemen, who had to go on living in the district. If the number and violence of riots did generally diminish, this was

83

in no small part because elites learned the importance of preventative measures, either through the Poor Law, or through the organisation of soup kitchens when prices were high, or trade was bad.[39] Because these antagonistic interests clashed within a set of shared assumptions, the struggle between them (war of position) turned as much on symbols as on the disposition of material goods. Thompson's analysis emphasises the performative dimension of a gentry/plebeian encounter within the constraining boundaries of the 'patrician' style of hegemony. The great freedom of agency, which had characterised *The Making of the English Working Class*, has been supplanted by roles that are partly prescribed. On both sides these roles were substantially scripted, and success hinged on the players' skill in enacting their respective parts. Gentlemen, who were becoming increasingly remote, 'met the lower sort of the people mainly on their own terms ... on the formalities of the bench; or on calculated occasions of popular patronage':

> Their appearances have much of the studied self-consciousness of public theatre. ... And with this went certain ritual appearances: the ritual of the hunt, the pomp of the assizes ... the segregated pews, the late entries and early departures at church ... the celebration of a marriage, a coming-of-age, a national festival. ... It is as if the illusion of paternalism was too fragile to be risked to more sustained exposure.[40]

'Such gestures', Thompson notes, 'were calculated to receive a return in deference quite disproportionate to the outlay.' When food prices rose, wages declined or enclosure beckoned, the gentry was perfectly content to imply that this was the fault of the middleman – the farmer, the miller, the Quaker grain merchant or the moneylending Jew. 'The credibility of the gentry as paternalists arose from the high visibility of certain of their functions, and the low visibility of others.'[41]

Patrician hegemony, popular culture and the law

This nuanced account of a struggle over custom, which allows circumscribed agency to both high and low, is perhaps the finest application of the Gramscian notion of 'hegemony' that any Marxist scholar (including Gramsci) has ever produced. But who exactly are the hegemons, and who are the hegemonised? For all the sophistication of his concrete analysis, Thompson never specifies the exact nature of the two poles that he posits to be in electromagnetic contention.

By subtitling his 1978 essay 'Class Struggle without Class', he seems to imply that the process of class formation has not yet begun in this early stage of agrarian capitalism. Yet his reversion to the language of 'gentry' vs. 'crowd' or 'labouring poor' suggests older, pre-capitalist classes adapting to an early capitalist world. These terms are 'vague', he admits, but then his solution is to undercut them by slipping into the even vaguer language of 'patricians vs. plebs'. Those words had served usefully as suggestive adjectives but, in his final revision of the essay(s), in 1991, Thompson turns them into nouns, leaving the implication that we really are dealing with a social structure resembling that of ancient Rome. 'A plebs is not, perhaps, a working class', Thompson acknowledges. 'The plebs may lack a consistency of self-definition', he then allows. But is consistency enhanced by the further assertion that 'I am therefore employing the terminology of class conflict, while resisting the attributes of identity to *a* class'?[42]

One understands why Thompson wants to avoid denominating either of his poles as 'pure' Marxist classes. But he runs the risk of rendering them meaningless if he cannot associate them with *some* definite social location(s) and with some *actual* social group(s). Had Thompson been willing to enter into dialogue with (rather than lampoon) structural Marxists who were then writing – for example, Perry Anderson, Gerald Cohen or Erik Olin Wright – he might have fastened on the concept of a 'social formation' to provide a solution to this problem.[43] Because eighteenth-century Britain was a complex society, at a transitional moment in capitalist development, both rulers and ruled comprised unstable compounds of shifting class fractions: landed gentlemen, aristocrats or mercantile capitalists on top; urban artisans, rural labourers or the semi-employed down below, with a host of expanding and shrinking intermediate groups in between.

Thompson's inability to reference the complexity of these combinations has the odd effect of leading him to treat eighteenth-century 'class' not as a relationship, but as a thing. His 'plebs' are most clearly limned, not when they are negotiating with their betters, but when they are standing fast against the market forces of privatisation, or opting out of the dominant culture, and creating a separate popular culture all their own. Alienated from the Church, which failed to address their predicament, he shows how they often reverted to a fragmentary folk religion (sometimes tinged with pagan survivals) embodied in the calendar of wakes and festivities that marked the change of seasons and the passage of years. Plebeian property was embedded in a 'grid of inheritance', which conveyed not only material goods or parcels of land, but a whole web of use rights, prerogatives and obligations that sought to transfer this cultural habitus from one generation to the next.[44]

In one of his more controversial articles, Thompson traced the vicissitudes of 'wife sale', a popular custom that was denounced by elite reformers as an example of the barbarism and backwardness of the plebs. In fact, Thompson argues, this custom was a form of popular divorce, which survived because the poor lacked any official means for sanctioning separation or remarriage. So far from being an example of patriarchal oppression, it was generally a humane practice that reflected personal choice, upheld community standards and provided community sanction to the decisions of individuals to rearrange their lives. In another essay, on 'Rough Music', Thompson analysed the English versions of charivari, in which community members assembled to humiliate transgressors, especially those deemed to be guilty of adultery, wife-beating, cuckoldry, or some other departure from sexual or gender norms. In many cases there was a quasi-judicial character to these proceedings. 'Rough music', in Thompson's view, 'belongs to a mode of life in which some part of the law belongs still to the community, and is theirs to enforce.'[45]

It was, however, one thing for the plebs to take the law into their own hands in the internal regulation of their own community. It was quite another being subject to the law of the ruling elite. The law, Thompson insists, has been badly misconstrued by orthodox Marxists, who would relegate it to the ideological superstructure, when it actually rears its imposing head 'at every bloody level' from superstructure to base. In eighteenth-century England, it 'was deeply imbricated within the very basis of productive relations', since it defined the terms of property – who owned it, on what terms, with what penalties for those who transgressed these rules. At the same time, it was the font of hegemonic legitimation, since it gave a universal gloss to grossly unequal power relations, whose inequalities were masked by the deeply rooted presumption that all were equal before the law. This idealised vision was a genuine product of seventeenth-century struggles against royal tyranny, when high and low had united to establish the law as a bulwark of liberty and a defence of property. With the intensification of capitalism and the taming of the crown during the early eighteenth century, property took precedence over liberty as the law increasingly showed its reactionary face. It now became an instrument of oppression, through which poverty was criminalised and the lower classes were rendered property-less. Stripped of their legal rights and customary prerogatives, these subaltern groups struck back. Transmuted by the law into criminals and transgressors, they took to poaching, smuggling, trespassing and purloining the goods and materials that they regarded as rightly their own.[46]

In a co-authored book, *Albion's Fatal Tree* (1975), Thompson and some of his leading students explored the ways in which 'a property conscious oligarchy' redefined 'through its legislative power, activities, use-rights in common or woods, perquisites in industry, as thefts or offences'. The most dramatic evidence for this process was the astonishing proliferation of capital penalties even for quite minor crimes against property.[47] The authors did not dispute conventional explanations: the lack of an adequate police force and the need to compensate for lax enforcement with intermittent brutality. Nevertheless, they insisted, the overwhelming emphasis on the sanctification of private property betokened more aggressive forms of class exploitation and an increasing criminalisation of poverty. In a particularly ingenious chapter, Thompson's student, Douglas Hay, argued that the intermittent application of the death penalty was a particularly useful tactic in shoring up the bulwarks of patrician hegemony. Selective application of pardons, sometimes proffered dramatically at the foot of the scaffold, 'put the principal instrument of legal terror – the gallows – directly in the hands of those who held power ... Discretion allowed a [usually private] prosecutor to terrorise a petty thief and then command his gratitude ... It allowed the class that passed one of the bloodiest penal codes in Europe to congratulate itself on its humanity'.[48]

Thompson's own major contribution to the study of eighteenth-century crime and punishment was published as a separate book, *Whigs and Hunters* (1975), which examined the origin of the 'Black Act' of 1723. This law criminalised deer hunting by those who were not upper-class licensees, and created over fifty new capital offences. Nocturnal marauding and cattle raiding were henceforth treated as hanging crimes, while failure to surrender after being accused of such offences guaranteed an automatic sentence of death. What precipitated this draconian law, whose brutal provisions were so disproportionate to any reasonable or actual threat? Thompson found the answer when he saw that all the prosecutors and enforcers of this newly implemented act were Whig MPs, cabinet ministers or wealthy sinecure holders, who envisioned royal forests as theirs for the taking. Under the leadership of Sir Robert Walpole, who was just then consolidating his hold on central government, they brazenly expropriated these vast tracts in the vicinity of London, either to exploit them as repositories of natural resources, or to privatise them as personal parks and pleasure grounds. 'Political life in England, in the 1720s had something of the sick quality of a Banana Republic', Thompson mordantly proclaims:

> This is a recognized phase of commercial capitalism when predators fight for the spoils of power and have not yet agreed to submit to rational or bureaucratic rules and forms. Each politician, by nepotism, interest and purchase, gathered around him a following of loyal dependents. The aim was to reward them by giving them some post in which they could milk some part of the public revenue: army, finances, the Church, excise.[49]

And yet, in the 'war of position' that was eighteenth-century English capitalism, this rank hypocrisy and outrageous corruption precipitated countervailing forces of judicial correction that ultimately restored the Law to its properly hegemonic role:

> If the law is evidently partial and unjust, then it will mask nothing, legitimize nothing, contribute nothing to any class's hegemony. The essential precondition for the effectiveness of law, in its function as ideology, is that it shall display an independence from gross manipulation, and shall seem to be just. It cannot seem to be so ... without, on occasion by actually *being* just.[50]

And so the same Law that sanctioned Walpole's swindles, and sent poachers swinging from Tyburn's fatal tree, also planted the seed of the 'freeborn Englishman', thus opening the door – when industrial capitalism built the structure – to the making of the English working class.

Conclusion

It is a measure of Thompson's high hopes for *The Making of the English Working Class* that he could commend his volume to a global readership in 1963, anticipating that 'causes which were lost in England might, in Asia or Africa, yet be won'. Twenty-eight years later, when he gathered his leading essays on the eighteenth century into another large volume, *Customs in Common*, he could hope, at most, for 'a new kind of "customary consciousness" in which once again, successive generations stood in apprentice relation to each other, in which material satisfactions remain stable (if more equally distributed) and only cultural satisfactions enlarge'. He added, however, 'I do not think this is likely to happen.'[51] This retrenchment of Thompson's political expectations during the 1970s and 1980s was clearly connected to a retreat in the power of the Left. Like other activist intellectuals who lived through the period, Thompson experienced these years as a difficult time, in which assumptions had to be questioned and verities had to be reassessed.[52] Painful as this process undoubtedly was, however, there was a significant payoff in the increasing sophistication and acuity of Thompson's historical work. *The Making of the English Working Class* had a tremendous impact because it seemed so perfectly in phase with the mood of the 1960s. For the same reason, however, its influence has somewhat faded in the decades since that mood collapsed.

By contrast, Thompson's studies of the eighteenth century remain fresh and exemplary because they explicitly contextualise the popular agency of that period in relation to the socioeconomic structures of early capitalism, within which that agency was inextricably enmeshed. Because agency in *The Making of the English Working Class* seems relatively untethered from such structures, the book could be more easily read as an inspiring tale, but it also became vulnerable to subsequent critics who drew attention to the questions it had neglected to ask:[53] what about those sectors of the working class which had eschewed the radical movement, which were indifferent to politics, unavailable for mobilisation, or which were openly loyalist?[54] In today's more sceptical climate, re-examination of the heroic makers of Thompson's working class has revealed a host of racial, ethnic and gendered exclusions on which the making of this class was based.[55] Because Thompson's eighteenth-century plebeians *are not* presented as universal exemplars, but as concrete actors constrained by the vicissitudes of time and place, they are not nearly so vulnerable to being deconstructed in this way. Because Thompson shows how their discourses were both constrained and also constructed by the structures of early capitalism, his account resonates more harmoniously with the assumptions of our postmodern age.

As the Gramscian 'war of [proletarian] movement' recedes ever further over the horizon, and the achievement of socialism grows ever more doubtful and remote, Thompson's account of the eighteenth-century 'war of position' may still have much to teach us about the prospects and possibilities of class negotiation and resistance in our own fully global capitalist age. It is unfortunate that Thompson's polemics against Althusserian structuralism have blinded us to these fruitful experiments in Gramscian structuralism. Some of the threads that Thompson first spun in his eighteenth-century studies have indeed been followed up by his students and other historians. Correspondingly, the advance of scholarship in other areas means that some of his assertions must now be revised. Nevertheless, many of the ideas and hypotheses that Thompson put forward in the 1970s remain open as promising avenues for historical explanation and empirical research. Moreover, these opportunities need not be restricted to historians who specialise in the field of eighteenth-century English social history. Historians of other times and places will be rewarded by reading (or rereading) Thompson. His sensitive explorations of the subtle dialectic between structure and agency can provide, if not a model, at least an inspiration. They reveal a master historian at work, and show some of the possibilities for applying theory to the complex, messy arenas of irrepressible human action and entangled human affairs.

Notes

1 See, e.g., the essays in H. Kaye and K. McClelland (eds), *E. P. Thompson: Critical Perspectives* (Cambridge: Polity Press, 1990); H. Kaye, *The British Marxist Historians* (Cambridge: Polity Press, 1984), pp. 167–220; B. Palmer, *E. P. Thompson: Objections and Oppositions* (London: Verso, 1994). See also A. M. Givertz, 'Interview with Bryan Palmer', *Left History*, 1:2 (1993), 110–20 and the memoir by P. Linebaugh, 'From the Upper West Side to Wick Episcopi', *New Left Review*, 201 (1993), 3–25.

2 E. P. Thompson, *The Poverty of Theory and Other Essays* (London: Merlin 1978).

3 E. P. Thompson, 'An Open Letter to Lezek Kolakowski', in *ibid.*, p. 396.

4 See, e.g., L. Alcoff and E. Mendieta (eds), *Identities: Race, Class, Gender and Nationality* (Oxford: Blackwell, 2002), pp. 136–8.

5 E. P. Thompson, *The Making of the English Working Class* (New York: Vintage, 1963), pp. 9–14. For Thompson's place in British Marxist historiography, see T. Koditschek, 'Marxism and the Historiography of Modern Britain: From Engels to Thompson to Deconstruction and Beyond', in T. Brotherstone and G. Pilling (eds), *History, Economic History and the Future of Marxism* (London: Porcupine, 1996), pp. 103–47; Kaye, *The British Marxist Historians*, pp. 167–200.

6 Thompson, *The Making of the English Working Class*, p. 9. It is important to understand that Thompson never denied the necessity of understanding social structures and how they work. 'I'm by no means a wholesale critic of structural Marxism', he insisted. 'No Marxist cannot be a structuralist in a certain sense.' M. Merrill, 'An Interview with E. P. Thompson', in MARHO, *Visions of History* (Manchester: Manchester University Press, 1983), p. 17.

7 Thompson, *The Making of the English Working Class*, p. 9. See also W. H. Sewell, Jr, 'How Classes are Made: Critical Reflections on E. P. Thompson's Theory of Working-class Formation' in Kaye and McClelland, *E. P. Thompson*, pp. 50–77.

8 Thompson, *The Making of the English Working Class*, pp. 17–185.

9 *Ibid.*, pp. 189–313.

10 P. Anderson, *Arguments within English Marxism* (London: Verso, 1980), pp. 33, 39. Thompson himself defended this omission on the grounds of having established a rough division of labour amongst the 'collective' of Marxist historians of Britain. 'I have comrades, I have associates, like John Saville and Eric Hobsbawm and many others, who are very sound economic historians. They are better at it than I am, and so I tend to assume that my work falls into place within a wider discourse.' Merrill, 'An Interview with E. P. Thompson', p. 22.

11 Thompson, *The Making of the English Working Class*, pp. 314–49.

12 *Ibid.*, pp. 349–400, especially pp. 368, 375. For the debate on the relationship between Methodism and radicalism in late eighteenth- and early nineteenth-century Britain, as it stood before Thompson's book, see E. Halevy, *A History of the English People in the Nineteenth Century*, 1, *England in 1815* (London: Benn, 1949 [1913]), pp. 410–28; E. J. Hobsbawm, *Labouring Men* (London: Weidenfeld & Nicolson, 1964), pp. 23–33. See also E. Halevy, *The Birth of Methodism in England* (Chicago: University of Chicago Press, 1971 [1896]); B. Semmel, *The Methodist Revolution* (New York: Basic Books, 1973).

13 Thompson, *The Making of the English Working Class*, pp. 401–47. See also C. Calhoun, *The Question of Class Struggle: Social Foundations of Popular Radicalism during the Industrial Revolution* (Chicago: University of Chicago Press, 1982).

14 Thompson, *The Making of the English Working Class*, pp. 451–602; Koditschek, 'Marxism and the Historiography of Modern Britain', pp. 112–14.

15 Thompson, *The Making of the English Working Class*, pp. 521–710.

16 *Ibid.*, pp. 711–832, quote on pp. 830, 831.

17 See, e.g., E. Hobsbawm and G. Rudé, *Captain Swing* (London: Lawrence & Wishart, 1969); J. F. C. Harrison, *The Quest for the New Moral World: Robert Owen and the Owenites in Britain and America* (New York: Scribners, 1969); P. Hollis, *The Pauper Press: A Study in Working Class*

Radicalism of the 1830s (Oxford: Oxford University Press, 1970); as well as the work of Thompson's wife, Dorothy Thompson, which ultimately led to *The Early Chartists* (London: Macmillan, 1971) and *The Chartists: Popular Politics in the Industrial Revolution* (New York: Pantheon, 1984).

18 Merrill, 'An Interview with E. P. Thompson', pp. 14–15.

19 'The Peculiarities of the English' was first published in *The Socialist Register* in 1965, and is reprinted in *The Poverty of Theory*, pp. 245–301. Even before he began this polemical essay, however, while he was waiting to receive proofs of *The Making of the English Working Class*, Thompson started work on what eventually became 'The Moral Economy of the English Crowd in the Eighteenth Century' (originally published in *Past and Present*, 50, 1971), reprinted in *Customs in Common* (New York: New Press, 1991), pp. 185–258. Circumstantial evidence indicates that he began 'Time, Work Discipline and Industrial Capitalism' at about the same time (originally published in *Past and Present*, 38, 1967, reprinted in *Customs in Common*, pp. 352–402). For details about Thompson's work on 'The Moral Economy', see *Customs in Common*, pp. 259–60.

20 P. Anderson, 'Origins of the Present Crisis', in *English Questions* (London, Verso: 1992), pp. 15–47. Thompson, 'The Peculiarities of English', pp. 245–301, quote on pp. 252–3.

21 Thompson's *The New Reasoner* published the earliest English translations of a few of Gramsci's prison letters in the late 1950s. (See www.amielandmel-burn.org.uk/collections/nr). Gramsci's ideas about hegemony, however, were largely unknown until 1960, when Gwyn Williams published 'The Concept of "Egemonia" in the Thought of Antonio Gramsci', *Journal of the History of Ideas*, 21:4 (1960), 586–99, which Thompson explicitly referenced in his 1964 critique of Anderson. Thompson also indicated that he had begun reading some of Gramsci's prison manuscripts in Italian, although his 'weak' linguistic skills dissuaded him from providing his own translations. For general analyses of the impact of Gramsci on British Marxists (especially historians), see G. Eley, 'Reading Gramsci in English', *European History Quarterly*, 14, London, SAGE (1984), 441–78; H. Kaye, *The Education of Desire: Marxists and the Writing of History* (New York: Routledge, 1992), 9–30; D. Forgacs, 'Gramsci and Marxism in Britain', *New Left Review*,176 (1989), 70–87. Perry Anderson's comprehensive account of Gramsci is 'The Antinomies of Antonio Gramsci', *New Left Review*, 100 (1976–77), 5–78.

22 Anderson, 'Origins of the Present Crisis', pp. 29–37; Thompson took particular umbrage at Anderson and Nairn's claim that the British working class had always exhibited a 'corporate' rather than a 'hegemonic' consciousness – a distinction which he insists runs counter to the usage of Gramsci, and would likely 'distract attention away from Gramsci's deeply cultured and original (if frequently ambiguous) insights'; 'The Peculiarities of the

English', pp. 275, 282–4. By the time he published *The Poverty of Theory*, however, in 1978, Thompson was willing to allow that 'it may be true (as he [Anderson] argued) that my account of Gramsci's usages of "hegemony" is inadequate', p. 404.

23 Thompson, 'Time, Work Discipline and Industrial Capitalism'.

24 *Ibid.*

25 E. P. Thompson, 'The Moral Economy of the English Crowd in the Eighteenth Century'. On Thompson's 'anthropological turn' see his 'History and Anthropology', in *Persons and Polemics: Historical Essays* (London: Merlin, 1994), pp. 201–27.

26 In 1991, Thompson surveyed the vast literature that had been spawned by his original essay up to that point in 'The Moral Economy Reviewed', in *Customs in Common*, pp. 259–351. See also J. C. Scott, *The Moral Economy of the Peasant: Rebellion and Subsistence in Southeast Asia* (New Haven, CT: Yale University Press, 1976), which argues that generic notions of 'moral economy' provide normative underpinning for communal values in most traditional peasant societies worldwide.

27 C. Hill, 'The Norman Yoke', in *Puritanism and Revolution: The English Revolution of the Seventeenth Century* (New York: Schocken Books, 1985), pp. 50–122; C. B. Macpherson, *The Political Theory of Possessive Individualism: Hobbes to Locke* (Oxford: Oxford University Press, 1962).

28 Thompson, 'The Peculiarities of the English', p. 258; L. Namier, *The Structure of Politics at the Accession of George III* (London: Macmillan, 2nd edn, 1957); J. H. Plumb, *The Growth of Political Stability in England, 1675–1725* (Macmillan: London, 1967); P. Laslett, *The World We have Lost: England Before the Industrial Age* (New York, Scribners, 3rd edn, 1984), pp. 22–52; H. Perkin, *The Origins of Modern English Society: 1780–1880* (London: Routledge & Kegan Paul, 1969), pp. 17–62. For reasons of space, I have deliberately excluded any discussion of Thompson's treatment of William Blake, or eighteenth-century Muggletonianism and Antinomianism, although they could be fitted into my overall argument.

29 B. Palmer, *The Making of E. P. Thompson: Marxism, Humanism and History* (Toronto: New Hogtown Press, 1981), pp. 83–101; Palmer, *Thompson: Objections and Oppositions*, pp. 107–25; Peter Searby and the Editors, 'Edward Thompson as Teacher: Yorkshire and Warwick', in J. Rule and R. Malcolmson (eds), *Protest and Survival: Essays for E. P. Thompson* (London: Merlin, 1993), pp. 18–23.

30 A. Gramsci, *Selections from the Prison Notebooks*, ed. and trans. Q. Hoare and G. Nowell Smith (New York: International, 1971), esp. pp. 229–39.

31 E. P. Thompson, 'Patrician Society, Plebeian Culture', *Journal of Social History*, 7:4 (1974), pp. 382–405. For Thompson's acknowledgement of Gramsci's influence on his work, see his preface to *Customs in Common*, pp. 10–11.

32 Thompson, 'Patrician Society, Plebeian Culture', pp. 382, 387.

33 E. P. Thompson, 'Eighteenth-Century English Society: Class Struggle without Class', *Social History*, 3:2 (1978), 133–65, quotes on p. 151. Both of Thompson's seminal essays on eighteenth-century English society (the first cited in n. 31) were later revised and combined into a single essay entitled 'The Patricians and the Plebs', in *Customs in Common*, pp. 16–96. This shift in usage from adjective to noun is significant, in my view, as betokening Thompson's late-life retreat from the categories of Marxism. It is consistent with an offhand comment he made that 'it would be strange, wouldn't it, if all we had been talking about through the centuries has been the struggle of the poor against the rich?', quoted in D. Thompson (ed.), *The Essential E. P. Thompson* (New York: New Press, 2001), p. x.

34 Thompson, 'Eighteenth Century English Society', p. 154.

35 *Ibid.*, p. 163. For an elaboration of this argument, see Thompson's contribution, 'The Crime of Anonymity', to the collection he co-edited with his students, D. Hay, P. Linebaugh, J. Rule and C. Winslow, *Albion's Fatal Tree: Crime and Society in Eighteenth-Century England* (New York: Pantheon, 1975), pp. 255–308. Thompson observes how anonymous letters show 'not the absence of deference in this kind of society, but something of its character and limitations: these workers do not love their masters, but, in the end, they must be reconciled to the fact that for the duration of their lives these are likely to remain their masters', p. 307.

36 Thompson, 'Patrician Society, Plebeian Culture', pp. 382–4.

37 Thompson, 'Custom and Culture' and 'Custom Law and Common Right', in *Customs in Common*, pp.1–15, 97–184, quote on p. 1.

38 Thompson, 'The Patricians and The Plebs', pp.16–96, esp. p. 74.

39 Thompson, 'Moral Economy of the Crowd'; J. Bohstedt, *The Politics of Provisions: Food Riots, Moral Economy and Market Transition in England, c.1550–1850* (Farnham: Ashgate, 2010), pp. 198–214, 236–8.

40 Thompson, 'Patricians and Plebs', pp. 45–6.

41 *Ibid.*, p. 43.

42 Thompson, *Customs in Common*, pp. 16, 56–7, 73.

43 G. A. Cohen, *Karl Marx's Theory of History: A Defense* (Princeton: Princeton University Press, 1978); E. O. Wright, *Class, Crisis and the State* (London: Verso, 1979); E. O. Wright (ed.), *The Debate on Classes* (London:Verso, 1989).

44 Thompson, *Persons and Polemics*, pp. 263–300.

45 E. P. Thompson, 'The Sale of Wives' and 'Rough Music', in *Customs in Common*, pp. 404–66, 467–538, quote on p. 530.

46 Thompson, *Poverty of Theory*, p. 96; E. P. Thompson, *Whigs and Hunters: The Origin of the Black Act* (New York: Pantheon, 1975), p. 261.

47 Hay *et al.*, *Albion's Fatal Tree*, p. 13. For a critique, see John Langbein, 'Albion's Fatal Flaws', *Past and Present*, 98:1 (1983), 96–120.

48 D. Hay, 'Property Authority and the Criminal Law', in *Albion's Fatal Tree*, pp. 17–64, quote on pp. 48–9.

49 Thompson, *Whigs and Hunters*, p. 197.

50 *Ibid.*, p. 263.

51 Thompson, *The Making of the English Working Class*, p. 13; *Customs in Common*, p. 15.

52 S. Hamilton, *The Crisis of Theory: E. P. Thompson, The New Left and Postwar British Politics* (Manchester: Manchester University Press, 2011), pp. 158–277; Palmer, *Thompson: Objections and Oppositions*, pp. 155–67.

53 The notion that *The Making of the English Working Class* offered a celebration of open-ended working-class agency entirely free from structural or circumstantial constraints is a misinterpretation (or at least a gross exaggeration) of Thompson's book, as I point out on pages 71–5 above, and in 'Marxism and the Historiography of Modern Britain', pp. 111–15.

54 See L. Colley, *Britons: Forging the Nation* (New Haven, CT: Yale University Press, 1992). For Thompson's response, see *Persons and Polemics*, pp. 321–31.

55 G. Stedman Jones, *Languages of Class: Studies in English Working Class History, 1832–1982* (Cambridge: Cambridge University Press, 1983), pp. 90–178; J. Scott, *Gender and the Politics of History* (New York: Columbia University Press, 1988), pp. 53–90; B. Taylor, *Eve and the New Jerusalem, Socialism and Feminism in the Nineteenth Century* (New York: Pantheon, 1983); A. Clark, *The Struggle for the Breeches: Gender and the Making of the British Working Class* (Berkeley: University of California Press, 1995); R. Chandavarkar, 'The Making of the English Working Class: E. P. Thompson and Indian History', in V. Chaturvedi, *Mapping Subaltern Studies and the Postcolonial* (London: Verso, 2000), pp. 50–71; S. Sarkar, *Writing Social History* (New Delhi: Oxford University Press, 2000), pp. 50–108.

5

The uses of literature:
Thompson as writer, reader and critic

Luke Spencer

Introduction

My purpose here is to examine in some detail Thompson's career-long commitment to literature and to the craft of writing. There already exist studies of his work which include – even foreground – recognition of Thompson's poetry, fiction, memoirs and critical essays as expressions of his evolving thought. Apart from giving due consideration to the full range of his output and to the crucial role within it of literary references and allusions, I also want to address a subject whose importance was indicated thus by Bryan Palmer in 1994: '[I]t was the style and persistently charged language of *The Making [of the English Working Class]*, in conjuncture with its emphasis in content on the self-activity of labouring people, that established its enduring political relevance.'[1] By focusing regularly on issues of style and lexical choice, I try to make clear some significant continuities and contrasts within Thompson's specifically literary output and between that and his major scholarly and polemical writings. It was Palmer again, among others, who drew attention nearly twenty years ago to Thompson's revelatory 'insertion of the poetic imagination into the discourse of Marxism'.[2] I hope what follows will offer some insights into how that insertion yielded, at its most productive, an exemplary poetics of radical engagement.

Soldiering and teaching

Talk of free-will and determinism, and I think of Milton. Talk of man's inhumanity, I think of Swift. Talk of morality and revolution, and my mind is off with Wordsworth's Solitary. Talk of the problems of self-activity and creative labour in socialist society, and I am in an instant back with William Morris.

'An Open Letter to Leszek Kolakowski'

Edward Thompson's writing life effectively began with the poems and prose pieces that came out of his experience as a young tank commander in North Africa and Italy in the latter stages of the Second World War. His *Collected Poems*[3] includes a couple of precociously competent poetic efforts from his schooldays, but it was the war that gave him something of colossal moral and historical importance to write about; and it helped him begin to bring his developing styles, in verse and prose, closely into line with the scale and significance of what he was witnessing. 'Overture to Cassino'[4] is a superb prose piece about the tragic and grimly farcical sides of war. Partly indebted to the Orwell of *Homage to Catalonia*, it is nevertheless richly evocative in its own distinctive way, especially in its use of the intercut first-person points of view of a platoon commander, a private soldier, an army doctor and even – briefly but movingly – a wife or girlfriend waiting helplessly back in England. Another strength is Thompson's deployment of ironic natural images to underscore the prevailing distortions. There are nightingales un-Keatsianly 'angry and frightened' at the noise of gunfire and a starving dog left homeless and uncared-for by the collateral death of its peasant owner. In 'Drava Bridge' Orwell's influence is again obvious, but with some modulations all Thompson's own:

> When we drove up to the mountains it was like coming to the gates of hell. I don't say that for effect. It was like coming to the gates of hell. The mountains stood up erect from the plain with black scarred faces. The sky was sagging with impending thunder and black, so that it seemed that some great tank was burning behind the mountains and belching a volume of coarse diesel fumes. And when the lightning at length came it was as if the flames had found the ammunition racks and flushed the cordite into a short white gasp, while overhead heavy guns argued our destiny. It seemed to us that there could be no way through when we were in the pass. It was like looking up the barrel of a gun when someone puts a round in and shuts the breech.
>
> When we came out of the pass it took us some moments to understand. This was when we first began to believe that the war had ended. Here were young green oak trees and beech woods. Here the grass was as green as an English water-meadow and the streams were clear and continually making laughter. Here were clean white villages and cattle swaying a loaded bag of milk. This was surely the richest plateau in

Europe, where men might trail their fingers in the fertile earth and multiply their wealth, and we might find rest from soldiering. It was like coming out of a long spell of action, and laying your cheek into the earth and smelling the roots of grasses before you are asleep.[5]

Thompson lets us see him reaching for suitable analogies in the first paragraph ('It was like ... it seemed ... it was as if ...'), but in the next one there is a sudden emergence into the sunlight of confident assertion. A final 'It was like' ironically echoes the earlier similes of threat and destruction, but in the service of an image of rest, renewal and a return to harmony with nature. In his early twenties Thompson is already showing himself capable of some memorable stylistic effects. He is already forming his own idiom in modulations of imagery and tone that are closer to fiction than to journalism. If this tempts him now and then into belletristic over-writing (e.g. those laughter-making streams), it's a price worth paying for passages as generally excellent as the one above.

Two poems from February 1945 show opposite facets of Thompson's youthful approach to poetry writing. 'Song for 1945'[6] is a rousing call to radical commitment as war and the wind of change from Europe demand an end to dithering on the sidelines of history. In contrast, 'Casola Valsenio: The Cat'[7] concentrates on a minor incident of war which gradually acquires enormous moral significance. First tolerated by Thompson and his tank crew, then shot because it gives away their position to the enemy, the stray cat of the poem's title uncomfortably challenges the emotional detachment instilled in the men by military discipline. Another pair of poems from 1945 deploy heavy irony to expose the murderous *Realpolitik* of a repressive regime in one case ('Untitled'), and in the other the vacuities of haute couture set against the harsh realities of occupation and liberation ('New Fashions'). The tonal virtuosity of his future polemics, and much of his historiography, is already confidently on display. With the end of the war would come a chance to consolidate and greatly extend his knowledge of both literary history and the potential uses of imaginative writing.

At the time of his 1948 appointment as a tutor for the newly-created Department of Extramural Studies of the University of Leeds, Thompson declared English literature to be his chief interest. This is hardly surprising, given both his wartime writing and the fact that he had just had two years (1945–47) at the University of Cambridge studying literature as well as social history. His first three years in the Leeds department were spent teaching literature exclusively and, until his departure for Warwick in 1965, his programme was never without at least one tutorial class in that subject. The early 1950s were a crucial transitional period which saw him combine literary criticism with painstaking historical research (and a tough political message) in his first book, *William Morris: Romantic to Revolutionary*. There, in tracing Morris's radical trajectory, he established his own credentials as a historian for whom the testimony of imaginative writing was permanently relevant. Yet, despite this decisive shift towards social history in his research, his regular tutorial work reflected a substantial continuing commitment to the value of literary studies. David Goodway has noted that 'in each of the three years 1959–62, the period when he was writing *The Making of the English Working Class*, he taught three literature classes and only one in social history'.[8] Coupled with his first attempts at imaginative writing, the shaping influence which this long pedagogic engagement with literature had on Thompson's outlook and style has been summed up thus by another commentator:

> Literature ... provid[ed] a special kind of utterance to which he repeat-edly returned. It was an arena of confrontation, a tool of social criti-cism, a badge of commitment, an expression of dissent, a defensive line, a bridgehead of cultural challenge, a special kind of code, a moral talisman, an infinitely powerful form of rhetoric, a place of retreat, and the source of a vision of the future that was always political but which also spoke against politics and beyond it.[9]

There are many points of purchase in such a comprehensive list of what literature and the criticism of it meant for Thompson as writer, teacher, historian and political activist. The discussion that follows will give close attention to some representative examples of how that 'special kind of utterance' was deployed by Thompson as cultural testimony and as a 'tool' for analysis, polemical argument and the activation of the moral imagination.

It was as an ex-member of the Leeds Extramural Department – as well as a by-then renowned historian – that Thompson delivered the 1967 Albert Mansbridge Lecture. His theme was 'Education and Experience' and he argued forcefully for education as a mutually enriching exchange between the teacher's formalised learning and the life experience of the student, typified by the best of extramural practice. (See chapter 2.) Although he readily identified his own disci-pline as social history, it was on literature that he relied for nearly all his examples of centuries-long shifts in the perceived value – or lack of it – of popular culture and of the sensibility of working people. Fielding, Coleridge, Hardy and Lawrence are adduced, alongside eighteenth-century 'peasant' poets like Stephen Duck, and there are glances at Goethe and Tolstoy. But Wordsworth is the key figure in Thompson's argument, for he is taken as representing a decisive shift away from patrician condescension towards a fuller recognition of 'the worth of the common man'.[10] As so often elsewhere in his work, Thompson bases his case on an idea of literature as a form of moral agency by which consciousness can be advanced beyond what is thinkable in the terms of established (i.e. mostly Establishment) common sense. Writers and their work are not to be regarded as merely the epiphenomena of historical circumstance; nor are artists of any kind to be seen as atomised individuals cut loose from surrounding cultural (including, of course, political) and economic conditions. Their true importance lies in their adaptation of pre-existing formal and stylistic resources in order to bear imaginative witness to – and, where possible, to modify – structures of feeling that are simultaneously personal to them and deeply communal.

Literature as agency

Edward was aware of a great variety of forms of literary expression not as 'illustrative' of the movements he was studying, but as an essential part of them.

Dorothy Thompson[11]

Thompson's interest in matters of form and style marries with his radicalism in the concept of agency. Early on in his writing life he admits that even the otherwise admirable William Morris can be convicted of having 'erred by divorcing art from the historical process as a whole' and of having 'not emphasized sufficiently the ideological role of art, its active agency in changing human beings, its agency in man's class-divided history'.[12] Such active participation by people in the shaping of their own minds and lives is a key analytical and organising principle of *The Making of the English Working Class* and one way Thompson measures its valency is by looking closely at how structures of feeling were articulated both through time and across any given historical moment. The across-time (synchronic) critical approach is cleverly applied in the section on William Cobbett in the final chapter of *The Making of the English Working Class*. Cobbett's strengths as a radical writer are highlighted through an extended comparison with his radical contemporary, William Hazlitt. An extract from the latter's *Political Essays* (1819) is cited to show that '[e]ven in his most engaged Radical journalism ... [Hazlitt] aimed his polemic, not towards the popular, but towards the polite culture of his time'.[13] His easy familiarity with the ruling-class world he attacks is pinned down to specific lexical choices and a certain tone, 'the drawl of the patrician Friend of the People';[14] and again, 'his style, with its sustained and controlled rhythms, and its antithetical movement, belongs to the polite culture of the essayist'.[15] (To be sure, one could equally stress – as Thompson does elsewhere and as Tom Paulin[16] has done in fine detail more recently – Hazlitt's insistent pushing against the ideological constraints endemic to the form he was working in; but Thompson's insight remains valid as far as it goes.)

Whereas Cobbett and Hazlitt, in their very different styles, were on the side of progressive social forces, a pairing of writers from the twentieth century gives Thompson a chance to examine an opposite trajectory, away from radicalism towards increasing denial and default. George Orwell's 1940 essay 'Inside the Whale', with its justification of Henry Miller's political quietism, is seen by Thompson as belonging to 'a similar pattern of default' as W. H. Auden's 'spiritual pessimism' in his end-of-decade valediction, 'September 1939'.[17] By the outbreak of war both men were convinced of the failure of progressive forces; yet, Thompson argues, Orwell's rejection of the possibility of progress is unfairly weighted against communism, with barely a mention of the crimes of Reaction or the positive achievements of radical initiatives like the Popular Front and the Left Book Club. The common point at which Auden and Orwell have converged is the refusal of progressive agency in favour of reactionary ventriloquism: '*1984* was the product not of one mind, but of a culture'.[18] Literary history is littered with such defectors, and Thompson names a fair few of them in this essay, from Coleridge and Southey to Dos Passos and Koestler. This kind of intertextual referencing is a vital aspect of the cultural contextualisation and dialectical argument by which Thompson's case develops. Like his great predecessor Hazlitt (and, one might add, Marx), Thompson deploys a wealth of quotation and allusion throughout his writing; but, whereas Hazlitt's prose moves always in the direction of confident assertions of categorical truth, Thompson's assertions are rarely categorical. Hazlitt's evidence is there to buttress his statements; for Thompson it is the other way around. Except when he is at his most polemical, Thompson's reasoning will rarely allow him to put the axiomatic cart before the analytical horse.

Thompson's insistence on literature as agency relies, of course, upon the ontological security of the author, an idea which it has been the business of much contemporary literary theory, from Barthes onwards, to discredit. His firm belief in authorial intention and the moral autonomy of imaginative writing puts Thompson squarely in the opposite camp to Barthes and Derrida; just as his defence of what he calls 'the empirical idiom' and of the value of personal experience in historical writing sets him against Althusser and Anderson. Yet it should be said that the Death of the Author does not of itself dispose of the case for agency, though the centre of gravity certainly shifts. However much the text delivered by literary theory may be the site of hegemonic ideology, another emphasis within the same theoretical spectrum has argued for its being also threaded through with unconscious fault-lines and fractures. Thus it may be read – indeed, demands to be read, according to many – as deeply subversive of established values, even (or especially) the ones it is ostensibly seeking to defend. Thompson was aware of this, as several of the readings quoted above make clear; but he always stressed the importance of literature being judged as *itself* and not as something else. Its imaginative insights and mode of expression were not reducible to this many discourses or to that much social determination.

Ideology and experience

No ideology is wholly absorbed by its adherents: it breaks down in practice in a thousand ways under the criticism of impulse and of experience.

The Making of the English Working Class, ch. 11

For all Thompson's sensitivity to the cultural contexts and aesthetic organisation of imaginative literature, he was occasionally willing to overlook crucial ideological distinctions in his eagerness to insist on the role of agency as such. John Goode has found him out in a serious misestimation of Yeats's 'The Second Coming', of which Thompson claims: 'it questions the values from which any adult politics should start'.[19] Goode rightly points out that Yeats's poem originated in 'post-Romantic disdain of practice' and that it is saturated in 'highly conservative values'[20] centred on a mythicised Anglo-Irish aristocracy. So far from setting some kind of benchmark for a mature understanding of politics, Yeats's position does not even qualify as 'adult'. But this kind of error is rare in Thompson's work. His judgements are usually securely grounded in historical detail and in a ready, if not always detailed, grasp of form and style.[21]

When Thompson applies himself to textual analysis the results are mostly persuasive and sometimes revelatory. Chapter 11 of *The Making of the English Working Class*, 'The Transforming Power of the Cross', contains some striking insights into the ideological function of Methodist theology and, in particular, how 'the perverted eroticism of ... imagery' in Methodist hymns directed the emotional energies of an increasingly work-disciplined labouring population into 'Sabbath orgasms of feeling' (406–7). After examining extracts from several hymns, Thompson turns his attention to Methodism's ambivalent attitude towards death: its lurid obsession with eternal punishment for sin and its simultaneous revelling in the idea of death as a welcome release from earthly hardship. He brings his argument to a climax by citing the work of two of literary history's most prominent heretics, Emily Brontë and William Blake: the life-denying Revd Jabez Branderham, from Lockwood's nightmare at Wuthering Heights, is taken to embody all that Blake so resolutely opposed. Brontë and Blake are perfect embodiments of the writer-as-agent: both are not merely bearing witness to the rise of Methodism and Evangelicalism as a cultural phenomenon; they are shaking moral fists at it in deliberate acts of imaginative insubordination.

Thompson the literary critic and cultural historian is at his best in 'Disenchantment or Default? A Lay Sermon', which was delivered as one of the Albert Schweitzer lectures at New York University in 1968. Arguing against an established view of Wordsworth as having become more of a poet the more he jettisoned his youthful radicalism, Thompson bases his case first of all on the evidence of 'actual lived historical experience'.[22] This reveals a Wordsworth rejecting the aridities of Godwinism, but only in order to turn towards 'real men and away from an abstracted man'.[23] What Hazlitt described as Wordsworth's levelling muse took the form it did because his Jacobinism enabled him to break with the prevalent condescension towards the experience of common people:

This creative moment might be defined as a Jacobinism-in-recoil or a Jacobinism-of-doubt. I must insist upon both sides of this definition. It is no good if we see only the recoil, or the doubt: yet so obsessed was a recent generation of critics with similar experiences of disenchantment in their own time, that this has been the tendency. The doubt is interesting and reputable; the affirmation can be discounted.

But it is exactly within this conflict – the moment when the received culture was challenged, all conventions were called into question, and the great humanist affirmations were abroad, but when sharp experience had shown that the florid periods of the platform Jacobin or the abstract periods of the *philosophes* were inadequate – it is exactly within this conflict that the great romantic impulse came to maturity.[24]

If 'recent critics' can be convicted (in the middle of the Cold War and in the aftermath of McCarthyism, let us remember) of conflating their own god-that-failed (communism) with the Godwin that failed Wordsworth, Thompson himself is able to see the continuity of affirmation in poems like 'The Ruined Cottage' and *The Prelude*. The dialectic of ideology and experience, of surviving ideals and the frightening excesses of politics on the ground with which Wordsworth and Coleridge were confronted cannot be fully understood, or its creative outcomes properly judged, if the persistence of the egalitarian impulse – especially in Wordsworth – is overlooked.

At this point in his lecture Thompson offers a crucial distinction between 'apostasy' and 'disenchantment'. He insists: 'There is nothing in disenchantment inimical to art. But when aspiration [towards liberty, equality, etc.] is actively denied, we are at the edge of apostasy, and apostasy is a moral failure, and an imaginative failure ... It is an imaginative failure because it involves forgetting – or manipulating improperly – the authenticity of experience: a mutilation of the writer's own previous existential being.'[25] The presence here of the words 'authenticity' and 'existential being' places this in its own cultural-historical moment: Thompson might just as appropriately have accused the apostate of 'bad faith'. However, his argument easily outlives, because it so effortlessly assimilates, what for some may be rejected as intellectual fashion. Only those who would downplay experience altogether – for example by relegating it to a secondary symptom of material forces and/or a conditioned reflex of hegemonic ideology – could fail to acknowledge the critical value of the dialectic Thompson proposes here. As long as Wordsworth was able to sustain some sense of it, his writing could still draw on a current of moral and emotional solidarity with the downtrodden. Coleridge was much quicker to oversimplify his own evolution and to dismiss his early radicalism as 'my squeaking baby-trumpet of Sedition'. Nevertheless, both poets ended up in apostasy and their work paid the price. Of disenchantment Thompson again insists: 'I cannot think that disenchantment is at enmity with poetry; one might as well suppose that honesty is so. I wish sometimes that Shelley's verse had been stiffened with a touch of it, that he had written an ode to the east wind.'[26] And to this Thompson adds a generous rider: even the apostates should not be written off, because they gave up the struggle to believe in a positive future for humanity when faced with the brute realities of struggle.

Thompson ends his 'lay sermon' (an ironic echo of Coleridge) by countering the twentieth-century apostasy of Auden with the example of an American poet, and personal friend, about whom he later writes at length in *The Heavy Dancers*. 'Homage to Thomas McGrath' forms the last and longest section of that book (279–337) and throughout it Thompson is at pains to pay tribute to McGrath's undeviating commitment to radical hopes and objectives. At one point, a long section of McGrath's poem 'Against the False Magicians' is quoted and discussed. Whilst the extract is too long to give here, the comments which follow it offer a characteristic instance of Thompson's critical practice:

> This poem is given an uncomplex dialectical structure. The thesis of the first verse (the wish-fulfilment of romanticism) is easy, fluent, uncluttered. The antithesis of the second verse (realism) opens with a memorable image: 'A warship can sink a circus at forty miles.' One remembers Mr Sleary's circus in *Hard Times* (which, however, was not in the end sunk by the batteries of utilitarianism); but today I always think also of the tanks rolling in to extinguish the Prague Spring. If realism surrenders to the contingent ('the chance and accident of our real world') then it betrays the privileged view of life of art has no terms for 'the potential' ('a view of life according to probability or necessity'), falling back in the end upon the lost fantasies of romance. In the final verse McGrath affirms the true magical properties of poetry ('the charm which the potential has'), moving through a commonplace pathetic image to the sustained and impassioned synthesis in which the reality of human spiritual forces is affirmed ('in a sense truer than the life we see lived all round us').[27]

Here Thompson moves easily from formal and stylistic features to a comparison with Dickens and a glance at the Czech uprising of 1968. His principal theme is how McGrath's poem manages its dialectical structure so as to achieve the final affirmation, not of the romantic dream of perfectibility, but of an enduring 'potential' about which poetry is especially able to speak – as long as it does not surrender its true magic to the tyranny of contingency.

Literature comes readily to hand as Thompson lays about him in 'The Peculiarities of the English', with here a clever inversion of Mr Podsnap's Little-Englandism, there an invocation of Elizabethan drama or Andrew Marvell, and elsewhere a lengthy quote from Smollett's *Humphrey Clinker* to illustrate the comedy of manners created by the conjuncture of different sources of wealth and status in eighteenth-century Britain. Pursuing Anderson and Nairn's failure to understand the true nature of historical change in Britain, Thompson offers this example of how lived experience does not readily submit to the tidy categories of theory:

> The Unitarians pushed God so far back into his Baconian heaven of first causes that he became, except for purposes of moral incantation, quite ineffectual. He was left alone (alas! to be fetched out later against the people as a furious Papa) while the bourgeoisie entered into their true inheritance – the exploitation of nature.
>
> It should not have happened this way. Heaven should have been stormed, *molte con brio*, and the fruits of knowledge should have been wrested from the clutches of priests. But happen this way it did. (The contrast between let us say, Zola on the one hand, and Hardy and George Moore on the other, or between Anatole France and E. M. Forster, points to a continuing difference in literary modes.)[28]

Thompson's reach extends well beyond the critique of a local theological emphasis to take in much wider, including European, cultural manifestations. Alongside theologians and philosophers, those inveterate moral witnesses the novelists are adduced, as Thompson points (and this only in parenthesis!) to hugely significant differences of outlook and approach – scientific or broadly metaphysical – regarding human nature and human society. And again writers are reckoned as important as scientists in his defence of empiricism:

> I cannot see empiricism as an *ideology* at all. Anderson and Nairn have confused an intellectual *idiom*, which for various historical reasons has become a rational habit, with an ideology. Bacon and Hazlitt, Darwin and George Orwell, may all have employed this idiom, but they can scarcely be said to have been attached to the same ulterior ideological assumptions.[29]

A little further on, he concludes:

The empirical idiom can favour insular resistances and conceptual opportunism. But it may also conceal acute intelligence and a conceptual toughness which is immanent rather than explicit; at best it has carried the realism of the English novel, and has served – notably in the natural sciences – as an idiom superbly adapted to the interpenetration of theory and *praxis*.[30]

This is one of the clearest expressions of Thompson's belief in the central historical relevance of imaginative literature. The empirical idiom has been as indispensable to the English novel as it has to the natural sciences; the moral imagination has proved as productive of humanly important evidence as the rubrics and procedures of the laboratory. Without constant testing against lived experience, theory is liable to spin off into the sort of dangerously alienated self-enclosure typified by Althusser.

Among the many complexly related crimes and misdemeanours of which Thompson accuses Althusser, the greatest is his systematic hostility to human agency, to people as subjects of their own history. Thompson surmises a situation in which we succumb to the coercive systematisations of Althusser and his followers: 'At last they extract from us a denial: a denial of human agency, creativity, a denial even of self. But, as we rise from their theoretical racks, we see, through the window, the process of history going on. "E per' si muove!" – and yet, *it does move!*'[31] The irony here is finely pointed: into the closed world of Theory breaks the recalcitrant voice of Galileo insisting on the validity of empirical observation. And where better to turn in pursuit of what experience can teach us than to imaginative literature? And what better exemplar of the writer-as-agent than this:

> Blake reminds us of a very old, sometimes reputable, sometimes arcane hermetic tradition – often a tradition of poets – which sought to articulate modes of apprehension appropriate to a reality which was always in flux, in conflict, in decay and in becoming. Against the 'single vision' of mechanical materialism, Blake sought, and succeeded, to think co-existent 'contrary states' and to marry heaven and hell.[32]

Here is a dialectical vision to rank with that of Marx, though of a very different kind. To both men history is a ceaseless conflict of contraries with no guarantee of a synthesis that will punctually deliver a fully human society. It is in the limitless investigative possibilities of dialectical vision, not in any mechanically generated resolutions, that its value lies. I shall return to it later in my discussion of Thompson's book on Blake.

Late poetry and The Sykaos Papers

Why shouldn't art try, by its **own** means of course, to further the great social task of mastering life?

Bertolt Brecht[33]

The influence of Auden is pervasive throughout Thompson's poetry. There is the defiant position-taking of 'The Place Called Choice' with its ringing humanist affirmations:

> First of all I declare
> That man is changed by his deeds,
> And all within his kingdom
> Is stone, water, air
>
> Transformed into a fire
> Lighting the moors and blown
> By every tempest higher
> Until air, water, and stone
> In the furnace of the mind
> Are changed into desire
> And all things are defined.

and, a little further on:

> It's time to speak one's mind.
> I'm sick of an 'anxious age'.
> I am fed to the teeth with the cant
> Of 'guilt' and original sin.[34]

Up to and including such late poems as 'History Lessons' and 'The Rectification of Names', Thompson can be seen combining and contrasting the resources of colloquial plain-speaking and various official discourses (politics, economics, technology) in a dialectic of dissent and sclerosis in which echoes of Auden's erudite bravado are ever-present. Furthermore, the intimate, wryly realistic but still defiantly tender side of Auden can be heard in 'Valentine' of 1957 which begins in much the same way, in both tone and setting, as Auden's 'Lullaby' ('Lay your sleeping head, my love'): 'Ten years your separate face / Has made its casual dent / Beside my own'. And the earlier 'Declarations of Love' (1952), dedicated to his wife, demonstrates Thompson's skill in blending the Auden voice ('My love, the earliest poets knew / That man was other than animals') with that of late Yeats:

I saw her bend over my son in the garden,
And the child turned suddenly and shouted at the snow.
That was enough to set these sensual rhythms swaying
Till all the rooms of reason rang: and I, above,
Saw words, like dancers, in their hundred motions go
Among the patterns which the fiddlers were playing,
And one recurring word came past, which I called 'Love'.[35]

Inescapably reminded of Yeats's 'Among School Children', as I think
we must be here, one is also conscious of Thompson confidently
commandeering 'influences' and keeping a clever intertextual balance
as he fashions a serviceable idiom for his own distinctive point of view.

And, of course, there is Blake, the most admired of all Thompson's
favourites. Yet there are few obvious echoes in Thompson's poetry,
though Blake's example is constantly invoked elsewhere in his work.
Blake's visionary inclusiveness may be regarded as a significant structural element in long poems like 'The First Emperor' and 'The Place
Called Choice'; but, if the Prophetic Books are present largely as an
organising principle, the *Songs of Innocence and Experience* have
surely contributed a very Blakean blend of formal conciseness and
resonant symbolism to short late poems like 'Art', 'Speech' and – last
of the *Collected Poems* – 'A Charm Against Evil', with its exhortation
to 'Let the dragons and the lions play. / Let us swallow the worm of
power / And the name pass away.'

The group to which these three short poems belong, *Powers and
Names* (1980), has a wry dedication to Szuma Chien, the victimised
Chinese historian of the second to first centuries BC, which points
to an oriental influence of the sort so successfully assimilated and
adapted by Brecht. If Blake stands behind a few of the poems, so does
Chinese poetry, the Japanese haiku and Far Eastern history and myth.
Thompson's ability to exploit his immensely wide-ranging literary
and world-historical knowledge was still functioning very effectively
in his final years as a poet.

That knowledge is abundantly present in Thompson's only
published novel, *The Sykaos Papers*.[36] Oi Paz, an intergalactic Gulliver,
crash-lands on Earth and goes through a series of encounters which
reveal to him the shortcomings of the human race. As with Swift, who
is Thompson's principal model here, the yardstick for most of the
offered judgements is Reason; but, whereas Gulliver is by turns the
judge and the judged – superior to Lilliputian folly yet found wanting
by the Brobdingnagians and the Houyhnhnms – Oi Paz is secure

in his own rationality, which is never seriously called into question when any major critical verdict is at issue.[37] Easy targets abound: 'I marvelled that any creatures could have turned a planet so clement into such a stinking dump.'[38] In particular, the threat of nuclear extinction gets a thorough satirical savaging in line with Thompson's current campaigning for END (for example, Oi Paz's 'Journal Entry 00226') and, near the novel's end, an all-out nuclear war is about to obliterate life on earth, watched from the moon by a helpless Helena Sage. Thompson has great fun playing with sci-fi clichés (Oi Paz repeatedly asks people to take him to their leader), and there are many comical Oitarian misunderstandings of everything from the meaning of being mugged and the taxation system to the mechanics of food ingestion and sexual intercourse. Misuses of the English language furnish the novel with some of its best comic moments. Oi Paz is in a state of chronic discourse maladjustment; he never gets the hang of how colloquialisms differ from polite speech, or how metaphors are distinguishable from literal statements. Even though he is physically attracted to Helena and fathers a child with her, he remains bemused by much of the vocabulary of human affection and commitment.

Throughout its nearly 500 pages the novel offers us some variations of narrative pace and point of view; but there are still too many *longueurs*, for example when Oi Paz virtually disappears from the scene during much of the 'Second Captivity' section and also when, in Sections 1–3, there is an inescapable sense of the plot being wholly subordinate to a procession of polemical targets. The novel raids the resources of science fiction and popular ethology like that in Desmond Morris's *The Naked Ape*, while at the same time exposing folly in ways derived from Swift and from essayists like Bacon and Hazlitt. Nevertheless, in the end one is left with a memory of many cleverly engineered moments of amusement and assent, but not much more. Even Oi Paz himself is not consistently handled: most of the time he is surprised and bewildered by what he witnesses; yet there are other times when he shows an unexplained familiarity with the smallest details of human technology or language or social behaviour. He also regularly forgets what he already knows, so that at one moment newborn babies appear to him to be 'so large as to scarcely be able to press a way' out of the womb, while a few lines later they are 'thrust pell-mell into the world ... raw and helpless' and 'not much larger than a hand'.[39] Some allowance should be made for an occasional lapse of concentration, especially in a writer as prolific as

Thompson; but lapses become much more prominent – and more of an obstacle to full engagement – when there is not enough psychological depth and narrative drive to compensate for them.

Blake and dialectical vision

Without contraries is no progression.

Blake, *The Marriage of Heaven and Hell*

Although his early death was responsible for Thompson's book on Blake being his last, there is also a peculiar aptness about it. Here, in this comparatively short study, are brought together the major critical ideas and practices identified in this discussion so far. In addition to his dialectical vision – and, changing the stress slightly but importantly, his visionary dialectics – Blake consistently exemplifies the highest and best of historical agency. No greater tribute could be paid him than the one with which Thompson concludes the book: 'Never, on any page of Blake, is there the least complicity with the Kingdom of the Beast.'[40] (The same could be said of Thompson himself, of course.) The Beast that Blake so consistently confronted was the State (including state religion, otherwise the Whore) in all its repressive, deformative aspects. In the *Prophetic Books* it is Urizen who personifies such power. One can see how Thompson had in mind the dead hand of Urizen in his portrait of the rule-dominated Oitaria in *The Sykaos Papers*, though that world also owes something to the Houyhnhnms and to the mechanistic determinism of Althusser's orrery. Now, despite the illness from which he would shortly die, Thompson showed himself in complete command of his source material, from the vast array of Blake-related studies to the most recondite of Dissenting tracts. Yet, for all the reach and depth of his scholarship, Thompson is characteristically concerned to take us with him, whether we are specialists or just interested amateurs. A typical aside is: 'I beg the impatient Blake reader to favour me with at least a temporary suspension of disbelief. I am not simply rambling on, wherever curiosity may lead me. I am engaged in a complex operation, teasing out strands which may lead on to other strands across 150 years.'[41] Such comradely appeals and patient explanations may, in part, be vestigial traces of the lecture series (Toronto, 1978) in which the book had its origin. Yet they also show the same blend of easy familiarity and intense intellectual concentration that we can identify again and again across the whole range of Thompson's work. Like the adult education tutor he once was, he treats his readers as co-workers to whom he is disarmingly frank about the tentativeness of his own thinking, 'teasing out strands which *may* lead on to other strands'.

And 'lead on' they do, as Thompson exhaustively discusses the century and a half of Dissenting, Antinomian, millenarian and other ideas that preceded and fed into the moment of Blake. An extended discussion of 'The Divine Image', from *Songs of Innocence*, brings into focus Blake's maverick version of Swedenborgianism by setting it against some leadenly orthodox Swedenborgian hymns of the Revd Joseph Pound. Further contextualising and clarifying evidence from Muggletonian and other sources takes us finally to the claim that the poem 'holds in tension and reconciles'[42] rival ideas of the nature of God. Such positions may have been irreconcilable at the level of contemporary theological debate, but, for the poet, 'a contradiction in thought, which derives from an acute tension of contrasting values, neither of which can be abandoned, can be wholly creative'.[43] Through the language and form of the poem the Blakean dialectic can hold such contraries in a productive equipoise from which can emerge a triumphant humanist imperative: 'all must love the human form / In heathen, Turk or Jew; / Where Mercy, Love and Pity dwell, / There God is dwelling too'. Thompson persuasively demonstrates that Blake's emphasis on the centrality of Love is interdependent with, and is actually enacted by, the reconciling power of the poetic imagination. There is nothing new about this idea as such; but Thompson gives it extra heft by his patient unpicking of the possible and probable strands of religious thought that Blake wove together in his inimitable way. Thompson the historian and Thompson the critic support and illuminate each other's work at all points.

A short chapter exploring the sectarian disputes behind *Songs of Innocence and Experience* leads us to an entire chapter on 'London'. This great poem makes a perfect object for Thompson's critical attention because, among many other things, it is easily understood without much prior detailed knowledge of the genealogy of Blake's ideas. Thompson is therefore able to analyse an absolutely seminal Blake text with less need for contextual elaboration and proportionally closer attention to matters of language and form. These he addresses by way of a stanza-by-stanza comparison of the poem's final version with earlier drafts. This immediately highlights the crucial substitution of 'charter'd' for 'dirty' in the two opening lines. The resonances of 'charter'd' are then traced in relation to both Whig ideology and Radical insistence on human rights: Paine's *Rights of Man* versus Burke's *Reflections on the Revolution in France*. Next come some thoughts on the alteration of 'see in every face I meet' to 'mark in every face I meet'. In his best tutorial style Thompson invites us to note the double repetition of mark as 'marks' in line four and to agree with him that 'the words beat upon us in subliminal ways: even in these biblically illiterate days we have all heard of "the mark of the Beast"'.[44] A biblical echo? An allusion to Virgil, as detected by one commentator? Thompson's interest is always in the *use* Blake makes of such intertextuality: '"The mark of the Beast" would seem, like "charter'd", to have something to do with the buying and selling of human values.'[45] A possible allusion to Ezekiel 9.4 is discounted after comparison of Ezekiel's vision with Blake's. To conflate the two would not be a creative balancing of contraries, but a 'direct contradiction of intention and feeling' about which Thompson is emphatic: 'Ambiguities of this dimension are not fruitful multipliers of meaning.'[46] Much more productive of meaning is a consideration of what Blake's radical and Dissenting contemporaries would have made of those 'marks'. This shift of perspective tends to support the Beast as the likeliest signified in the minds of a Dissenting readership steeped in the language of Revelation.

In a luminously clear analysis of the poem's second stanza, Thompson begins with 'mind-forg'd manacles' and proceeds to a passage that can easily be taken to exemplify his critical style:

How then are we to read 'ban'? F. W. Bateson, a confident critic, tells us 'in every execration or curse (*not* in every prohibition)'. I can't share his confidence: one must be prepared for seventeen types of ambiguity in Blake, and, in any case, the distinction between a curse and a prohibition is not a large one. The 'bans' may be execrations, but the mind may be encouraged to move through further associations, from the banns before marriage, the prohibitive ethic constraining 'lawless' love ('"Thou Shalt Not" writ over the door') to the bans of Church and State against the publications and activities of the followers of Tom Paine. All these associations are gathered into the central one of a code of morality which constricts, denies, prohibits and punishes.[47]

The opening question is typical, with its unifying appeal to a common pursuit. Then there is the quoted voice of a critic whose categorical certainty offers a useful foil for Thompson's more hospitable inclusivity. A joking allusion to Empson's *Seven Types of Ambiguity* gently mocks a lack of alertness in Bateson's reading, while the rest of the paragraph brings together a formidable list of plausible associations which, for all its nod towards tentativeness ('may be ... may be'), turns out to be just as confident as Bateson's more limited one. The remaining discussion, of stanzas three and four, may not at every point satisfy the more exacting literary specialist (for example, Thompson misses an important ironic sense of 'appals'), but the strategy of comparing the poem's final version with earlier drafts and other Blake poems continues to pay dividends. Above all, it yields the remarkable judgement that 'London' is 'a literal poem and it is also an apocalyptic one; or we may say that it is a poem whose moral realism is so searching that it is raised to the intensity of apocalyptic vision'.[48] He goes on to examine Blake's management of the transition from visual to auditory imagery and the cumulative impact of all that is seen and heard in the poem; but he also notices the way Blake's simple human archetypes (infant, soldier, harlot) extend a very specific social scene into something redolent of a more general condition. There is a dialectical balance even at the level of *tone*, with the 'voice of indignation ... held in equilibrium with the voice of compassion',[49] so that we realise that this urban hell is populated 'not so much by our fellow-damned as our fellow-sufferers'.[50] There is a solidarising commonality of experience, rather than a series of isolated individual fates. Blake's dialectical vision encompasses everything without sacrificing local tensions or the sense of a predicament in which, with whatever grotesque ironies, we all share. In this way he goes beyond not only the glaring injustices of the State, with its palaces, churches and prisons, but also beyond the limiting materialist rationality espoused by radicals like Tom Paine and the London Corresponding Society.

Conclusion

It's time to speak one's mind.

'The Place Called Choice'[51]

Edward Thompson's deepest instincts were democratic. From his wartime experience in the army, through his years in adult education, to his many interventions in moral campaigns and intellectual debates, his style was always and invariably that of someone anxious to join with others in – if nothing else – the solidarity of shared conversation. He did not think of himself as a different sort of writer when he was practising social history, or literary criticism, or political polemics – or, for that matter, preparing teaching notes or making poems. All writing was a means of engaging with oneself and other people, a salutary assertion of the individual moral will and of an inescapable mutuality as much as an invigorating tussle with language and form. He could turn his hand to many things; but the essential challenge was always the same: to oppose with all his strength the forces of reaction and defeat. As things stand in the world at present, the force of his example is not likely to diminish.

Notes

1 B. D. Palmer, *E. P. Thompson: Objections and Oppositions* (London and New York: Verso, 1994), pp. 92–3.

2 *Ibid.*, p. 74.

3 E. P. Thompson, *Collected Poems* (Newcastle-upon-Tyne: Bloodaxe, 1999).

4 E. P. Thompson, *The Heavy Dancers* (London: Merlin Press, 1985), pp. 203–25.

5 *Ibid.*, p. 232.

6 Thompson, *Collected Poems*, p. 38.

7 Thompson, *The Heavy Dancers*, pp. 227–8; Thompson, *Collected Poems*, p. 39.

8 D. Goodway, 'E. P. Thompson and the Making of *The Making of the English Working Class*', in R. Taylor (ed.), *Beyond the Walls: 50 Years of Adult and Continuing Education at the University of Leeds 1946–1996* (Leeds: University of Leeds, 1996), p. 134.

9 A. Croft, 'Edward Thompson the Literature Tutor', in Taylor, *Beyond the Walls*, pp. 154–5.

10 E. P. Thompson, *Education and Experience* (Leeds: Leeds University Press, 1968), reprinted in Thompson, *The Heavy Dancers*, pp. 4–32, p. 11.

11 D. Thompson, 'Foreword' in E. P. Thompson, *The Romantics: England in a Revolutionary Age* (Suffolk: Merlin Press, 1997), p. 1.

12 E. P. Thompson, *William Morris: Romantic to Revolutionary* (New York and London: Pantheon and Merlin Press, 1977), p. 657.

13 E. P. Thompson, *The Making of the English Working Class* (Harmondsworth: Penguin, 1968), p. 821.

14 *Ibid.*, p. 822.

15 *Ibid.*

16 See T. Paulin, *The Day-Star of Liberty: William Hazlitt's Radical Style* (London: Faber & Faber, 1998), *passim*. It should be noted that Paulin takes issue with Thompson by stressing Hazlitt's Radical credentials and in particular his knowledge of 'common life'. *Ibid.*, p. 241.

17 E. P. Thompson, 'Outside the Whale', in E. P. Thompson (ed.) *Out of*

Apathy (New Left Books, 1960), reprinted in E. P. Thompson, *The Poverty of Theory* (London: Merlin Press, 1978), pp. 1–33, p. 13.

18 *Ibid.*, p. 22.

19 Thompson, *The Heavy Dancers*, p. 4.

20 J. Goode, 'E. P. Thompson and "the Significance of Literature"', in H. J. Kaye and K. McClelland (eds), *E. P. Thompson: Critical Perspectives* (Cambridge: Polity Press, 1990), pp. 183–203, p. 199.

21 To claim, as Michael Fischer has done, that Thompson 'is not a close reader of texts' ('The Literary Importance of E. P. Thompson's Marxism', *English Literary History* 50:4 [Winter 1983], 826) may be plausible in the purest poststructuralist sense of close reading; but it surely fails to recognise the readerly intelligence and stylistic acuity I'm discussing in this chapter.

22 E. P. Thompson, 'Disenchantment or Default?: A Lay Sermon', reprinted in Thompson, *The Romantics*, pp. 33–74, p. 34.

23 *Ibid.*, p.34.

24 *Ibid.*, p. 37.

25 *Ibid.*, p. 38.

26 *Ibid.*, p. 68.

27 Thompson, *The Heavy Dancers*, p. 289.

28 Thompson, *The Poverty of Theory*, pp. 60–1.

29 *Ibid.*, p. 63.

30 *Ibid.*, p. 64.

31 *Ibid.*, p. 300.

32 *Ibid.*, p. 305.

33 B. Brecht, 'Alienation Effects in Chinese Acting', in J. Willett (trans.) *Brecht on Theatre* (London: Eyre Methuen, 1978), p. 96.

34 This and the previous extract, Thompson, *Collected Poems*, pp. 64–5.

35 *Ibid.*, p. 71.

36 E. P. Thompson, *The Sykaos Papers* (London: Bloomsbury, 1988).

37 To be sure, the reader grows increasingly aware of the limitations of the Oitarian mind-set. Oi Paz may be a Poet, but he shares with Swift's talking horses an inflexible rationality which, in its intolerance of mess or muddle, cannot see the creative side of inconsistency.

38 Thompson, *The Sykaos Papers*, p. 79.

39 *Ibid.*, pp. 156–7.

40 E. P. Thompson, *Witness Against the Beast: William Blake and the Moral Law* (Cambridge: Cambridge University Press, 1993), p. 229.

41 *Ibid.*, p. 31.

42 *Ibid.*, p. 160.

43 *Ibid.*, p. 159.

44 *Ibid.*, p. 179.

45 *Ibid.*, p. 180.

46 *Ibid.*, p. 181.
47 *Ibid.*, p. 184.
48 *Ibid.*, p.187.
49 *Ibid.*, p. 189.
50 *Ibid.*, p. 190.
51 Thompson, *Collected Poems*, p. 65.

Part II

Policy, theory and peace campaigns

6

Thompson and socialist humanism

Kate Soper

Introduction

My first encounter with the writings of E. P. Thompson was not *The Making of the English Working Class*, but *The Poverty of Theory and other Essays*. As a graduate student of Marxist philosophy at the time, taught and surrounded by convinced Althusserians and feeling much peer pressure to conform, though unpersuaded by structuralist anti-humanism myself, I remember the pleasure and relief with which I read this work (and the chiding I received in some quarters for my enthusiasm). It was not that I could endorse all its argument, for it struck me that there were many places where Thompson had miscon-strued Althusser's position or argued mistakenly or feebly against it.[1] But here for the first time I felt in the presence of a truly powerful and sympathetic contemporary Marxist voice. A voice, moreover, that was calling one to action and not merely advising one of academic recti-tude. And then there was the wit, the passionate polemic, the frisson of the writing in itself. Here was someone to read and read again, simply for the pleasure of it – and I did.

Over the following decade, in response to the deployment of Soviet SS-20 and NATO cruise and Pershing missiles in the European 'theatre of war', I, like many other lapsed CND-ers, became heavily involved in the resurgent peace movement, and was especially influenced by the rallying cry of Thompson's pamphlet, *Protest and Survive*, and the non-aligned 'Beyond the Blocs' politics of END (which I joined early, subsequently becoming a member of the Coordinating Committee and, for a time, Chairperson). It was during this period, when I was working quite closely with both Edward and Dorothy Thompson in END, that I went back to Thompson's earlier New Left writings, and eventually wrote a synoptic view of his 'socialist humanism' conceived as a constant, if continuously revised, thematic of his historical and political argument.[2] At the time of its writing, although Gorbachev had come to power in the USSR, and there had been some easing of Cold War hostility, there was little sense that within a year or so the Berlin Wall would have crumbled and the bloc division of Europe be fast breaking down. Nor did I foresee how soon the whole philosophy and politics of 'socialist humanism' would come to seem, if not exactly outdated, certainly bereft of much of its immediate theoretical pertinence and political connection. The reasons for this, and its implications, will be discussed in more detail later. Suffice it to say here, that the issues raised by this shift bear on the more general question of the purposes of the re-engagement with Thompson's work to be found in this volume.

It can be said, of course, that its aim is obvious, namely, to commemorate the publication, fifty years on, of Thompson's magnum opus. Yet Thompson himself might well have queried this rationale on the grounds that the justification to return to his legacy should be more than commemorative or a matter of 'historic interest': that it should lie in its abiding relevance to the present or message to the future. Or, if preferred, because 'historic interest', in his conception, should always be construed as implying, in its very scrutiny of the past, some form of critique of the present or instruction for the future. If this is indeed the case, then we must ask how we are to understand that instruction and critique today in the case of Thompson's argument on 'socialist humanism': a phrase naming a theoretico-political stance, both of whose terms are sounding fairly archaic in the ears of most younger academics and cultural critics, and certainly not much found together on their lips, or on those of left-wing activists generally. In short, what relevance, if any, does Thompson's 'socialist humanism' have for us today? Since no answer can be given to this question, and certainly none of positive import, without examining his argument more fully, I shall seek at this point to provide some historic overview on this.

As Thompson himself acknowledged, the term 'socialist humanism' has had an ambiguous history.[3] Many and various are the parties that have laid claim to it.[4] But for Thompson it always referred to a libertarian communism and positive neutralism that was as opposed to Stalinism in Soviet dominated Europe as it was to 'Natopolitanism' in Western Europe. Its core themes, as expressed and defended by him in the 1950s, were the rejection of the antithetical 'philistinisms' of social democracy and Stalinist Communism; the insistence that the sole route to genuine socialist emancipation lay on a course between the two; and the affirmation of human moral autonomy and powers of historical agency. Together, these provided the unbroken thematic thread of all Thompson's writings. The early study of William Morris and the critique of Stalinism in the 1950s, the wrestlings with Labour movement reformism in the 1960s, the quarrel with Althusser, the assaults upon the erosion of civil liberties and the manufacture of consensus in the late 1970s, and – perhaps most pressingly of all – the denunciation of Cold War stasis and the 'exterminist' logic of the arms race in the 1980s, were part of a singular project designed to rescue the 'moral imagination' from 'philistinism' (the disposition to accept and defend any existing reality as immutable necessity), and thus to check the mindless drift towards the obliteration of all human culture.

In charting Thompson's 'socialist humanism' one is therefore charting both a moment in his political thinking (one which also belonged to a larger moment of European history) and the conceptual framework within which that thinking was cast. But while the framework proved a constant, Thompson did not show himself disposed to cling to the early formulas of his 'socialist humanism' as if their ritualistic repetition could ward off all diabolisms, whether of left or right. On the contrary, they were modified and reformulated as new circumstances came into being, requiring different emphases, struggles and polemic. Sulk in his tent as he did at times, Thompson also always emerged again to renew the dialogue, to take issue again with history and to put veteran arguments to work for new campaigns. In this sense, his socialist humanism has a history of development within its relative fixity of outlook.[5]

Out of Stalinism

The inaugural date of socialist humanism, so Thompson maintained, was 1956. In reaction to the revelations of Stalin's crimes made at the Twentieth Congress of the CPSU and the subsequent Soviet invasion of Hungary, the term, he tells us,

> arose simultaneously in a hundred places, and on ten thousand lips. It was voiced by poets in Poland, Russia, Hungary, Czechoslovakia; by factory delegates in Budapest; by Communist militants at the eighth plenum of the Polish Party; by a Communist premier (Imre Nagy), who was murdered for his pains. It was on the lips of women and men

coming out of gaol and of the relatives and friends of those who never came out.[6]

In Britain the key factors were the mass resignation from the CP occasioned by the suppression of the Hungarian revolt, and the subsequent regrouping of former communist dissidents and others into the 'New Left'[7] (see chapter 8).

Disillusionment with Soviet communism was not, it should be said, the sole motive behind these developments – which were inspired also by fears of a wholesale rejection of socialist argument. Abhorrence at what 'Marxism' had come to encompass, anxiety lest disenchantment might lead to its complete abandonment: these were the impulses of the New Left in general and of Thompson's argument in particular. In line with this, they saw their task in actively political terms: the aim was to build a nationwide campaigning base for socialist renewal (hence the importance attached to the formation of the network of New Left clubs).[8] Rather in contrast to this emphasis, the socialist humanist revolt on the continent was much more closely associated with a flowering of Marxist philosophy based on a reappraisal of Marx's debt to Hegel, and an awakened interest in his early texts. New readings of Hegel were of critical importance in this process,[9] as was the influence of the 'humanist-Hegelian' Marxism first developed in the inter-war years by Gramsci, Korsch and, above all, Lukács.[10]

Though the general claim of these humanists was that they were doing no more than reassert the authentic Marxist dialectic of human beings as both 'made' by historical circumstances and active in their making, it was inevitable, given the mechanistic orthodoxy to which they were reacting, that they placed the stress on the active and creative component. At times, this brought them close to a denial of economic or ideological determination altogether, a denial associated in the existentialist argument with a tendency to recast relations of production as interpersonal relations, and thus to put in question the whole idea of 'unwilled' social forces possessed of their own dynamic and exigency. At the same time, and incompatibly in some ways, there was an emphasis on *alienation*, a process associated with the failure of individuals to perceive the social source of the value of commodities (fetishism) or to understand the true nature of social relations and institutions (ideology).

The tension between these emphases was reflected in a certain polarisation of Marxist humanist argument. On the one hand, a more

Hegelian–Lukácsian school of thinking pointed to the importance of generalised processes of reification and alienation as the 'theft' of our humanity, but encountered difficulties in consequence when it came to specifying the means of escape from these. (Thus Lukács was led to posit a hyper-organic collectivity – the proletariat in its 'ascribed' consciousness – as the universal 'subject' of history, and to view its project in directly Hegelian terms as the realisation of an immanent historical reason.) The existentialist tendency, on the other hand, emphasised the irreducibility of conscious, or 'lived' experience, and insisted upon the intelligibility of history as aggregated human praxes. This was an argument that respected the claim that history is made by real men and women rather than by hypostatisations. But it had difficulties in reconciling that claim with the historical materialist insistence on 'alien' or 'unwilled' social forces possessed of their own intrinsic order.

Nearer to the existentialist pole than to the Hegelian–Lukácsian in the stress it placed on conscious experience, Thompson's position should nonetheless be distinguished from both, not only on account of its sharper political focus and moral passion, but also by his reluctance to engage in the debates on philosophical anthropology that preoccupied his continental counterparts. But there was no way he could avoid the philosophical problems posed by juxtaposing 'humanism' and 'socialism' as if these were two clearly complementary impulses of a single *political* strategy, and no sooner had Thompson formulated the argument for this than the charge of idealism – and thus evasion – was laid against it from both sides of the political fence. The more liberal critics suggested that 'socialist humanism' was all very fine as an aspiration, but Stalinism had made clear the impossibility of any such route to communism, and commitment to the latter had therefore to be rethought. The more 'Stalinist' argument was that it was simply unrealistic to suppose that a movement committed to the interests of a particular class could hope to proceed to its goals without offending against a 'humanist' regard for all individuals 'as such'. In short, a class-based morality was incompatible with any humanist ethic, and the linking of the two purely verbal: 'socialist humanism' offered no guide at all on the crucial issue of the means that communists could justifiably use in pursuit of their ends.[11] Thompson's general line of reply was that the charge of 'contradiction' in his argument was inappropriate, since the appeal was not to a seamless theoretical unity but to a certain sensibility or instinct: we know very well what we are talking about when we call for a more democratic and humanist socialism, and we also have a pretty good idea what sort of practices conform to it; but to attempt any rigid specification of those principles and practices would be to betray the very spirit of flexibility which they oppose to communist dogma.[12]

That said, it cannot be denied that a 'socialist' recognition of the class-conditioned nature of experience and affectivity is in uneasy tension with Thompson's 'humanist' appeals to a more universal and apparently 'natural' moral sense. The problem can be formulated thus: if this morality is genuinely universal (i.e. to be human is to be possessed of it), then how do we explain evil except as a form of corruption accountable to social conditioning? But so to explain it would appear to deny the essential element of moral autonomy central to the 'humanist' case. If, on the other hand, we take the view that individuals are morally autonomous, and thus good or bad 'in themselves', it is not clear why 'humanists' should be so concerned to defend the principles of the moral equality of persons. Nor can we allow, it would seem, for the possibility of moral error. An inherent moral sense of the kind invoked here by Thompson may be the only guide in the end as to what is right and wrong. But it can never be a guarantee against our acting badly; at least not if we accept that the consequences of our acts, and not merely our beliefs about them, have to enter into consideration of their ethical status. Yet to acknowledge that individuals can make moral 'mistakes' is to allow that moral consciousness must be open in some sense to forces it cannot grasp and to which its response is 'irrational'. (And, in fact, some recognition of this was implicit in Thompson's treatment of Stalinism as an 'ideology'. For this was to imply that it was not so much a deformed moral character but the grip of false ideas that drove the Stalinists to their crimes.)

In *The Poverty of Theory* Thompson was to circumvent the whole issue of conflict regarding the irreducibility of 'lived experience'[13] by arguing that concepts offering explanation in terms of a 'genetics' of self-mystification had very limited value. Thus he wrote:

> while historians may find these notions suggestive in certain areas, as in the study of ideologies, they would argue – I certainly will argue – that, in more general application, they are the product of an overly-rational mind; they offer an explanation in terms of mystified rationality for *non*-rational or irrational behaviour and belief, whose sources may not be educed from reason.[14]

The possibility of systematic misunderstanding of social relations along lines argued for by Marx was here more or less ruled out. Experience is itself a form of truth, and if we 'handle' it irrationally, that is not due to misconstruction of its causes or consequences but to our own intrinsic (affective, moral) being. Here again, then, as in the 1950s articles, the individual's 'moral character' is presented as a kind of base-line grounding the assertion of human agency which lies at the heart of the socialist humanist critique of Stalinism.

Part of the reason, one supposes, for Thompson's resistance to the idea of 'self-mystification' is that it appears to rely on the idea that consciousness can be moulded by forces that it cannot know. This was very much Sartre's objection to the Freudian Unconscious, and it is curious that Thompson seemed so little inclined to recognise any intellectual kinship here. For Sartre was not of the party of the anti-humanists, as Thompson was wont to imply,[15] but at one with Thompson in rejecting the idea of 'unconscious' forces which are excluded from experience while determining its content. According to Sartre, 'lived experience' is all there is; consciousness is translucent and the individual capable in principle of total self-understanding. Yet 'lived experience' is also a 'mystery in broad daylight',[16] since it has no means to express what it 'sees'. It is thus always 'simultaneously present to itself and absent from itself.'[17] Chary though Thompson was of seeking explanations for 'irrational' behaviour, it is surely something closer to this Sartrean conceptual framework that is needed to do justice to that favourite of Thompson's quotes from Morris – that men and women are the 'ever-baffled and ever-resurgent agents of an unmastered history'. Indeed, one might almost claim that Sartre's *Critique of Dialectical Reason* is an extended gloss on that remark; in other words, that it is a sustained attempt to theorise (through the concepts of 'lived experience', 'the group', 'seriality', 'the practico-inert', 'alterity', etc.) the Vico–Marx–Engels–Morris–Thompson conception of history as a humanly created but largely unauthored (in the sense of unintended) process.

What is more, Sartre insisted that this is a process in which action is both conditioned and free (by which he means that it is able to transcend or 'totalise' existing experience). 'Subjectivity', as he wrote, 'is neither everything nor nothing; it represents a moment in the objective process (that in which externality is internalised), and the moment is perpetually eliminated only to be reborn.'[18] Out of the ashes of the 'practico-inert', the phoenix of human freedom continually rearises – or so Sartre would have us believe. Is this so very different from Thompson's faith in the ever possible resurrection of the 'moral imagination' from the deadening processes of bureaucratisation, state encroachment, the arms race and media manipulation? (In a letter responding to my earlier article, Thompson expressed some limited agreement on this, writing that he found the comparison with Sartre 'especially valuable and convincing.')[19]

Out of neo-Stalinism

It was, of course, precisely because he felt a need – two decades on from 1956 – to reaffirm this 'moral imagination' and to rescue it from the deadening effects of Althusser's structuralist Marxism, that Thompson wrote *The Poverty of Theory*. Younger readers of his book, he told them, were not the 'post-Stalinist' generation they fondly imagined themselves to be. On the contrary, Stalinism as *theory* and attitude still weighed 'like an alp' on the brain of the living: the agenda of 1956 was still to be completed; the 'post-Stalinist' generation yet to be born.[20] Thompson proceeded to call for 'relentless war' upon the Althusserians, for they were the latest representatives of that current of Marxism against whose inhumanity and irrationalism the agenda of 1956 had been originally drawn up. The book ends, in effect, with a call to all Marxist intellectuals to come out of their academic ivory tower to renew, in 1978, the programme of the (old) New Left sketched in the original 'Epistle' of 1957.[21] In *The Poverty of Theory*, then, all the main themes of the socialist humanist polemic against Stalinism were re-enacted but in the form of an attack upon its theoretical legitimation rather than directly upon its practice. As might be expected, the argument converged in an assault on Althusser's anti-humanist denial of agency. But directly associated with that, and equally repugnant to Thompson, was the downgrading of ethical protest to the status of ideology. This was, indeed, an important move to contest, for not only was it the means by which Althusser was able to assimilate the humanist defence of morality to 'moralism' (the view – clearly mistaken – that moral argument will in itself bring about political transformation), it was also the charge that Perry Anderson was to lay against the old New Left in general in their response to 1956.[22] Anderson, indeed, suggested at one point that it was the central point from which radiated all the critical differences between the earlier 'socialist humanists' and the new grouping, led by himself, which took over the editorial direction of the *NLR* in 1962. Reading through his charting of their disagreements on historiography, Marxism, philosophy, internationalism and political strategy, a series of antinomies and equations impresses itself upon one: moralism versus historical materialism equals empiricism versus rationalism equals humanism versus anti-humanism equals reform versus revolution equals the parliamentary road versus (probably violent) class struggle equals the Labour Party versus international communism. In short, the issue of 'moralism' appeared to carry a heavy load.

But whatever the strains and stresses of the socialist humanist argument, it is simply not true that Thompson and the old New Left were guilty of 'moralism' in the sense of supposing political action to be exhausted in moral protest. In his discussion of '1956', one cannot help feeling that Anderson uncritically adopted the same reductive attitude to moral criticism that Thompson justly objects to in Althusser. And elsewhere in *Arguments Within English Marxism* Anderson states explicitly that he does not think Thompson's engagement with communist morality can be reduced to a mere 'moralism', or that we can dispense with moral critique.[23] One can note also that some new and different dialogues were to emerge a little later, whether or not they properly represent the synthesis Anderson calls for. One index of this was the publication of *Exterminism and Cold War* in 1982: among those paying tribute to Thompson's 'key' essay was the allegedly arch 'neo-Stalinist', Étienne Balibar.[24]

Out of apathy

In 1960, Thompson looked back upon the 1950s as a decade of apathy in which only the alarm call of CND had seriously disturbed public complacency. Capitalism had been left to rot on the bough and Britain was overripe for socialism. Yet never had the orthodox labour movement shown itself less concerned to foster the immanent growth.[25] Along with this gloomy retrospection went a distinct change of emphasis. The call was not for communist renewal[26] but for a socialist 'revolution' in Britain, and it was directed primarily at members and fellow travellers of the Labour Party rather than to disaffected communists. It was as if accounts had been settled with Stalinism, and the immediate task was to correct the flight from humanism of 'Natopolitanism', not communism. And although Thompson intended the abolition of capitalism to be the aim of a new working-class consciousness, less cloth-cap and orthodox in outlook, the emphasis now fell on the role of socialist intellectuals in its creation:

> we can *fix* this new working-class consciousness and give it goals. More than that, I am saying that it is the constant business of social- ists to endeavour to fix this consciousness, since – if we do not do it – the capitalist media will 'fix' it for us. Political consciousness is not a spontaneous generation, it is the product of political action and skill.[27]

Here then, in the articles of the early 1960s, we encounter the same difficulties in sustaining the 'ambiguous' dialectic of 'socialist humanism', but now viewed, as it were, from the opposite pole: where the former stress on the irreducibility of experience had the cost of not making proper sense of the notion of cultural conditioning, the later stress on the openness of consciousness to manipulation put in question the faith in moral autonomy. But these were aspects of any socialist analysis sensitive to the problems posed by the transfor- mation and break-up of the traditional working class under condi- tions of relative material comfort. The New Left was not alone with its dilemmas, nor was Thompson the only Marxist at the time to be accused of abandoning faith because he questioned the continuing validity of some of its categories. At around the same time, in the USA, Herbert Marcuse (of whom Thompson has been markedly critical), was writing:

> *One-Dimensional Man* will vacillate throughout between two contra- dictory hypotheses: (1) that advanced industrial society is capable of containing qualitative change for the foreseeable future; (2) that forces and tendencies exist which may break this containment and explode this society. I do not think that a clear answer can be given. Both tendencies are there, side by side –and even the one in the other.[28]

Both these 'tendencies' were registered turn by turn in Thompson's writings of the period. On the one hand, 'revolution' is said to be in prospect and the continued possibility of socialist transformation justified by reference to 'the long tenacious revolutionary tradition of the British commoner'.[29] On the other hand, we are reminded of how easily the revolutionary impulse is contained and defused by the 'fixing' of popular consciousness and the systematic manipulation of opinion. At the same time, and overarching any such sociological accounting, we are offered an argument of an altogether different and more deeply pessimistic temper, one that invites us to think in terms of the failure of the socialist project as such:

it is not Stalin, nor Khruschev, nor even Gomulka who must be seen to have failed, so much as the entire historic struggle to attain a classless society with which the particular, and more or less ephemeral, systems of Communist Party organisation and doctrine have been associated. What must be seen to have 'failed' is the aspiration itself: the revolutionary potential – not within Russian society alone – but within *any* society, within man himself.[30]

Here, revolution is no longer presented as an issue of rulers and ruled nor even of 'oligarchs' and 'people'. It is rather that human nature in some more collective, trans-class, even trans-historical sense has 'betrayed' itself, and we are all – exploited and exploiters, manipulated and manipulators – to blame.

The note of pessimism continued to sound throughout the 1960s[31] and into the writings of the 1970s, where a deep and sometimes even despairing concern with the encroachment of state power, the erosion of civil liberties and above all with the sclerotic effects of the Cold War, came to take precedence over the defence of Marxism or the advocacy of revolution. Maybe even, Thompson suggested at one point, we have been passing through a counter-revolution.[32] Together with pessimism went a relative retreat from political action and, it has been said, a lessening of interest in the affairs of the communist nations. Anderson claims, pointing in particular to Thompson's low profile during the Vietnam Solidarity Campaign, that 'when the challenge of '56–'58 faded, his interest correspondingly waned'.[33] But to suppose, as Anderson implies, that this represented a falling-off of socialist commitment is disingenuous. For the issue had never been purely one of strategy alone, but concerned the extent to which the existing 'socialist' nations could still be conceived as providing any sort of model for socialism. Thompson was always opposed to US imperialism and favoured the overthrow of capitalism; but by the 1950s he had also become very wary of all political organisations and strategies that would bring him into alignment with the Soviet Union. This indeed, was the real significance of 1956: that it marked the beginning of Thompson's long and unswerving pursuit of a non-aligned programme for socialist renewal. 'Socialist humanism' thus understood does not simply amount to a Eurocommunist endorsement of the parliamentary road to socialism; it was also distinguished by its hostility to the methods and ideologies of both the superpowers, and by its demand for the transcendence of the bloc system as such.

Out of Cold War

In the early 1980s, as the peace movement burgeoned again in response to the agreement on the Intermediate-Range Nuclear Forces
Treaty (INF) deployment, this demand for an end to the Cold War
and the dissolution of the blocs assumed central political importance.
It became the major theme of all Thompson's political writings in the
decade, and the core of the political agenda to which he was to devote
unremitting energy for the remainder of his active life.[34]

But sounded as it was with new urgency and with a definition that
reflected the specific historical moment, the 'out of Cold War' politics
of the 1980s must also be seen as a continuation of a central motif of the
1950s 'socialist humanism'. From the beginning, in fact, Thompson's
major fear was that the Cold War would pre-empt all moves towards
an authentically democratic socialism in Eastern Europe: a fear that
issued in numerous warnings of the repercussions this would have on
socialist projects in the West, and reminders of the common interest
of the opposed Soviet and US elites in repressing popular initiatives.[35]
It is true that nothing in the earlier argument matched the bitter-
ness and irony with which he was in his later 'exterminist' writings
to illustrate this 'mirroring' of Soviet attitudes in Western postures.[36]
But the call of these writings – for END, for a movement 'beyond the
blocs', for active British neutrality and the uncoupling of Europe from
superpower domination, for solidarity with independent peace initiatives in Eastern Europe, and for resistance to pro-Sovietism in the
Western movements – this was of the same logic that lay behind the
initial demand for a 'socialist humanism' as a mid-course between the
opposing but complementary philistinisms of Soviet socialism and
complacent anti-communism.

In more marked contrast, perhaps, was the quality of the response
to the rallying-call of the early 1980s. Anyone involved in the early
days of the peace movement renaissance is likely to have felt the
historical significance of Thompson's opening of the classic disarmament argument to the European dimension and the politics of
the Cold War and in particular, perhaps, of the 'moment' of *Protest
and Survive*,[37] with its insistence on the importance of consolidated
pan-European opposition to the warmongers, its visionary sense of
the alternative to their 'degenerative logic', and its signalling of the
emergence of the 'All-European Appeal for END'. Individuals do not
make history, but some more than others help it on its way, and to

Thompson must go some of the credit for pushing it towards the END end rather than the other end.[38]

Paradoxically, however, it was the ending of the Cold War which led some to call into question the adequacy of the 'exterminist' thesis, with its emphasis on the role played by social movements and citizen initiatives in furthering these changes in international relations. The 'exterminist' vision, it has been suggested, with its portrayal of the blocs as locked into reciprocal antagonism, formulated the dynamic of arms accumulation and of peace-movement opposition in terms that excluded the possibility of state-led initiatives (of the kind evidenced in the INF agreement) to break the impasse.[39]

This argument seems to imply, however, that in stressing the role of social movement activism and 'citizens' détente', END politics was operating some sort of historical veto on more official forms of intervention: had these alternative distraints on the arms race been obviously forthcoming at the beginning of the 1980s, no one would have been more pleased than Thompson and his fellow campaigners (who would probably have cast doubt themselves, in the light of it, on the appropriateness of the 'exterminist' image). Secondly, it mistakenly portrays END politics as exhausted in unofficial inter- or trans-bloc citizens' dialogues when in fact a great deal of energy went into pressurising East European officialdom and influencing Western governmental and opposition parties precisely with a view to bringing about some state-led defence and foreign policy initiatives. Thirdly, it tends to a hypostatisation of the 'State' as an 'agent' constantly outmanoeuvring peace movements and other naive forms of citizen protest in the pursuit of an overarching and always perfectly coherent historical rationality. In reality, states muddle along much as do social movements (and the former can sometimes be wrong-footed by the latter). But finally, all these other mistaken tendencies derive from the fundamental error of interpreting Thompson's arguments about 'exterminism', the mirroring of the blocs and the self-sustaining dynamic of the arms race in too literal a fashion. The 'exterminist' account was surely never offered as a finished conceptual analysis, but rather as a heuristic formula, and above all as a parable to capture the political imagination at a moment when the maximum mobilisation of opposition to the deployment of INF was clearly called for.

That the first measure of nuclear disarmament came about through state negotiation is therefore by no means an embarrassment to the 'exterminist' thesis, or its falsification. Or it is not unless it is assumed that either the thesis was a profession of nihilism (when, in fact, as everyone knows it was a summons to humanist resistance), or else that it implied that the 'people' themselves would physically dismantle the weapons systems without the mediation of any governmental or institutional forces at all, which is plainly absurd. Moreover, it is certain that the new directions of Soviet defence and foreign policy in the 1980s were assisted rather than disabled by the non-aligned policies pressed for by Thompson and his END supporters – and this came to be acknowledged even in Soviet official circles at the time.[40]

What, then, of the other more directly 'socialist humanist' aspect of Thompson's END politics? The suggestion, that is, that democratic socialist developments in both halves of Europe were blocked by the Cold War and advanced by its erosion. In Eastern Europe the record is complex and chequered. In the countries of the former Soviet Union market forces have replaced a state-planned economy, and citizens formally enjoy voting rights and other personal freedoms that were lacking under the old regime. But these moves have gone together with the squeezing out of socialism, rather than its human- istic flourishing. Most of the newly created wealth has flowed into the pockets of a tiny elite, and there is now massive corruption and extensive rigging of elections, notably in Russia itself – where Vladimir Putin is currently both strongly opposed by the Commu- nist Party, and is himself appealing to the 'spirit of Stalin' to justify his hardline domestic and foreign policy stance. Meanwhile, in the West neo-liberal policies have continued to retain the command established in the earlier part of the 1980s, especially in Britain and the USA. If we think, moreover, of the values for which Thompson and the New Left stood in the 1950s – anti-nuclear, anti-nationalistic, anti-capitalist and anti-consumerist – then we must acknowledge that the direction of the Labour Party has been opposed to them for some fifty years now, and probably never showed fewer signs of reversing this tendency than at the point where some minimal progress was being made on disarmament and the democratisation of socialism in Eastern Europe. Indeed, the leadership of the Labour Party celebrated the INF agreement by signalling its desire to ditch the one commit- ment that had brought it more into line with New Left demands – that of unilateral nuclear disarmament. And since then, of course, it has dropped Clause IV, thus ending any lingering constitutional commit- ment to begin to dismantle capitalism (indeed doing much in govern- ment to advance neo-liberal economic policies).

Socialism, then, as understood by Thompson, no longer figures strongly in the argument of any of the major UK political parties, nor has it recently featured much in hegemonic politics elsewhere in Europe, either West or East, although this may now be set to change somewhat. (And, of course, outside the mainstream, socialism has been well represented in left-wing social movement politics.) In this sense, Thompson's belief (if it was a belief rather than an optimism of the will) that the ending of the bloc system might or could usher in a democratised politics in both halves of Europe and a 'third way' economic order that, if not quite a humanistic socialism, would at least have transcended the worst abuses of both capitalism and communism, has certainly not proved accurate.

The irony of this situation is that, in the years since Thompson's death, the destructive nature of capitalism, economically, socially and environmentally, could hardly have been more plainly exposed across Europe, and indeed globally. Its current crisis, the most serious since the 1930s, and still unfolding in unpredictable ways, has certainly now caused some misgivings about continuing as we are. But mainstream parties have offered little more than feeble expressions of hope that the greediest financiers will content themselves with a little less. And despite the obvious irrationalities of the uncritical commitment to 'growth', it is clung to as the panacea for all evils. Only by stimulating the economy, so it is argued, by producing and persuading people to consume more, by fixing credit at rates that might allow them to borrow and hence buy more, can we hope to spend our way out of a crisis largely precipitated by the dynamic of borrowing and spending. There is very little mainstream discussion of what might be gained by pursuing a less work-driven and acquisitive way of life. We are held captive, it seems, to a consumerist version of well-being that excludes all other ideas of how to live and prosper.[41] The end of capitalism is indeed in this sense rather more difficult to envisage than the end of the world;[42] and 'exterminism', as a pointer to where the coming Cold Wars and conflicts over energy and other resources may ultimately take us, arguably remains a concept of considerable relevance. So, too, does the distinction Thompson was making back in 1985, when he spoke of the need for the 'whys' of the people to be reasserted against the 'hows' of the media experts, who

> go on and on, in these frames, to the point of tedium, with the *how* questions only. How do we get inflation down? How should we cut

up the defence budget between Trident and the fleet? A national 'consensus' is assumed – but in fact is manufactured daily within these frames ... For example, all political discourse must assume that we're agreed on the need for economic growth, and the only problem is to find the party which can best fix it. But across the world people are asking questions of *why* and *where*? Do we have the right to pollute this spinning planet any more? To consume and lay waste resources needed by future generations? Might not nil growth be better, if we could divide up the product more wisely and fairly?[43]

Thompson may here again have proved rather too optimistic in his assessment of the public mood. And shifting to a steady-state economy is, in any case, a daunting prospect, given the integrated structure of modern existence and the dependencies of national economies on the globalised system. It is an index of the depth of our collective alienation, that we scarcely know how to begin to achieve it. But it is nonetheless a form of denial to suppose that we can continue with current rates of expansion of production, work and material consumption over this century, let alone into the next. Indeed, the ecological crisis is so alarming and capitalism so clearly unhelpful in countering it, that one has to hope that the various oppositional campaigns and protest movements of the present day, fragmented, marginal and limited in their political demands as they currently are, can consolidate over time to form a stronger, more coherent and articulate global, eco-socialist political front.

Thompson was always ahead of his day in his support for such a politics, and were it to prevail it would no doubt go some way to realise his early aspiration to a union of the wisdoms of Marx and William Morris.[44] But at the present time, it is very unclear who would be the agents or constituencies involved in any such formation. Working-class sympathies are scarcely very markedly in favour of socialism, let alone of any version of it that would seriously challenge conventional views in affluent societies about the role of work in our lives and its economic rewards, about the requirement for upward mobility and ever-improving living standards, about time expenditure, pleasure and personal fulfilment. Nor, relatedly, is there any longer the kind of audience of organic intellectuals that Thompson and his colleagues in university adult education and the New Left Clubs had inspired (and themselves relied upon for the coherence of their political vision). Certainly, there are some new, mainly 'socially networked', commu-nities of opposition that might substitute for this absence of earlier forms of agency, but how they might translate into any more institutional and pervasive form of politics remains to be seen.

Moreover, on the 'humanist' front things have also shifted, and much social movement energy and cultural theory in recent decades has gone into exposing and subverting the pretensions to universal representation of Enlightenment humanism. Feminists have been justifiably critical of the gender-blindness of both liberal and socialist humanisms, given their roots in an inherently masculinist conception of subjectivity and agency.[45] And Thompson has himself been criticised for his abstraction from gender in his historical writings, and his (at times) somewhat grudging response to the analyses and demands of his feminist contemporaries.[46]

Postcolonial theory and cultural analysis have also in recent times criticised the forms of cultural imperialism associated with the Western humanist tradition.[47] It is true that many of the more cogent critiques of Enlightenment humanism are immanent in the sense that they are critical, not of humanistic ideals in themselves, but of their too partial and ethnocentric application. The postmodernist emphasis on respect for personal 'difference' and cultural autonomy against the assimilative dynamic of some humanist discourse and practice is to that extent itself implicitly humanist in outlook. But we must recognise, too, its important role in exposing humanism's globalising pretensions to this critical scrutiny, and in rendering this a more complex and contested area of theory than in Thompson's time.

However, if Thompson's humanist argument now looks in certain respects dated and in need of qualification, its core philosophical emphases remain of abiding relevance. Thompson's objections to the deterministic and politically disabling arguments of Althusserian Marxism should be defended as a still pertinent counter to the anti- and now predominantly post-humanist forms of thinking in our times. Today, the structuralist discourse of humans as 'bearers' of trans-individual social forces beyond their access or comprehension has given place to a post-humanist emphasis on the role of technology in human formation, but without any significant alteration in the overall view of humans as subject to generative systems that deny them any fixity of being and are viewed as essentially beyond their cognitive mastery or control.[48] This perspective tends to dispute the existence of cognitive forms (consciousness, rationality, language use) exclusive to human nature and to treat belief in such human exceptionality as ontologically mistaken and ecologically regrettable.

Given this outlook, it is hardly surprising to find that the primary post-humanist demand is not for human beings to assume moral responsibility, but for an ever more comprehensive mapping of their practices and subjectivities. In other words, academic re-description of our conditioning by technology is presented as if it could substitute for an ethico-political programme of action. For those who would today take issue with this type of post-humanist explanation (and the fatalism or political quietism it can justify), Thompson's humanist argument still offers a needed polemical resource. Moreover, for all its theoretical difficulties, his appeal to the moral subject, and to the power of concerted human action to make history, proved catalytic in ways too easily ignored or denied by current anti- or post-humanist forms of counsel. The importance to transformative practice of his kind of inspirational summons should neither be discounted theoretically nor underestimated politically. Indeed, without an understanding of the dialectic of agency and process of the kind sustained in Thompson's argument on 'socialist humanism', it is difficult to see what force to give to the idea of politics at all.

Notes

1 See P. Anderson, *Arguments Within English Marxism* (London: Verso, 1980), pp. 122–57; and K. Soper, 'Socialist Humanism', in H. J. Kaye and K. McClelland (eds), *E. P. Thompson: Critical Perspectives* (Cambridge: Polity Press, 1990), pp. 204–32, pp. 214–17. I shall be drawing on this article in what follows, and am grateful to Polity Press for permission to quote from it.
2 Soper, 'Socialist Humanism'.
3 E. P. Thompson, *The Poverty of Theory and Other Essays* (London: Merlin Press, 1978), p. 326.
4 Cf. L. Althusser, *For Marx* (Harmondsworth: Penguin, 1969), pp. 221–2, 236–41; and see below.
5 Scott Hamilton draws a comparable distinction between his 'hardcore' and 'softcore' ideas in *The Crisis of Theory: E. P. Thompson, the New Left and Postwar British Politics* (Manchester: Manchester University Press, 2011), *passim* and pp.269–72.
6 Thompson, *The Poverty of Theory*, p. 322. Cf. 'Socialist Humanism, an Epistle to the Philistines' (henceforth 'Epistle'), *New Reasoner*, 1 (Summer 1957), 103–43.
7 Both journals of the 'New Left' in the period, the *New Reasoner*, and the more academically orientated *Universities and Left Review*, professed

allegiance to 'socialist humanism'. For a fuller account, see J. Saville, *Memoirs from the Left* (London: Merlin Press, 2007), pp. 101–28.

8 Cf. Thompson, *The Poverty of Theory*, p. 326.

9 Those of the Frankfurt Institute theorists before the war and the very influential lectures given by Alexandre Kojève in France in the 1930s deserve particular mention.

10 See also E. Fromm (ed.), *Socialist Humanism* (London: Allen Lane, 1965).

11 His most incisive liberal critic was Charles Taylor in his 'Marxism and Humanism', *New Reasoner*, 2 (1957). In the same issue, Harry Hanson charged him with 'romanticism' and 'utopian socialism'.

12 Thompson, 'Epistle', p. 128; 'Agency and Choice', *New Reasoner*, 5 (1957), p. 103.

13 Interestingly enough, Thompson refers us to Maurice Merleau-Ponty when he invokes this term (*The Poverty of Theory*, p. 366), but employed not so much as a technical term of phenomenology, but as more or less equivalent to the ordinary concept of 'experience', which in the 1950s articles and elsewhere in *The Poverty of Theory* he seemed to find quite adequate.

14 Thompson, *The Poverty of Theory*, p. 357.

15 Cf. *ibid.*, p.104. (But Sartre wrote as a fellow 'socialist humanist' in *New Reasoner*, 1 (1957), 87–98.)

16 Cf. D. Archard, *Consciousness and the Unconscious* (London: Hutchinson, 1984), pp. 50–2.

17 J-P. Sartre, *Between Marxism and Existentialism*, trans. J. Mathews (London: New Left Books, 1974), p. 42.

18 J-P. Sartre, *Search for a Method*, trans. H. E. Barnes (London: Methuen, 1963), p.33 n.

19 Letter of 4 September 1990 (written from his hospital bed). He added: 'I have always been an amateur theorist, and too often have expressed over-hasty opinions, grounded upon inadequate study. Impatient impressionism, seduced by the colour of polemical metaphors, is the hallmark.'

20 Thompson, *The Poverty of Theory*, pp. 331–3.

21 *Ibid.*, p. 383.

22 *Arguments*, pp. 116–20.

23 Cf. Anderson, *Arguments*, p. 157; cf. p. 206. Cf. Thompson's own, conciliatory assessment in his interview with Michael Merrill in H. Abelove *et al.* (eds), *Visions of History* (New York: Pantheon, 1983), pp. 16–17.

24 É. Balibar, 'The Long March for Peace', in *Exterminism and Cold War*, ed. New Left Review (London: Verso, 1982). The editors wrote here of Thompson's intellectual role in the revival of the peace movement as 'an act of public service with few comparisons in the recent history of any country' (p. ix). Thompson's 'Notes on Exterminism: The Last Stage of Civilisation' appeared originally in *New Left Review*, 121 (1980). Cf. P. Anderson, *Spectrum* (London: Verso, 2005), p. 180.

25 Thompson, *Out of Apathy*, pp. 9–10.

26 *Ibid.*, p. 11.

27 E. P. Thompson, 'Revolution Again!', *New Left Review*, 6 (1960), p. 28; cf. Thompson, *The Poverty of Theory*, p. 21.

28 H. Marcuse, *One Dimensional Man* (London: Routledge & Kegan Paul, 1964), p. xv. For Thompson's differences with Marcuse, see Thompson, *The Poverty of Theory*, pp. 141–2, 174.

29 Thompson, *Out of Apathy*, p. 308.

30 Thompson, *The Poverty of Theory*, p. 11.

31 Thompson did, however, continue to press for a gradual and non-violent 'revolutionary' transition to socialism in his 'The Peculiarities of the English' (1965; subsequently included in *The Poverty of Theory* collection.). He was also a contributor to the New Left 'May Day Manifesto' which urged a similar policy in 1968. See R. Williams (ed.), *May Day Manifesto 1968* (Harmondsworth: Penguin, 1968). For the French 'events' of May 1968 Thompson did not express any great enthusiasm, either at the time or subsequently.

32 Thompson, *Writing by Candlelight* (London: Merlin Press, 1980), p. 252. Thompson's pessimism at this stage is noted by S. Hamilton, *Crisis of Theory*, p. 257 and P. Mandler, 'Written by Candlelight', *Dissent*, Spring 1993.

33 Anderson, *Arguments*, p. 151. Thompson was to remain resistant to any 'canonisation' of the VSC and wrote that he dissented 'sharply from the analysis of Anderson and others which tends to demote CND (pacifist, neutralist, middle-class "failed")', Thompson, *Exterminism and Cold War*, p. 33, n.48.

34 For further discussion of Thompson's involvement with the peace movement from the late 1940s until the end of his life, see chapter 9 in this book.

35 The role of the Cold War in crushing socialist initiatives both East and West is one of the major themes of Thompson's article, 'The New Left', *New Reasoner*, 9 (1959), and was repeated in 'Outside the Whale' the following year. Cf. also 'Agency and Choice', p. 94; *Universities and Left Review*, 4 (1958) and 'The Doomsday Consensus', in *Writing by Candlelight*, p. 273, where Thompson himself remarked on the persistence of his warnings since 1958.

36 Though cf. Thompson, *The Poverty of Theory*, p. 168, where the failure of '1956' is said to be in part a failure imposed by the West. This is echoed in his call for European nuclear disarmament in 1980: 'The hawkism of the West directly generated the hawkism of the East ... On the Cold War billiard table, NATO played the cruise missile ball, which struck the Afghan black, which rolled nicely into the Russian pocket' (*Writing by Candlelight*, p. 278).

37 This was first issued as a pamphlet in 1980 by CND and the Bertrand Russell Peace Foundation, and later included along with writings by other authors in the Penguin of the same name (Harmondsworth, 1980). Nothing here should be taken to imply that Thompson was the sole initiator of the END idea or unaided architect of its organisation. For an account of the origins of the 'European Campaign', see James Hinton, *Protests and Visions* (London: Hutchinson/Radius, 1989), and for a sense of the role of the Bertrand Russell Peace Foundation, see K. Coates (ed.), *Détente and Socialist Democracy* (Nottingham: Spokesman Books, 1975); *Listening for Peace* (Nottingham: Spokesman Books, 1987); *The Most Dangerous Decade* (Nottingham: Spokesman Books,1984); and 'A Political Life', Ken Coates interviewed by George Lambie, 'Resist Much, Obey Little', T. Simpson (ed.), *The Spokesman* 116 (2012), pp. 19–46.

38 Cf. the closing words of *Protest and Survive*: 'The acronym of European Nuclear Disarmament is END. I have explained why I think that the arguments of Professor Howard are hastening us towards a different end. I have outlined the deep structure of deterrence, and diagnosed its outcomes as terminal. I can see no way of preventing this outcome but by immediate actions throughout Europe, which generate a counter-logic of nuclear disarmament. Which end is it to be?'

39 For an elaboration of some of these themes, see S. Bromley and J. Rosenberg, 'After Exterminism', *New Left Review*, 168 (1988).

40 Cf. the interview with Tair Tairov of the Soviet Peace Committee, *END Journal*, 36 (Autumn 1988).

41 For more on the arguments for 'alternative hedonism', see the introduction and bibliographies in K. Soper, M. Ryle and L. Thomas (eds), *The Politics and Pleasures of Consuming Differently* (London: Palgrave, 2009).

42 Cf. Fredric Jameson, who cites 'someone' as the author of the thought, but himself suggests, possibly more alarmingly, that 'we can now revise that and witness the attempt to imagine capitalism by way of imagining the end of the world', *New Left Review*, 21 (May–June 2003).

43 *The Heavy Dancers* (London: Merlin Press, 1985), p.3. (The title essay from which this quotation comes was first delivered as a television talk in 1982.)

44 For his 'green' sentiment, see: 'Postscript' to *William Morris: Romantic to Revolutionary* (2nd edn, London: Merlin Press, 1977); his Introduction to R. Bahro, *Socialism and Survival* (London: Heretic, 1978), pp. 7–8, and his tribute to Lucio Magri in *Exterminism and Cold War*, p. 347.

45 The bibliography of feminist critique of Enlightenment humanism is very extended. For a brief synoptic overview, see K. Soper, 'Liberalism, Feminism, Enlightenment', in M. Evans (ed.), *The Edinburgh Companion to Contemporary Liberalism* (Edinburgh: Edinburgh University Press, 2000), pp. 197–207.

46 Cf. J. Wallach Scott, *Gender and the Politics of History* (New York: Columbia University Press, 1988). See also chapter 1 in this book, pp. 9–10.

47 Although given Thompson's record as an internationalist and cultural critic, there is little to suggest he would have resisted this development.

48 Influential texts of post-humanism include N. K. Hayles, *How we Became Posthuman: Virtual Bodies in Cybernetics, Literature and Informatics* (Chicago: Chicago University Press, 1999) and C. Wolfe, *What is Posthumanism?* (Minneapolis: University of Minnesota Press, 2009).

7

Thompson's concept of class:
the flesh and blood of self-emancipation

Nina Power

Few writers have ever done as much to place the lived experience of
the working class at the forefront of their work. Thompson is justly
renowned for his celebration of ordinary men and women and his
vivid portrayal of struggle across the ages. It may seem paradoxical,
then, to try to extract something like a 'concept' or a 'theory' of class
from Thompson's work, especially bearing in mind the arguments
he makes against Althusser and Althusserianism in *The Poverty of
Theory*. Nevertheless, as a way of intervening in current debates about
the nature and composition of the working class, there is much to be
learned from attempting to conceptualise, with the greatest possible
respect for his anti-theoreticism, a notion of class from Thompson's
writings. This chapter will attempt to synthesise a concept of class
from specific texts by Thompson and to explain why the continuation of Thompson's project is both relevant and necessary for today's
debates regarding class and class struggle.

The problem with theory

Thompson was, and with good reason, highly suspicious of theory
or anything that attempted to abstract from the real experiences and
historical details of the lives of those who struggled, and continued to
struggle, against capitalist oppression. His splenetic 1978 *The Poverty
of Theory: or an Orrery of Errors*, which took the structuralism of
Louis Althusser to task, remains one of the great polemics of the late
twentieth century, harking back to Marx's 1847 attack on Proudhon
in *The Poverty of Philosophy*. What Thompson saw as Althusser's
'closed system' and denial of history was infuriating and dangerous to
Thompson (and others), because it seemed to simply cut out the 'real

people' and the 'real context' that Thompson sought in all of his work to understand, defend and celebrate. As against theoretical readings of class as a kind of 'framework', Thompson states: 'I do not see class as a "structure", nor even as a "category", but as something which in fact happens (and can be shown to have happened) in human relationships.'[1] As Ellen Meiksins Wood writes in defence of Thompson's concept of historical materialism, as opposed to what she calls the 'geological' model of class (with all that this implies – stasis, depth, ossification): '[Thompson]'s subversive genealogy of capitalist principles, tracing capitalist practices, values and categories to their systemic roots in specific relations of production and exploitation, restores not only the historicity of capitalism but also its contestability.'[2] Reading Thompson gives us an astonishingly vivid, non-judgemental image of resistance and the desire for liberty, and the genuine possibilities of a truly historical materialism. As he puts it in his most famous text: 'I am seeking to rescue the poor stockinger, the Luddite cropper, the "obsolete" hand-loom weaver, the "utopian" artisan, and even the deluded follower of Joanna Southcott, from the enormous condescension of posterity.'[3]

What, then, would be the purpose of trying to extract a systematic notion of class from Thompson's work? None, if all we would be doing was sucking the life out of his work in the name of a frozen pile of concepts. However, there are moments where Thompson himself takes a step back, as it were, to discuss the conceptual dimensions of the use of 'class' as a category and as a guiding concept. The strong position he takes in *The Making of the English Working Class* in favour of 'class' rather than 'classes', of class as a 'historical phenomenon, unifying a number of disparate and seemingly unconnected events, both in the raw material of experience and in consciousness,'[4] is revisited, in particular, fifteen years later in 'Eighteenth Century English Society: Class Struggle Without Class?', where Thompson directly addresses again his notion of class, albeit as a 'preamble, a thinking aloud,'[5] and cautions that 'It is easy to suppose that class takes place, not as historical process, but inside our own heads.'[6] The anti-idealism, the historical materialism, through which Thompson endeavours to remain faithful to Marx (but only because Marx's methodology and politics are so manifestly important), is laid out in some detail in his crucial 1978 essay, and much of my discussion of Thompson's 'concept' of class will be drawn from this text, as well as negatively through his polemic from the same year against Althusser and structuralism. The chapter

will also draw upon the attention paid by Wood to Thompson's definition of class as part of an attempt to defend his consistent attempt to
understand the concept historically, and to argue against any 'theory'
or philosophy that would understand it statically or sociologically.
Thompson's notion of class – as a process, as relational – is, and cannot
but be, part of an ongoing argument in the philosophy of history. This
chapter also attempts to examine some of the strengths of Thompson's
concept of class as a historical category by examining its use in his
own work and similar notions in the work of others (in particular,
the perhaps surprising overlaps between Thompson's notion and the
work of Jean-Paul Sartre in his 1960 text, the *Critique of Dialectical
Reason*), and to revisit some of the criticisms and problems identified
in Thompson's work as identified by G. A. Cohen and Perry Anderson
in 1978 and 1980, respectively, before concluding with a brief suggestion as to Thompson's relevance to today's discussion and practice of
class and anti-capitalist politics.

Thompson's concept of class: against stasis

Without wishing to become too abstract from the outset and to end
up accidentally introducing 'categories of stasis',[7] it is useful to clarify
a little what we mean by 'concept' when talking about Thompson and
the way in which it fits into his definition and guiding framework –
namely, historical materialism. In this respect, as in several others,
his polemic against Althusser, positivism, idealism, neo-religious
thinking and structuralism pushes Thompson towards a 'concept
of concepts' as such, within his broader understanding of history as
process. Despite this initial seeming abstraction, this is important as
it allows us a general insight into the overriding concept of 'class' as
mobilised by Thompson throughout his work. Indeed, it is the notion
of class, in particular and above all, that operates as a consistent
guiding principle from the early work on William Morris to the later
work on customs. This is what Thompson says about concepts, quoted
here at relative length so as to allow a close reading at the outset:

> The investigation of history as process, as eventuation or 'rational
> disorder', entails notions of causation, of contradiction, of mediation,
> and of the systematic organisation (sometimes structuring) of social,
> political, economic and intellectual life. These elaborate notions
> 'belong' within historical theory, are refined within this theory's proce-
> dures, are thought within thought. But it is untrue that they belong *only*

145

within theory. Each notion or concept, arises out of empirical engagements, and however abstract the procedures of its self-interrogation, it
must then be brought back into an engagement with the determinate
properties of the evidence, and argue its case before vigilant judges in
history's 'court of appeal.' It is, and in a most critical sense, a question
of dialogue once more.[8]

Thompson's description of concept formation is a defence of the
dialogue between empirical engagement and theoretical process,
and one cannot operate without the other. 'The homeland of Marxist
theory', he writes, 'remains where it has always been, the real human
object, in all its manifestations.'[9] The concept of 'class' is thus something
that emerges out of an empirical engagement: the 'making' of the
English working class indicates that the formation is a process and
the end result less a fixed outcome than a kind of regulative principle,
taken in great part (and in the first place) from the empirical quality of
the historical experience of men and women itself. Class is a concept,
but this 'concept' is the very opposite of a pure theoretical construct.
It guides empirical and political work and is open to revision, yet it
has a consistency of its own. This is what Thompson is so keen to
stress in his defence, against Althusser and others, of 'historical logic'.
Concepts such as class are generalisable because there are so many
historical examples to draw upon, and in turn these concepts are
brought to bear on the evidence not so much as 'models' but rather as
'expectations':

> [Concepts] do not impose a rule, but they hasten and facilitate the
> interrogation of the evidence, even though it is often found that each
> case departs, in this or that particular, from the rule ... [t]his provokes
> impatience in some philosophers (and even sociologists) who consider
> that a concept with such elasticity is not a true concept, and a rule is
> not a rule unless the evidence conforms to it, and stands to attention
> in one place.[10]

Thompson's defence of the elasticity of historical logic allows for
structuring principles – class, as in our discussion here – that do not
themselves become structures. But as Thompson recognises, part of
the ubiquity of the term, its common currency and its ability to move
from discipline to discipline, its weight as a subjective and cultural
self-description ('I'm working-class'), as well as a quasi-objective
quantitative description ('these people are working-class because they
have to sell their labour power in return for a wage'), has meant that,

as Thompson puts it: 'No historical category has been more misunder-stood, tormented, transfixed, and de-historicised than the category of social class.'[11] It is necessary that he define in more detail exactly what he means, and why the notion of class at work in historical logic, and historical materialism in particular, avoids these still-prevalent tendencies.

Thompson's 1978 piece, 'Eighteenth-Century English Society: Class Struggle without Class?' ('better described as an argument than as an article'[12]), deals in some detail with the challenge of historical 'proof' as against the seemingly more rigorous methods of positivism and falsification (defended by, amongst others, Karl Popper[13]). Thompson's claims from the outset defend a notion of historical process in which 'in any given society we cannot understand the parts unless we understand their function and roles in relation to each other and in relation to the whole ... the "truth" or success of such a holistic descrip-tion can only be discovered in the test of historical practice.'[14] The problem confronting Thompson, and no doubt one that historians, particularly those writing as 'Marxists' of one stripe or another, have encountered and continue to encounter, is the counter-accusation of imprecision and imposition: can concepts such as class (or 'capitalist', 'bourgeois', among other examples that Thompson uses here) really *clarify* what is specific to a particular time, location, people and event? How can historians, typically associated with work of minute detail and archival research, use categories that are also extremely general categories (even if these categories can sometimes be derived from the research or are terms that people often use to describe their own situa-tion)? Class is precisely such a term, and even if Thompson describes the project of *The Making of the English Working Class* as a 'work of analysis into a particular moment of class formation',[15] his use of class in the singular and the attempt to define it, however minimally, however fairly to the subjects of his study ('Class is defined by men as they live their own history, and in the end, this is its only definition'[16]), he cannot avoid the demand to explain his use of the term. Partly this is a contextual question, as accusations of empiricism, lack of rigour, and so on, were being levelled at history as a discipline at this time (and it is interesting to note that Thompson treats Althusser and Popper's criticisms of historicism together, facing down two enemies from very different conceptual backgrounds). Partly, too, Thompson wants to clarify his own historical practice. The Preface to *The Making of the English Working Class*, he says, was composed at the end of the writing of the book and thus arises out of 'both historical and theoretical practice'.[17] Thompson states that he still upholds the same conclusions, but 'perhaps these should be re-stated and qualified'.[18] So how exactly is 'class' defined by Thompson in the later essay?

It is, above all, a 'historical' category: 'it is derived from the observation of the social process over time'.[19] 'We know about class', Thompson states, 'because people have behaved in class ways.' We are reminded here of the spirited defence in *The Making of the English Working Class* of the absolute *reasonableness* (as in, not *the* right to protest but *how* right it is to do so) of forms of dissent that are so often – in the eighteenth century as now – dismissed as acts of madness: riots, uprisings, prison breaks and so on ('these historical events disclose regularities of response to analogous situations'[20]). Thompson's defence of the patterns of class have a political and geographical significance beyond that of class defined by a particular frame (for example, the 'English' working class): 'at a certain stage (the "mature" formations of class) we observe the creation of institutions, and of a culture with class notations, which admits of trans-national comparisons'.[21] Thompson's desire for these 'trans-national comparisons' is hugely significant, in the sense that it avoids a culturally specific notion of class, and acknowledges the global interconnectedness of all those struggling against both national oppression and the cross-border and highly uneven exploitation of multinationals. Perry Anderson's criticism that there is 'little sustained acknowledgement of the international dimensions of English working-class history'[22] in *The Making of the English Working Class*, is undermined by Thompson here, but it is in fact a refrain repeated from Anderson's earlier text, 'Origins of the Present Crisis', where he takes both 'nerveless' historians and sociologists to task for refusing to carry out 'structural' or 'totalising' studies of contemporary Britain or any 'serious' global history of British society in the twentieth century, and criticises Marxist historians (including Thompson) for confining themselves to the 'heroic periods' of English history (the seventeenth and eighteenth centuries).[23] Thompson's earlier response, in 1965, addressing both Tom Nairn and Perry Anderson, in turn attacks what he perceives as their theoretical thirst for 'a tidy Platonism' whose method 'concentrates attention upon one dramatic episode – the Revolution – to which all that goes before and after must be related; and which insists upon an ideal type of this Revolution against which all others may be judged'.[24] The battleground for the arguments that Thompson and Anderson make again in *The Poverty of Theory* and the 1978 essay on class, and *Arguments Within English Marxism*, was already laid out more than a decade earlier, and Thompson's expansion of his concept of class in admitting 'trans-national comparisons' can be perhaps understood in the light of Anderson's accusations of parochialism.[25]

However, there is a caveat in Thompson's words here: the emphasis is on 'comparisons', not homogeneity or patterns. To jump too quickly to talk of stages and levels of class-consciousness is to reduce the specificity of struggle in different places and times. Any attempt to impose a theory of class development must avoid reducing these patterns and comparisons to a single story. Here is when, Thompson suggests, 'models or structures are theorised that are supposed to give us objective determinants of class'.[26] Here is where the tendency to ossify class into a static, rather than relational and processual entity, emerges. Thompson identifies two versions of this tendency, the sociological and the heuristic. In the former, class becomes a 'literal quantitative measurement' and in the latter, class becomes 'what people *think* they belong to in response to a questionnaire'. Either way, once again, 'class as a historical category – the observation of behaviour over time – has been expelled'.[27]

It is worth pausing for a moment to observe the relevance and specificity of what Thompson is proposing and opposing: the two notions of class he identified here remain utterly prevalent in most discussions of the topic, even among the Left (Thompson in fact notes this in 1978: 'class as a static category has taken up occupation within very influential sectors of Marxist thought as well'[28]). Discussion of 'false consciousness' and the alternative proposal by one vanguard or another that a better 'consciousness' is to be substituted is clearly based, argues Thompson, on a static model of capitalist productive relations and leads, we could say, to a kind of implicit methodological moralism (this class *is* such-and-such but it *ought* to be like this). Thompson is surely right that these temptations to static or moral definitions are problematic (although Anderson thinks that Thompson has bent the stick too far in *The Making of the English Working Class*: 'It comes as something of a shock to realise, at the end of 900 pages, that one has never learnt such an elementary fact as the approximate size of the English working class, or its proportion within the population as a whole'). This results, Anderson suggests, in a 'disconcerting lack of objective coordinates'.[29] Similarly, Thompson's focus on the working class will offend anyone looking for a historical account of different classes (for example, understood as upper, middle and lower, to use a conventional frame) in the late eighteenth and early nineteenth centuries.

Thompson's desire to remain as close as possible to the experience of those he describes in the process of their 'making' and to avoid static, sociological formulations is perhaps, on occasion, taken too far. But he is surely right that the objective facts regarding how many people work in what sector in a particular period tells us nothing about what this means, and also nothing about what class resistance, subversive activity and antagonism might look like. But is Thompson's approach so unique? Although he has a tendency to polemically dismiss theory or philosophy, particularly that emanating from across the channel, Thompson does grudgingly admit in *The Poverty of Theory* that some of Jean-Paul Sartre's work in the early 1960s (*The Critique of Dialectical Reason*) shares some perhaps surprising parallels with Thompson's own project:

> We may be helped at this point by Sartre, whose thought I cannot (as a good Englishman) always follow in its subtlety – nor always assent to – but whose understanding of history, and whose relation to political reality, is altogether superior, at every point, to that of Althusser.[30]

Thompson proceeds to quote an argument made by Sartre in an interview (translated into English in 1971) where Sartre states that 'neither time itself nor, consequently, history, can be made the object of a concept'. Thompson responds:

> Sartre's argument conforms closely to my own earlier argument as to the approximate and provisional nature of historical concepts, as to their 'elasticity' and generality ('classes', 'class struggle'), as to their character as exceptions rather than as rules. It conforms also to vigilant rejection of the closed and static concept or analogy in favour of the open and the shaping, formative one: as, by replacing 'law of motion' by 'logic of process', and by understanding determinism, not as pre-determined programming or the implantation of necessity, but in its senses as the 'setting of limits' and the 'exerting of pressures'. It means retaining the notion of structure, but as structural actuation (limits and pressures) within a social formation which remains protean in its forms.[31]

While Thompson's mention of his own proximity to Sartre remains tantalisingly brief, the former's reflection on the latter's project forces Thompson to speak directly in the language of concepts: the image of 'structural actuation' and the language of limits and pressures provide a fluid image of class development, but not an image so liquid as to escape all specificity and determination. The movement of class is parallel to the movement Thompson wants to see between theory and content in historical work in general: 'theory will be nothing but a thin enigma unless it is fattened on the content of substantive historical analysis.'[32] It is a pity Thompson did not pursue his felt similarities with Sartre further, as there is a real analytic and political problem at the heart of the relationship between structure and process which invokes the central tendency at the heart of Sartre's earlier, more explicitly existentialist work in *Being and Nothingness*, namely, the question of *agency*. And not only agency as such (who or what directs action?), but the even trickier problem of collective agency (how do groups act together?). Trying to understand both individual action and directed collective behaviour (rebellions, for example) is the problem that preoccupies Sartre in the 1960s and touches on questions that history must ask itself. Anderson poses the problem in the following way:

> If fundamental historical processes, the structure and evolution of whole societies, are the involuntary resultant of a duality or plurality of voluntary forces clashing with each other, what explains their *ordered nature*?[33]

In other words, how does class superimpose itself upon, or how does it shape, individual action into a collective form? We are reminded of Marx's great aphorism from the *Eighteenth Brumaire*: 'Men make their own history, but they do not make it just as they please; they do not make it under circumstances chosen by themselves, but under circumstances directly encountered, given and transmitted from the past.'[34] But defining class in the present seems, on the face of it, much harder to establish than simply pointing to those historical circumstances we can identify. Getting the balance between where action comes from and what the context might be is singularly difficult – swing too far in favour of individual will and you leave yourself open to the problem of explaining how anyone ever does anything collectively, rather than as clashing individual forces; focusing too much on the structures ('circumstances') threatens to eliminate agency altogether and make men and women pawns in some sort of larger game – that of history itself. Thompson had already stated in 1965 that '[t]o reduce class to an identity is to forget exactly where *agency* lies, not in class but in men',[35] but there is clearly something unsatisfying about this description, whilst it nevertheless also rings true. What would be the use of talking about class *at all* if what we really meant was the action taken by individual men and women? The questions that guide the late work of Sartre – How do uprisings occur? What makes a group cohere? How can we understand shared purpose? – are philosophical versions of the structuralism/agency debate over class as it appears in the work of Thompson and Anderson. In Sartre's description of his own 'progressive-regressive method' in the methodological account of his later work, he frames the problem as a threefold choice: we reduce everything to 'identity', thus substituting mechanistic materialism for dialectical materialism; or we turn the dialectic into a 'celestial law' in which history unfolds idealistically (and here are interesting parallels with Thompson's polemical description of the mechanical 'orrery' of Althusser's errors); or we 'restore to the individual man his power to go beyond his situation by means of work and action'.[36] Sartre's 'solution' is ultimately very close to Thompson's own. It is not surprising, then, given the proximity of Sartre and Thompson's concerns (if not exactly a shared language), that attempts have been made to use both thinkers together to look back at collective political action by members of the working class. James Holston's *Ehud's Dagger: Class Struggle in the English Revolution* makes explicit and parallel use of both thinkers in order to make two simultaneous arguments (based on Sartre's progressive–regressive method): 'not simply the bare thesis that the English Revolution was a class struggle, but also the argument that this class struggle took a particular shape partly because of the complexly determined and determining projects of working people'.[37] If Sartre's later work is partly an attempt to compensate for the overly individuated image of the existentialist 'project' in work and to explain instead those times where action is taken collectively, he also reaches a rather similar conclusion to Thompson as regards the best *method* to achieve this as Thompson: man, states Sartre, rather poetically, is 'Universal by the singular universality of human history, singular by the universalizing singularity of his projects', and as such, 'he requires simultaneous examination from both ends'.[38] Sartre and Thompson have the same desire to avoid falling into the traps of rendering all agency completely voluntary and individualised, but also to escape from quantitative traps or teleological fallacies.

Sartre's work in the 1960s is, like Thompson's, explicitly anti-sociological and anti-determinist. When Anderson criticises Thompson for not fully exploring the question of agency, we can ask, in the light of

Thompson's 1978 essay on class whether Anderson is fair, particularly given an important section in the same essay by Thompson where he argues that the real focus of his work is less class as such, but more 'class struggle': 'class-struggle', he writes, is 'the prior, as well as the more universal, concept'.[39] In a reformulation of Marx's aphorism from the *Eighteenth Brumaire*, Thompson argues that 'people find themselves in a society structured in determined ways (crucially, but not exclusively, in productive relations)', they experience exploitation (or 'the need to maintain power over those whom they exploit'). The identification of antagonism, shared interests and struggle is the process that comes to generate self-awareness and self-identification as a class ('in the process of struggling they discover themselves as classes, they come to know this discovery as class-consciousness'.[40]) The attempt to first identify who or what comprises a class is to mistake the stages of historical class-formation: classes do not pre-exist the struggle they emerge from. Sartre's move in his own work away from the image of existentialist man 'condemned to be free' towards a non-sociological analysis of group-formation (Sartre talks about the 'group-in-fusion' as a collective subject united in goal and purpose, but forever haunted by the possibility of betrayal) is close to Thompson's insistence on process, but in a primarily philosophical rather than historical register.

To return to the earlier discussion of class understood as process and relation, Thompson highlights the crucial dimension of *antagonism* in the formation of class. This is why the title of Thompson's most famous work, *The Making of the English Working Class*, should be understood, in Sartrean terms, as a 'progressive–regressive' description: the English working class are 'made' by exploitation and antagonism but they also 'make themselves'. The 'problem' of the division between structure and agency is addressed and at least partly resolved if this double movement, which is at the same time always a relationship, is kept in mind at all times, both as a method and as a description of what class is at a certain point and in a particular place. The possibilities for seeing patterns across different periods and places stem not from the imposition of a 'structure' to read class, but from the ability to see how class (and class struggle) makes history by making itself. As Wood puts it: 'the great strength of Thompson's conception of class is that it is capable of recognising, and giving an account of, the operations of class in the absence of class consciousness'.[41]

But why, then, are so many critics so keen to argue that Thompson is missing something fundamental when it comes to class? It certainly cannot be to do with the *content* of Thompson's analyses, which provide us with one of the richest, if not the richest, account of the flesh and blood of emancipation, and the experience, suffering, failure and courage of the working class. Again we come back to the question of *structure*. G. A. Cohen, in *Karl Marx's Theory of History: A Defence*, takes umbrage with Thompson precisely on this question, attacking him for his repeated attacks on and dismissals of structural under-standings of class. Cohen ultimately argues that Thompson is too reductive in his understanding of what is meant by 'structure'. Cohen argues that 'structural' accounts of class are not simply the static, sociological and agency-denying lumps of conceptual framework that Thompson so decries, or at least are not in opposition to accompanying descriptions of process.[42] Cohen's is a different attempt to overcome the structure/agency opposition, by expanding structure to encom-pass agency. But the stronger point here is the explanatory neces-sity, according to Cohen, of economic structure (which, as Althusser would say, determines 'in the last instance'). Without this framework, Cohen suggests, distinct sorts of explanation are liable to be confused. Thompson's account of class might end up confusing self-description ('we struggled because …') with what really happened ('class struggle arose because …'). Sometimes, Cohen argues, the concept of structure must be kept if we are attempting to abstract the economic dimen-sion, in particular, from the processes that constitute it.

In his bid to preserve and dignify the empirical experience of class struggle, does Thompson ultimately throw the structural baby out with the voluntarist bathwater? Anderson concurs with Cohen in arguing that Thompson's definition of class is ultimately 'far too voluntarist and subjectivist',[43] but Wood in turn defends Thompson, suggesting that his work is already performing the kind of manoeuvre that Cohen, Anderson and others believe is absent: '[w]here Thomp-son's critics see structures *as against* processes, or structures that *undergo* processes, Thompson sees structured processes'.[44] The point made above regarding the order of class formation through struggle is also made central in Wood's account of Thompson's contribution: 'Class *formations* and the discovery of class consciousness grow out of the process of struggle, as people "experience" and "handle" their class situation'.[45]

Wood's sympathetic reading is, I would suggest, closest to what Thompson seems to intend, particularly in the more conceptual 'Class Struggle' essay from 1978. Thompson ultimately avoids reinstating the structure/agency opposition as Cohen arguably does through his attack on Thompson (Cohen at least reinstates a hierarchy of structure over agency). Thompson's concept of class is ultimately best understood, perhaps with some help from Sartre, as a *method* for allowing every dimension of class struggle to be seen as equally important, in process and in relation, all at once: after all, if it is not clear what it is like to struggle, and why class struggle is so important, we will not understand what we are struggling for *now*, or what people were struggling for *then*. Thompson's deft touch with the theoretical dimensions of his concept of class allow him full scope for describing the real experience of class formation and the real experience of the historically marginalised – and indeed those marginalised by 'History'. The men and women who populate his books are comprehensible because Thompson lets them speak for themselves, without condescension. Yet their experiences are also collective processes precisely because Thompson does not presuppose the existence of class as a static block, but rather attempts to describe its formation. As Wood puts it: 'His primary concern ... is to focus attention on the complex and often contradictory historical processes by which, in determinate historical conditions, class *situations* give rise to class *formations*.'[46]

Conclusion

One of the challenges facing any definition of the working class today can be helpfully aided by Thompson's method: before we decide what the working class is, how big it is and what it 'should' think, we should remember to think always in terms of processes and relations, rather than static categories and unhelpful aggregates, and to avoid the trap of political hand-wringing ('why don't people think the right way about their situation?'). To pay attention to antagonism and collective opposition, no matter how minute, obscure or dead-end, is one of the fundamental lessons Thompson teaches his readers.

One of the most important questions regarding Thompson's concept of class, or, to nuance it, his concepts of class-*struggle* and class-*formation*, is to ask what it makes us understand and what we can learn from his lengthy and serious analyses. Put more in terms of the effects generated by his writing, we can ask whether Thompson creates an image of the world in which struggle is real and whether its relevance to today's antagonisms and battles is made abundantly clear even in the most pure 'historical' moments of his work. In my view, Thompson succeeds in this task admirably: the 'concept' of class that flows through his writing is as vivid and as flexible as one could possibly hope for. Above all, his descriptions and accounts in *The Making of the English Working Class* and elsewhere generate a sense of optimism, even where rebellions are brutally crushed and passions are dissipated. Thompson's perpetual attempt to avoid static, socio-logical accounts of class is in part due to his desire to keep these struggles alive, to avoid diminishing the sacrifices made by real individuals working together to counteract the oppressive and exploitative forces of capitalism and the ruling class. Thompson's 'concept' of class is as alive as the men and women of his texts, and as complex yet forceful as the rebellions and uprisings they created.

Notes

1 E. P. Thompson, *The Making of the English Working Class* (Harmondsworth: Penguin, 1963), p. 9.

2 E. Meiksins Wood, *Democracy Against Capitalism: Renewing Historical Materialism* (Cambridge: Cambridge University Press, 1995), p. 13.

3 Thompson, *The Making of the English Working Class*, p. 13.

4 *Ibid.*, p. 9.

5 E. P. Thompson, 'Eighteenth-century English Society: Class Struggle without Class?', *Social History*, 3:2 (1978), 133–65, p. 133.

6 *Ibid.*, p. 147.

7 E. P. Thompson, *The Poverty of Theory: An Orrery of Errors* (London: Merlin Press, 1978), p. 128.

8 *Ibid.*, p. 58.

9 *Ibid.*, p. 60.

10 *Ibid.*, p. 62.

11 *Ibid.*

12 Thompson, 'Eighteenth-century English Society', p. 133.

13 See, e.g., K. Popper, *Conjectures and Refutations* (London: Routledge, 2002 [1963]).

14 Thompson, 'Eighteenth-century English Society', p. 133.

15 This is how Thompson describes the project of his earlier book in 'Eighteenth-century English Society', p. 146.

16 Thompson, *The Making of the English Working Class*, p. 11.

17 Thompson, 'Eighteenth-century English Society', p. 147.

18 *Ibid.*, p. 147.

19 *Ibid.*

20 *Ibid.*

21 *Ibid.*

22 P. Anderson, *Arguments Within English Marxism* (London: New Left Books and Verso, 1980), p. 36.

23 P. Anderson, 'Origins of the Present Crisis', *New Left Review*, 23 (January–February 1964), 26–53, p. 27.

24 E. P. Thompson, 'The Peculiarities of the English', in R. Miliband and J. Saville (eds), *Socialist Register*,1965 (London: Merlin Press, 1965), pp. 311–62, p. 32.

25 See also Anderson's response to Thompson's mid-1960s criticisms in 'Socialism and Pseudo-Empiricism', *New Left Review*, 30 (January–February 1966), 2–42.

26 Thompson, 'Eighteenth-century English Society', p. 147.

27 *Ibid.*

28 *Ibid.*, p. 148.

29 Anderson, *Arguments Within English Marxism*, p. 33.

30 Thompson, *The Poverty of Theory*, p. 147.

31 *Ibid.*, pp. 147–8.

32 *Ibid.*, p. 149.

33 Anderson, *Arguments Within English Marxism*, p. 51; original emphasis.

34 K. Marx, *The Eighteenth Brumaire of Louis Bonaparte* (London: Lawrence & Wishart, 1934), p. 10.

35 Thompson, 'The Peculiarities of the English', p. 358; original emphasis.

36 J-P. Sartre, *Search for a Method*, trans. H. E. Barnes (New York: Vintage Books, 1963 [1960]), p. 99.

37 J. Holston, *Ehud's Dagger: Class Struggle in the English Revolution* (London: Verso, 2002), p. 93.

38 J-P. Sartre, *The Family Idiot: Gustave Flaubert 1821–1857*, trans. C. Cosman (Chicago: University of Chicago Press, 1981 [1971]), p. ix.

39 Thompson, 'Eighteenth-century English Society', p. 149.

40 *Ibid.*, p. 149.

41 Wood, *Democracy against Capitalism*, p. 79.

42 G. A. Cohen, *Karl Marx's Theory of History: A Defence* (Princeton, NJ: Princeton University Press, 1980), p. 87.

43 Anderson, *Arguments Within English Marxism*, p. 40.

44 Wood, *Democracy Against Capitalism*, p. 79; original emphasis.

45 *Ibid.*, p. 80.

46 *Ibid.*, p. 83.

8

Thompson and the early New Left

Michael Newman

The year 1956 was the historical 'moment' that led to the emergence of the New Left as an international phenomenon, with both innovative forms of thought and the rediscovery of aspects of Marxism that had been suppressed during the years of Stalinist domination. Although it failed to achieve sufficient 'take-off' to challenge the ascendancy of communism and social democracy, the ideological breakthrough had a lasting radical effect, fuelling further phases of political and social contestation, including the era of 1968 and the subsequent growth of new social movements.

In Britain, at the beginning of 1956, there appeared to be few openings for the Left. The previous year the Conservative Party had been re-elected to power and Hugh Gaitskell had become Labour Party leader. In intellectual terms, revisionism also appeared to be dominant, with John Strachey's *Contemporary Capitalism* and Anthony Crosland's highly influential work, *The Future of Socialism*, both published in 1956.[1] And then quite suddenly in the autumn a new political space opened up. Krushchev's speech in February to the Twentieth Congress of the Communist Party of the Soviet Union (CPSU), in which he denounced Stalin's crimes, had led to turmoil in the communist world, culminating in the brutal Soviet repression of the Hungarian uprising in November. The outcry against this was reinforced by the mass protests against the simultaneous British and French military aggression against Egypt, in collaboration with Israel. This was followed in May 1957 by the testing of the first British hydrogen bomb and the subsequent establishment of CND. Since there was so much similarity between the New Left and CND in their ethos, political culture and objectives, there was a symbiotic relationship between the two and both movements grew until 1960, when a unilateralist resolution was passed (against the leadership's wishes) at the Labour Party conference (see chapter 9). This was the zenith for the New Left, with 45 clubs and a combined membership of 3,000.[2]

The embryonic new movement was underpinned by its journals. The NR, edited by Edward Thompson and John Saville, first appeared in the summer of 1957, building on the dissident publication, *The Reasoner*, which they had launched in July 1956 in an attempt to generate debate within the CP. The NR would remain closely associated with the opinion of ex-Communists, with Ralph Miliband, who joined in 1958, the only member of its editorial board who had not previously been in the CP. In February 1957, the second New Left journal, the *ULR*, began publication, initiated by four editors – Raphael Samuel, Gabriel Pearson, Stuart Hall and Charles Taylor – whose average age was 24. Although there were differences between the two journals, there was also considerable co-operation between them and a merger – to create the *NLR* – took place at the end of 1959, when the potential for a new movement appeared to be at its greatest, bringing nearly 10,000 subscribers to the new journal. However, the reversal of the unilateralist commitment at the 1961 Labour Party Conference had a knock-on effect on the New Left. A meeting near Stockport in July 1961 brought matters to a head, with many of the clubs, which were themselves divided, focusing on a common target – the journal – and claiming that they were being ignored by the centre.[3] This acrimonious meeting was probably the moment at which the New Left went into terminal decline as a political force, but the tensions had been obvious ever since the merger of the two journals.[4]

An unwieldy board had been established, which included the editorial members of both original journals with some additional members. Thompson chaired this board and subjected Stuart Hall, the first editor of the *NLR*, to enormous pressure.[5] In June 1960 Thompson resigned (and was replaced by Saville) and, although he was persuaded to rejoin the board, he remained deeply critical.[6] In the aftermath of the Stockport conference, Saville, normally a steadying influence, resigned and Thompson resumed his previous position. By now the *NLR* was also in debt and at the end of 1961 Hall resigned as editor. The key task was to restructure it in straitened financial circumstances, and a string of further resignations took place. Three editors, formally associated with the *ULR* – Samuel, Dennis Butt and the 23-year-old Perry Anderson – were charged with producing the next issue of the journal. However, when this finally arrived, it was twice as long as expected and £1,000 over budget.[7] After heavy criticism from the board, Butt and Samuel resigned in March 1962, but Thompson persuaded Anderson to stay on and in May implored him to accept the board's continuing supervisory control of the journal.[8] However, the *NLR* was now deeply indebted, with a sharp decline in subscriptions (to 3,000). Anderson was able to supply the necessary funds and simultaneously recruited Robin Blackburn and Tom Nairn as part of a so-called 'team' to take over the journal. The change of theoretical direction that ensued led to the final break-up of the *NLR* and by April 1963 all the editorial members of the former *NR* Board had resigned. The *NLR* would establish itself as an internationally renowned organ of Marxist scholarship, but it never constructed – or attempted to construct – a political or social movement of the kind sought by the early New Left, which is the focus of this chapter.[9]

The early New Left in Britain included many intellectual 'heavyweights', but Thompson certainly played a pivotal role because of his intellectual prowess, personal charisma and the enormous amount of time and energy he devoted to the project. Yet his contribution remains controversial. The first criticism, which is largely justified, is that he was often highly temperamental and 'difficult' with his colleagues in the embryonic movement.[10] Not only was he suspicious of the *ULR* group, whom he regarded as too eclectic, middle-class and 'metropolitan', but he often tested the patience of his closest associates, including John Saville, and was certainly partly responsible for the failure to foster effective collaboration, particularly after the merger. A second criticism is focused upon the conception of 'socialist humanism', which he formulated in this period, and which was later dismissed by Perry Anderson and by those sympathetic to the 'anti-humanist' Althusserian school of Marxist theory.[11] From such perspectives, Thompson's views came to be regarded as outmoded, pre-theoretical and moralistic.[12] These claims are refuted very effectively by Kate Soper (see chapter 6). A third criticism is that Thompson's thinking was directed more towards the past than the present and future. This is perhaps implied in some important recent work emphasising policy-relevant contributions in the sphere of political economy by such figures as John Hughes, Michael Barratt Brown and Kenneth Alexander, who have been less celebrated in most histories of the early New Left than Thompson, and the cultural theorists, Raymond Williams and Stuart Hall.[13] It is certainly true that Thompson's sphere was in defining general ideas rather than in detailed analysis and policy proposals, but both types of contribution seem equally important. However, Thompson's ideas have also been criticised on the grounds that they were tainted by his preoccupation with the CP during the Stalinist period. Michael Kenny thus suggests that Thompson's thinking constituted 'a historically specific project which enabled sections of the British intelligentsia to escape the confines of Stalinist Marxism'.[14] His argument, in effect, is that his work lacked contemporary relevance and could not therefore provide a theoretical basis for understanding the problems that the Left was to confront in the years ahead.

This chapter challenges this view. It argues that, despite the undoubted significance of his past, Thompson was not locked into a mindset of the 'ex-Communist', but was constantly thinking and evolving. It begins with a brief summary of his political evolution and then examines his ideas on a number of related themes. His overall contribution is evaluated in the concluding section.

From dissident communist to New Left theorist

In his final contribution for *The Reasoner* Thompson included this personal note:

> I recall a 'Christmas message' from my brother, which he wrote after meeting Communist partisans, in December 1943:
> 'There is a spirit abroad in Europe which is finer and braver than anything that tired continent has known for centuries and which cannot be withstood. You can, if you like, think of it in terms of politics, but it is broader and more generous than any dogma. It is the confident will of whole peoples, who have known the utmost humiliation and suffering and who have triumphed over it, to build their own life once and for all'.[15]

The crime of Stalinism, Thompson continued, had 'crabbed and confined this spirit', but had never killed it.[16] Of course, this was a very selective interpretation of the essence of Communism, but after leaving the CP Thompson still believed that it could be recovered. He thus suggested that the 'liberal Gods' were those of justice, tolerance and intellectual liberty, 'but not the humanist Gods of social liberty, equality, fraternity', which remained on the communist side, and that 'is why – although I have resigned from the Communist Party

– I remain a Communist'.[17] At this stage, his thinking on some other issues also appeared somewhat 'frozen'. In spring 1957 he suggested that this was a moment 'not only for "re-thinking", but above all for *re-affirmation*' of 'the thought which is central to Socialism ... that man is capable not only of changing his conditions, but also of transforming himself'.[18] He warned against joining the Labour Party, where too many intellectuals got swallowed up in short-term political practicality and 'cease to think as socialists'.[19] He insisted that 'the working people of Britain could end capitalism tomorrow if they summoned up the courage and made up their minds to do it' and attributed their lack of will to do so to their disappointment with the Soviet Union and their unwillingness to risk giving their allegiance to a 'vanguard' that would establish the dictatorship of the proletariat.[20] In these circumstances, the main task was to re-establish the open circuit that had existed in the 1930s between a significant group of intellectuals and the most politically alert section of the labour movement, which he defined largely in terms of CP-backed popular-front organisations and networks. The implication was that the answers to the problems were already known – it was largely a matter of *promulgating* them.

Although Thompson continued to reaffirm his debt to communist traditions and values – for example, in the final issue of the *NR* – [21] this discourse partially masked important shifts in his thinking. By the summer of 1958 he accepted some of Charles Taylor's criticisms of Marxism in relation to humanism, agreeing that a critique of Stalinism must also involve a critique of the values of Marxist communism.[22] A year later, talking for the NR group as a whole, he noted that since 1956 'we have altered some opinions', tending to see Marxism 'less as a self-sufficient system, more as a major creative influence within a wider socialist tradition'.[23] By 1960 he was also expressing irritation 'with some of the members of "Marxist" sects who pop up at Left Club meetings around the country to demand in a your-money-or-your-life tone of voice whether the speaker is a Marxist',[24] and he called instead for a co-operative examination of particular practical and theoretical problems. There was also a *partial* shift in his attitude to the Labour Party. By the summer of 1959 he insisted that it would be futile and counterproductive to attempt to offer an alternative faction, party or leadership to those currently holding the field,[25] and he recognised that the majority of the New Left were also active members of the Labour Party and trade-union movements. And in January 1961, when he read a late draft of Miliband's Parliamentary Socialism,[26] he clearly thought it too negative in arguing that the Labour Party as a whole had never followed a socialist strategy. He thus told Miliband that he had not paid sufficient attention to the diversity of the party in historical terms, ignoring the 'movement at the bottom', including local government, that his impatience with the 'welfare state myth' led to a lack of sympathy where there were real gains; and that the history of Bradford, Poplar and parts of South Wales and Scotland demonstrated socialist initiatives that could not be equated either with liberal reformism or bureaucratic piecemeal collectivism.[27] He certainly had no illusions about the Labour Party, but believed it necessary to draw on its whole record at all levels in the attempt to understand future possibilities.

I now turn to the development of some of his ideas as a result of engagement with the New Left. One major topic was that of 'revolution', which incorporated various themes about transition, power, bureaucracy and the nature of socialism. He published two articles on such questions in 1960,[28] but he developed much of his thinking on them two years earlier in correspondence with Ralph Miliband. This was initiated in April 1958 when Saville (on behalf of the Editorial Board of the *NR*) asked Miliband to write an article providing a contemporary perspective on the difference between the evolutionary and revolutionary conceptions of a socialist transition.[29] Miliband responded cautiously, on the grounds that no such transition was even on the agenda, and his subsequent synopsis included little about the key issues that Thompson had wanted him to address.[30] Thompson now set out his own thinking. Miliband, he argued, was too traditional in his understanding of a revolutionary model, in which there was a 'cataclysmic' view of a transition based on the assumption of a dramatic crisis preceding a seizure of power. In this model, the period of 'transition' was also seen as a sharp break leading to distinct forms of economic and social organisation, with correspondingly distinct forms of political institutions. Against this, he suggested incorporating some features of a reformist approach, normally associated with evolutionary socialism, into the political framework of a revolutionary model. This recognised that the Western labour and trade-union movements had been strong enough to build up certain features of socialist society within the overall economic and political framework of capitalism. These included restrictions on the free labour market, social legislation and increasing state control over a major portion of the economy, with elements of social ownership. In Thompson's view, four important consequences followed from this. First, the problem of transition was no longer a simple seizure of power; secondly, nationalisation of a preponderant section of the economy would not necessarily bring about a transition; thirdly, transition needed to be redefined in order to understand how existing forms of nationalisation and state control could lead to both resistance from above *and* heightened working-class consciousness, militancy and democratic participation; and finally, the transition might not therefore be cataclysmic, but immanent within the present situation. The overall policy, he suggested, should be to probe capitalist power by using reformist tactics within an overall revolutionary strategy. Ultimately, there would no doubt be a crisis, which needed to be anticipated with appropriate planning, but a constructive 'reform-by-reform' appeal should be made to working people so that they would be led by their own daily experience to recognise the moment of transition when it came. It was also necessary to propagate models for the future, with the main question no longer that of socialism or capitalism, but of the *kind* of socialism. He concluded:

> What it seems to add up to is a trend of thought which says: we agree that socialism – in the sense of public ownership – is inevitable, and (as opposed to private ownership) generally desirable: it is coming anyway … What we doubt is whether it *matters*. Megalithic industrial society, with its accompanying bureaucracy, is too big for any of us to influence much in any direction. The individual has got to make his own life somewhere in the interstices of the industrial machinery, despite the state, whether a board of directors or a board of technicians or a board of black-coated trade union bureaucrats are running it.[31]

The two articles in 1960 elaborated on many of these ideas. Recognition of the need to displace the dynamic of the profit motive in order to attain a 'Society of Equals' was, he argued, a distinguishing feature of the socialist tradition, but nationalisation was not the only alternative to private ownership, and he also suggested co-operative and municipal forms of ownership. Once again he claimed that there was no automatic relationship between social ownership and either socialist institutions or moral dispositions, but he also insisted that it was mistaken to appeal to morality or values outside the context of power. While a revolution of some kind was necessary, he regarded the classic debate between 'reformism' and 'revolution' as sterile. The countervailing forces of democracy meant that there was a precarious equilibrium within capitalism that could be tipped back towards authoritarianism, but could also 'be heaved *forward*, by popular pressures of great intensity, to the point where the powers of democracy cease to be countervailing and become the active dynamic of society in their own right.'[32] Such a revolution was far more likely to be peaceful than in the recent past because the 'advances of 1942–48 *were* real, because the socialist *potential* has been enlarged, and socialist forms, however imperfect, have grown up "within" capitalism.'[33] However, the point of breakthrough was not one more shuffle along an evolutionary path, for a transition in class power was necessary and the breaking point needed to be found. A revolutionary culmination would involve

> the making of revolution simultaneously in many fields of life. It involves the breaking-up of some institutions (and the House of Lords, Sandhurst, Aldermaston, the Stock Exchange, the press monopolies and the National Debt are among those which suggest themselves), the transformation and modification of others (including the House of Commons and the nationalised Boards), and the transfer of new functions to yet others (town councils, consumers' councils, trades councils, shop stewards committees, and the rest).[34]

The immediate task was the elaboration of a democratic revolutionary strategy. This demanded a break with 'parliamentary fetishism', for most popular gains had been won in the first place by direct action, although this did not mean establishing alternative institutions or working entirely outside the political system. 'But, in the last analysis, the context will dictate to the politicians, and not the reverse. And socialists must make the context.'[35] He was also conscious of the international dimensions of such a shift, including the likelihood of US sanctions in the event of a withdrawal from NATO, but suggested that Britain was perhaps best placed to bring about such a transition because the equilibrium within capitalism was the most precarious and the labour movement the least divided, while the democratic socialist tradition was stronger than elsewhere.[36] Finally, he recalled the 'long and tenacious revolutionary tradition of the British commoner', affirming that while everyone knew its weaknesses, 'its strengths, its resilience and steady humanity, we too easily forget.'[37]

Thompson's text provoked a wide range of criticisms, from various viewpoints, which he attempted to deal with in 'Revolution Again'. But a key question was why he used the term 'revolution' at all. As he acknowledged:

The word 'revolution' is like a bell which makes some salivate approval or disapproval according to the conditioned response ... [S]ome said: 'Revolution: Apocalyptic, Marxist pipe-dream, opiate of the intellectuals, nostalgia for Chartism, utopian rhetoric, etc.' Others said: 'Revolution? I go for that – down with the lot, Bomb, Establishment, mass media, Shell building and all – roll on the day!'[38]

Yet although he agreed that for most people the concept suggested, at best, a very remote contingency or, at worst, an exercise in scholasticism, he defended its use against alternative concepts, clearly viewing this as a matter of real importance.[39] For he appeared to believe that his conception of 'revolution' not only transcended the conventional distinction between evolutionary and revolutionary forms of socialism, but that this also needed to be *recognised* if a potentially revolutionary opportunity was to be grasped. His correspondence with Miliband is again helpful in revealing some of his underlying assumptions.

In private, Miliband provided detailed criticisms of 'Revolution', affirming his own belief in a *necessary* relationship between the base and superstructure.[40] Thompson was adamant in rejecting this:

Using these terms, I think it is true that there is a relationship: that is, that the basis defines and confines the possible variations of superstructure; and that therefore you cannot have a socialist superstructure on a capitalist basis. But from that point we lead either to a tautology (a socialist basis must give rise to a superstructure which is socialist because this is in the definition of the basis) or we have a very much vaguer and more challenging statement: that a socialist basis gives rise to a great variety of possible socialist superstructures, some of which would embody values which we customarily consider (as socialists) to be desirable while others we might (from the usual ethical tradition of socialism) abhor. I do not think that a socialist basis necessarily gives rise to a *democratic* superstructure.[41]

Miliband also again expressed reservations about how fruitful it was to speculate on the 'transition', but Thompson insisted that this was necessary because a revolutionary situation was constantly imminent:

one important part of realising this, redirecting the energies of the Labour movement to take advantage of it, is to break with the evolutionary and also the errors in the revolutionary model. Therefore it is not only important but could be a theoretical task of prime importance. I am suggesting there is a way open ... which we cannot see because our theoretical glasses have got misted up. There was a cataclysmic revolution lying around in Russia in 1916-7 but it took Lenin to see it. I am suggesting that there may be a new kind of revolution lying around in Britain in 1969 or 1974, and that [it] won't get it unless I can prod Miliband or some other potential theorist to see it.[42]

With hindsight Thompson's belief in a potentially revolutionary situation may seem wildly optimistic. Even some of those who are generally very sympathetic to his work have been baffled by it, suggesting that it revealed his inability to make serious political calculations.[43] Certainly, crucial aspects of his analysis – for example, on structural dimensions of power and the State – were missing and he was conscious of this. However, he was also saying something very important about the relationship between consciousness and change. As he argued in another essay,[44] the *belief* that all the obstacles meant that transformation was impossible led to a particular form of apathy that served dominant interests very well. However, once collective discontent was expressed outside the authorised institutional channels the vulnerability of the existing system could be exposed – as he believed had been the case with the success of CND in 1960. This meant that there were, in his view, integral links between rejecting the view that incremental change was the only realistic outlook, identifying the necessary changes for transition, defining a model of socialism and achieving a 'revolution'.

Thompson's analysis of social class also developed in this period – largely in response to contributions by others on the New Left that he believed to be misconceived. Unfortunately, he was also often defensive in relation to positions that he associated with the *ULR* group and sometimes expressed his reservations quite brutally. This was particularly the case in 'Commitment in Politics' in spring 1959 when, by implication, he came very near to accusing the new generation of being 'anti-working-class'.[45] He warned that certain attitudes could be corrosive in the socialist movement:

These attitudes seem to me to stem from an ambiguity as to the place of the working-class in the struggle to create a socialist society: a tendency to view working people as the *subjects* of history,[46] as pliant *recipients* of the imprint of the mass media, as *victims* of alienation, as *data* for sociological enquiry: a tendency to under-estimate the tensions and conflicts of working-class life, and the creative potential – not in the remote future but here and now – of working people: a tendency to assert the absolute autonomy of cultural phenomena without reference to the context of class power: and a shame-faced evasion of that impolite historical concept – the class struggle.[47]

167

Three of Thompson's criticisms, which were partly aimed at a contribution by Stuart Hall in the previous edition of *ULR* and at Richard Hoggart's *The Uses of Literacy*, were particularly important.[48] The first was that there needed to be a greater emphasis on *history*, for this would demonstrate that many of the attitudes and phenomena attributed to the current situation had also existed in previous eras. Secondly, he contested the suggestion that materialism in itself, or forms of morality that accompanied it, or the kinds of media that were absorbed, necessarily led to passive acceptance of the capitalist system. This led to his third point – that progressive change always came about through an active minority. These were important arguments but, as Madeleine Davis has argued, the vehemence of his attack may have cut short a debate on a key issue.[49] And yet, paradoxically, Thompson's own attitude to class was much less traditional than he implied. This was indicated in a brief passage in the same article:

> I hope we may become a little less self-conscious ourselves about status and class, and cease to play the game of the Establishment by drawing an abstract line between the 'real working-class' of heavy industry, and the teachers, the technicians, the draughtsmen, the white-coated and the rest.[50]

A few months later he rejected Alasdair MacIntyre's criticism of the New Left for its failure to focus on the 'point of production' as the basic antagonism in society, arguing that there was not just *one* such antagonism at the place of work, 'and a series of remoter, more muffled antagonisms in the social or ideological "superstructure", which are in some way less "real"'.[51] Rather, there was a class-divided society, in which conflicts of interest, and conflicts between capitalist and socialist ideas, values and institutions took place all along the line. The notion of a 'point of production' was, in any case, more ambiguous than it seemed, for it was not clear what teachers and health-service workers produced. Furthermore, if the trend was towards a greater proportion of the workforce in secondary, rather than primary productive operations, it would surely follow from MacIntyre's theoretical framework that the socialist base would be weakened? Against this, Thompson asked whether ideologies really originated at the point of production or 'by much more complex processes of conditioning within a class culture'.[52]

His views on class were closely related to his conception of revolution and he argued that a revolutionary strategy could not 'and must not rely exclusively upon the explosive negatives of class antagonism':

> And this is the more easy to envisage if we cease to draw that imaginary line between the industrial workers and the rest. The number of people who are wholly and unambiguously interested in the defence of the *status quo* is small ...
> Alongside the industrial workers we should see the teachers who want better schools, scientists who wish to advance research, welfare workers who want hospitals, actors who want a National Theatre, technicians impatient to improve industrial organisation ... It is the business of socialists to draw the line, not between a staunch but diminishing minority and an unredeemable majority, but between the monopolists and the people – to foster the 'societal instincts' and inhibit the acquisitive. Upon these positives, and not upon the debris of a smashed society, the socialist community must be built.[53]

He argued that there was a danger of the working class splitting down the middle, with the 'old' working class, grouped round the pits and heavy industries of the North and Scotland, holding on to its traditional values and forms of organisation, while younger workers identified with the ideology of 'classlessness'. It was also true that

> if fewer people think or affirm that they are working-class, this expresses a cultural reality which cannot be argued away by dragging in the term 'false consciousness'; it indicates an important *fact* about the consciousness of people who – so far as objective determinants are concerned – remain working people. Socialists may argue that the common interests which unite the 'old' and 'new' are vastly more important than those which divide them; but the fact will remain that many working people are scarcely conscious of their class identity and very conscious of their desire to escape the narrowing features of class.[54]

However, he insisted that it was not inevitable that differences in consciousness would lead to fragmentation, and it was up to the Left to fight for new ways to redefine the common good in terms of a society of equals, with renewed emphasis upon the values of community.

Thompson's tendency simultaneously to develop his own thinking while attacking others was also apparent in his last major contribution before the break-up of the early New Left – his critique of the work of Raymond Williams in a two-part review article, which considered both *Culture and Society* (1958) and *The Long Revolution* (1961).[55]

In many respects, Thompson and Williams had much in common. They were of the same generation, both worked in university adult education, and both had been members of the CP, though Williams's membership had lapsed in the 1940s. Furthermore, both rejected the traditional Marxist interpretation of the relationship between base and superstructure and tended to stress the primacy of experience and consciousness in defining social class. Yet at this stage there were also some important differences between them. Williams had been politically isolated during the period in which he was developing his ideas and was deeply influenced by T. S. Eliot and Frank Leavis, although he was attempting to provide a critical alternative to their views.[56] And although *Culture and Society* was immediately viewed as a key work by much of the New Left, Williams was particularly influential in *ULR* circles and was rather disparaging about the *NR*, which he regarded as 'still too involved in arid fights with the Party Marxists', with some of its essays giving the impression that nothing had changed.[57] Thompson in turn feared that Williams was 'writing off' the socialist tradition rather than seeking a more satisfactory version of Marxism.[58] His critique was clearly intended to provide this.

Culture and Society traced the idea of culture from the Industrial Revolution onwards, attempting to demonstrate that this was a democratic idea in opposition to the disintegrating effects of capitalism and to both classical liberalism and to the Eliot–Leavis tradition of elite culture. However, he rejected the Marxist claim that the cultural realm was necessarily bourgeois and would be replaced by a proletarian culture after a revolution.[59] *The Long Revolution* had a more pronounced socialist emphasis, reflecting Williams's engagement with the New Left, and in this work he attempted to formulate a whole theory, with his own conceptual terminology. The 'long revolution' denoted three interrelated revolutions in industry, democracy and culture that had taken place over the previous two hundred years, but he insisted that there was no necessary primacy in any one of these transformations. Instead he suggested that all were part of a seamless social whole. Within the sphere of culture itself, he distinguished between three levels. First, from an anthropological perspective, culture signified the meanings, values and institutions of a society, which Williams often termed a 'whole way of life'. Secondly, it conveyed a body of intellectual or imaginative work representing creativity; and thirdly, each society designated aspects of such work in an ideal form, which was regarded as a 'cultural heritage'. In his view, the key tasks were to establish the relationships between these three levels and to develop a theory of culture based on this. In attempting to do so he further distinguished between 'social character' and 'structure of feeling'. 'Social character' referred to a system of values and ideals taught formally and informally, while 'structure of feeling' characterised the inner experience of individuals sharing a common way of life, and was revealed in a concrete form in cultural artefacts, particularly through the arts. Focusing on England in the 1840s, he sought to demonstrate the way all this operated in practice. Whereas a conventional Marxist analysis would stress the class conflict of the period, Williams viewed it in terms of the interaction between three social characters, each of which experienced distinct structures of feeling. The middle class was dominant and put its stamp on society as a whole, but this was tempered by the differing structures of feeling emanating from both the aristocracy and the working class. This interaction produced a distinct social process, which could not therefore be identified in any simple way with the dominant class.[60]

Williams's two books were complex and the argument was sometimes obscure, but he was certainly breaking new ground (at least in a British context) in highlighting the multidimensional interrelationships between culture and other social processes and in insisting that the Left needed to understand and grapple with these if it was to advance politically. Thompson appreciated the importance of what Williams was attempting and paid tribute to it, but he also thought that his view of culture was tainted by the influence of Eliot and Leavis. Whereas Williams appeared to regard it as integrative, as denoted in the term 'a whole way of life', Thompson regarded it as a 'whole way of struggle' and stressed the variety of cultures within any society. Whereas Williams tended to regard cultural developments as relatively autonomous, Thompson was concerned that this meant that they could appear to be detached from class power and conflict. In Thompson's view, any theory of culture

> must include the concept of the dialectical interaction between culture and something that is *not* culture. We must suppose the raw material of life-experience to be at one pole, and all the infinitely complex human disciplines and systems, articulate and inarticulate, formalised in institutions or dispersed in the least formal ways, which 'handle', transmit, or distort this raw material to be at the other. It is the active process – which is at the same time the process through which men make their history – that I am insisting upon.[61]

Thompson's review opened up some important theoretical debates about the relationships between culture and power. However, his objective was also political. Because Williams was the most influential non-Marxist in the New Left, Thompson argued that a dialogue about power, communication, class and ideology was necessary.[62] So far, he suggested, no synthesis had been achieved and he feared that a preoccupation with culture as an apparently autonomous sphere might divert attention from wages, welfare and the political realm, and that ambiguities in *The Long Revolution* could reinforce the weaknesses that he saw in the New Left. Yet he also thought that some of Williams's conclusions offered the basis for a synthesis in a formulation proposed by Alasdair MacIntyre about the 'mode of production' being 'a kernel of human relationship from which all else grows'.[63] Both might then accept that the mode of production and productive relationships determine cultural processes in an *epochal* sense; that when we speak of the capitalist mode of production for profit we are indicating at the same time a 'kernel' of characteristic human relationships – of exploitation, domination, and acquisitiveness – which are inseparable from this mode ... Within the limits of the epoch there are characteristic tensions and contradictions, which cannot be transcended unless we transcend the epoch itself: there is an economic logic *and* a moral logic and it is futile to argue as to which we give priority since they are different expressions of the same 'kernel of human relationship'. We may then rehabilitate the notion of capitalist or bourgeois culture in a way that owes much to Marx but also much to Weber, Morris, Veblen, Tawney and others who have studied its characteristic patterns of acquisitiveness, competitiveness, and individualism.[64]

And this, he concluded, could also lead to the rehabilitation of the notion of a 'socialist culture' ultimately growing from and being sustained by a co-operative mode of production for use and a corresponding kernel of co-operative relationship.[65]

This very public critique of Williams's work was probably not the best way to forge harmonious relations within the New Left at a particularly difficult juncture in its history, and Thompson later claimed that Stuart Hall had persuaded him to publish the piece.[66] Williams did not respond to it, but almost twenty years later confessed that he had found it hard, particularly as he was being attacked so fiercely by the Right at the time.[67] Yet he also accepted that Thompson's critique, with its emphasis on culture as 'a whole way of struggle', had forced him to rethink some of his ideas. Later, Williams would also adopt Gramsci's concept of 'hegemony' and, reflecting on *Culture and Society* and *The Long Revolution*, he declared:

in understanding cultural hegemony and in seeing it as the crucial dimension of the kind of society which has been emerging since the war under advanced capitalism, I felt the need to break both from mainline Marxism and even more from the traditions of social democracy, liberalism and Fabianism which had been my immediate inheritance.[68]

As Dworkin has pointed out, Williams's later use of the Gramscian concept of hegemony implicitly acknowledged the force of the critique by Thompson, whose central argument was that Williams had failed to highlight the role of culture in relation to class struggle.[69] At the same time, the engagement with Williams's work perhaps also sharpened Thompson's own ideas about the relationship between the base and superstructure, for the synthesis that he suggested would be developed in *The Making of the English Working Class*.[70] His attempts to develop a flexible, revisionist Marxist position were thus particularly creative just as the early New Left plunged into its terminal crisis.

The disintegration of the first New Left and Thompson's legacy

The kind of movement to which many of the participants of the early New Left had aspired had probably not been possible at the time. The ascendancy of the Labour Party had not been seriously challenged, and once the politically astute Harold Wilson became leader in February 1963, the party regrouped and narrowly won the October 1964 general election. Nor had the social conditions really existed for a new movement to take root. Certainly, there were significant changes in contemporary Britain in the new era of decolonisation, 'protest' films and theatre and popular teenage culture, but the short-term breakthrough had largely been brought about by the resonance of the nuclear issue. CND and the New Left Clubs also tended to be based on the same social groups – particularly the newly enlarged cultural, intellectual and student sectors. The links with working-class movements remained quite weak and tended, above all, to be through workers' education in trade-union colleges and research departments, extramural and WEA adult education, and links with a few significant trade-union leaders.[71]

Yet even if the collapse of the early New Left as a movement was largely explicable in terms of the wider social and political environment, Thompson could never come to terms with what had happened. He remained bitter about the new direction taken by the *NLR* under Perry Anderson's control, and would revisit the dispute in three major essays and in an historic debate in a church in Oxford in December 1979.[72] He also chose a path of relative isolation, declining the invitation by Saville and Miliband to join them in founding the *Socialist Register* – the annual that would most closely follow the tradition of the *NR*.[73] He collaborated with Raymond Williams, Stuart Hall and others in producing the May Day Manifesto, actively supported the student sit-in at Warwick in 1970, and continued to denounce injustices in British society, but he did not again become involved in any sustained political activity until he returned to play the leading role in END (see chapter 9).[74] Perhaps he had invested so much in the early New Left that he was 'burnt-out' by the experience. However, there were almost certainly other aspects to all this.

After 1956 Thompson had made a colossal effort to establish a form of Marxist socialism that was open and flexible. He was quite wrong to imply – as he subsequently did – that the group that came to dominate the *NLR* was 'Stalinist'.[75] However, from 1962 onwards the journal was written in an authoritative style that suggested that theoretically sophisticated forms of Marxism could reveal a truth that was not available to those who followed the so-called empirical tradition of the British Left. This provoked Thompson into launching a public polemical attack on Anderson and Tom Nairn. Anderson's response was excoriating – a scathing and sometimes humiliating forensic exhumation of Thompson's contributions.[76] Thompson tried to shrug this off, but the attack was surely wounding. In any case, his retreat into relative isolation meant that his main theoretical interventions about the contemporary world now tended to be negative, rather than building on the more positive ideas that he had been developing. How then should Thompson's contribution to the early New Left be evaluated?

Much of the criticism of his theoretical writing focused on the conception of socialist humanism and, as Kate Soper suggests (see chapter 6), this sometimes emphasised impersonal forces and structures to an absurd degree. However, it is reasonable to argue that Thompson's emphasis on the subjective realm needed to be complemented by other approaches stressing structural categories and explanations to a greater extent than he normally did. Similarly, it should be noted that his work omitted any serious consideration of the economy and the possibilities that capitalism might develop in new ways rather than collapsing in crisis.[77] More specifically, there were also some weaknesses in his ideas on the themes discussed in this chapter. First, and most obviously, his claim that Britain had particular advantages as the location for a significant advance by the Left was never substantiated and perhaps rested more on hopes than evidence. This relates to a second weakness: his assumptions about the country and its people.

Much has been written about Thompson's identification with Blake, Morris and English radicalism, but there were also some deeper, and probably unconscious, assumptions. The power and brilliance of his historical writing about the formation of the working class was unparalleled, but his romanticism about elements of the past sometimes implied a particular form of identity. 'We are', he said, 'a Protestant people', and he related this to a distrust of system-building and a preference for pragmatism.[78] Of course, the struggle against Catholicism was profoundly important in the development of British political culture, but this definition of 'Englishness' was unlikely to attract the growing numbers of religious and ethnic minorities in the population. Similarly, while Thompson emphasised the radical tradition, others would tend to associate Britain with less appealing features of its history. For example, Stuart Hall's preoccupations in the era centred on anti-imperialism and the failure of orthodox Marxism to deal adequately with such issues as ethnicity, race and racism.[79] Again, while Thompson viewed London and the 'metropolis' with suspicion and associated socialism and the working class with the 'provinces', Hall recalled that, as a Jamaican in 1950s Britain, he felt instinctively more at home in the socially anonymous metropolitan culture than elsewhere.[80] Thompson's underlying assumptions were naturally shaped by his generation and background, and he virtually ignored the fact that Britain was now changing fast through migration patterns. His stress on a particular form of English identity did not therefore have resonance for everyone on the Left. As Anderson observed, Thompson's internationalism was active and generous, but he nevertheless sometimes expressed a form of cultural nationalism.[81]

And perhaps this was related to his concerns about the new directions that the *NLR* was taking just before the break-up, with its increasing attention on developing countries and postcolonial theories. While he (and others) were justified in warning against uncritical 'third-worldism', his attitude may have also reflected a reluctance to accept new theoretical approaches emanating from quite different contexts from his own, including, for example, that of Frantz Fanon in *The Wretched of the Earth*.[82]

There were also other weaknesses. He tended to react too sharply to theories or analyses that he felt were deviating from socialism. He sometimes therefore appeared to condemn studies of youth culture, or riots, or perceptions of class or consumer capitalism, as if any focus on such issues was a diversion. Thompson also shared in a *collective* failing – the attitude to women, who were not generally regarded as the active subjects of history and did not play a leading role in the early New Left (see chapter 1). In general, it was only in the later 1960s, with 'second-wave feminism', that a major change took place. Yet Thompson – perhaps because of Dorothy Thompson's role – was not entirely gender blind. For example, he joined her in mounting a sharp critique of an article on the Welfare State by John Saville, which had viewed this simply as a buttress of capitalism. Certainly, it was Dorothy Thompson who paid particular attention to its impact on women,[83] but Thompson himself criticised Miliband for adhering to a notion of 'real socialism', which was too limited and ignored the dimensions concerning child care, maternity services, education and a wide range of welfare.[84] Thompson's position on gender was not particularly advanced, but this was also the case with most of the early New Left.

Yet, despite the criticisms, his contribution remains outstanding. Apart from his conception of socialist humanism, which was in many ways the foundation for the more specific ideas discussed in this chapter, his attempt to apply his independent, revisionist form of Marxism to the questions of class, transition and the concept of socialism, as well as to wider issues of power in material and cultural forms, remains very instructive and often prescient. In all this he was seeking a new form of synthesis. Did he achieve this? His own words about C. Wright Mills, seem appropriate in this context:

> I must say plainly that I don't think he achieved this synthesis. Nor would he have made any such claim. Nor will it enhance his reputation if the claim is made on his behalf.[85]

Thompson regarded himself as an historian, rather than a political theorist, and his contributions were necessarily too brief and ephemeral to have constituted a work of synthesis. His writings were produced at breakneck speed in an attempt to provide a new sense of direction. In some ways, the current impasse of the Left may also make some of the ideas appear dated. Does it really make sense, one may ask, to speculate about the nature of a (non-violent) socialist revolution when we now appear to be regressing towards an increasingly harsh form of capitalism? Yet there is surely continuing relevance both in Thompson's insistence on the need to combine immediate reforms with a long-term vision and his emphasis on the relationship between consciousness and transformation. He also recognised the changes in the composition of the working class, with the relative decline in blue-collar work, and insisted on the need for the Left to find some way of uniting the apparently disparate groups behind a new political programme. Similarly, he was a pioneer in realising that socialism as well as capitalism could pursue 'some maniacal teleological worship of economic growth' and subordinate other human values to this end,[86] and also that the problems of bureaucracy and impersonal power needed to be addressed with the same sense of priority as those of ownership. Of course, he did not resolve such questions but, as Miliband once told him, his work 'does force debate and thought, in areas which most people tend to leave alone'.[87] This is still the case today.

Notes

1 J. Strachey, *Contemporary Capitalism* (London: Gollancz, 1956); C. A. R. Crosland, *The Future of Socialism* (London: Cape, 1956).

2 S. Hamilton, *The Crisis of Theory: E. P. Thompson, the New Left and Postwar British Politics* (Manchester: Manchester University Press, 2011), p. 98.

3 *Ibid.*, p. 100.

4 M. Kenny, *The First New Left: British Intellectuals After Stalin* (London: Lawrence & Wishart, 1995), p. 28.

5 Hamilton, *The Crisis of Theory*, pp. 96–7.

6 Kenny, *The First New Left*, pp. 35–6.

7 *Ibid.*, p. 29.

8 Letter from Thompson to Anderson, 23 May 1962 (copy of letter in the author's possession given by the late Dorothy Thompson).

9 There is much controversy about the extent of the continuities between the early and later New Left. See D. Thompson, *Pessimism of the Intellect? A History of New Left Review* (London: Merlin Press, 2007), pp. 39–43.

10 Kenny, *The First New Left*, pp. 34–8.

11 P. Anderson, 'Socialism and Pseudo-Empiricism', *New Left Review*, 1:35 (January–February 1966), pp. 2–42.

12 However, Perry Anderson apologised and withdrew some of his earlier criticisms in *Arguments within English Marxism* (London and New York: Verso, 1980), pp. 139–75.

13 M. Davis, 'Arguing Affluence: New Left Contributions to the Socialist Debate 1957–63', *Twentieth Century British History* (first published online 2 September 2011), doi:10.1093/tcbh/hwr033 (accessed 24 April 2012).

14 Kenny, *The First New Left*, p. 83.

15 E. P. Thompson, 'Through the Smoke of Budapest', *The Reasoner: A Journal of Discussion* (November 1956), quoted in D. Widgery, *The Left in Britain 1956–1968* (Harmondsworth: Penguin, 1976), pp. 71–2.

16 *Ibid.*

17 E. P. Thompson, 'Socialism and the Intellectuals', *Universities and Left Review*, 1 (Spring 1957), 31. All issues of *Universities and Left Review* and *The New Reasoner* have been made available online by the Barry Amiel and Norman Trust on www.amielandmelburn.org.uk/collections/ulr and www.amielandmelburn.org.uk/collections/nr.

18 *Ibid.*, p. 36.

19 *Ibid.*, p. 34.

20 E. P. Thompson, 'Socialist Humanism: An Epistle to the Philistines', *New Reasoner*, 1 (Summer 1957), 141.

21 E. P. Thompson, 'A Psessay in Ephology', *New Reasoner*, 10 (Autumn 1959), 7–8.

22 E. P. Thompson, 'Agency and Choice – I', *New Reasoner*, 5 (Summer 1958), 96.

23 Thompson, 'A Psessay in Ephology', p. 8.

24 E. P. Thompson, 'Revolution Again! Or Shut Your Ears and Run', *New Left Review*, 1:6 (November–December 1960), 21.

25 E. P. Thompson, 'The New Left', *New Reasoner*, 9 (Summer 1959), 16.

26 R. Miliband, *Parliamentary Socialism: A Study in the Politics of Labour* (London: Allen & Unwin, 1961).

27 Letter from E. P. Thompson to R. Miliband, undated January 1961 (copy in the author's possession with permission of the late Dorothy Thompson).

28 E. P. Thompson, 'Revolution', *New Left Review*, 1:3 (May–June 1960), 3–9; also published in E. P. Thompson (ed.), *Out of Apathy* (London: Stevens & Sons and New Left Books, 1960); Thompson, 'Revolution Again!'

29 Letter from J. Saville to R. Miliband, 11 April 1958 (Miliband papers, University of Leeds library).

30 Letter from R. Miliband to J. Saville, 18 April 1958 (Miliband papers); 'Synopsis for an article on 'Socialism and the Labour Party', sent by Miliband to Saville, 2 May 1958 (Miliband papers).

31 Letter from E. P. Thompson to R. Miliband, 12 June 1958 (Miliband papers).

32 Thompson, 'Revolution', p. 7.

33 *Ibid.*

34 *Ibid.*, p. 8.

35 *Ibid.*

36 *Ibid.*, p. 9.
37 *Ibid.*
38 Thompson, 'Revolution Again!', p. 18.
39 *Ibid.*, p. 29.
40 Letter from R. Miliband to E. P. Thompson, 1 April 1960 (Miliband papers).
41 Letter from E. P. Thompson to R. Miliband, 13 April 1960 (Miliband papers).
42 *Ibid.*
43 D. Dworkin, *Cultural Marxism: History, the New Left and the Origins of Cultural Studies* (Durham, NC and London: Duke University Press, 1997), pp. 65, 72.
44 E. P. Thompson, 'At the Point of Decay', in E. P. Thompson (ed.), *Out of Apathy.*
45 E. P. Thompson, 'Commitment in Politics', *Universities and Left Review*, 6 (Spring 1959), 50.
46 In the context of these criticisms, it must be assumed that Thompson intended to put 'objects of history'.
47 *Ibid.*, p. 51.
48 S. Hall, 'A Sense of Classlessness', *Universities and Left Review*, 5 (Autumn 1958), 26–32; R. Hoggart, *The Uses of Literacy: Aspects of Working Class Life* (London: Chatto & Windus, 1957).
49 Davis, 'Arguing Affluence'.
50 Thompson, 'Commitment in Politics', p. 54.
51 E. P. Thompson, 'The Point of Production', *New Left Review* 1:1 (January–February 1960), 68.
52 *Ibid.*
53 Thompson, 'Revolution', p. 8.
54 Thompson, 'Revolution Again!', p. 27.
55 E. P. Thompson, 'The Long Revolution' (Part 1), *New Left Review*, 1:9 (May–June 1961); 'The Long Revolution' (Part 2), *New Left Review*, 1:10 (July–August 1961).
56 Dworkin, *Cultural Marxism*, pp. 88–9.
57 R. Williams, 'The British New Left', *Partisan Review*, 27 (Spring 1950), 344, quoted in Dworkin, *Cultural Marxism*, p. 62.
58 Thompson, 'Long Revolution' (Part 1), p. 30.
59 Dworkin, *Cultural Marxism*, pp. 88–92.
60 *Ibid.*, pp. 93–5.
61 'Long Revolution' (Part 1), p. 33.
62 'Long Revolution' (Part 2), p. 37.
63 A. MacIntyre, 'Notes from the Moral Wilderness 1, *New Reasoner*, 7 (Winter 1958–59), 98.
64 Thompson, 'Long Revolution' (Part 2), p. 38.
65 *Ibid.*, p. 39.

66 E. P. Thompson, 'The Politics of Theory', in R. Samuel (ed.), *People's History and Socialist Theory* (London: Routledge & Kegan Paul, 1981), pp. 397–8.
67 R. Williams, *Politics and Letters* (London: New Left Books, 1979), p. 134.
68 R. Williams, 'You're a Marxist, Aren't You?', in B. Parekh (ed.), *The Concept of Socialism* (London: Croom Helm, 1975), pp. 231–41, quoted in Kenny, *First New Left*, p. 241.
69 Dworkin, *Cultural Marxism*, p. 104.
70 *Ibid.*
71 M. Rustin, 'The New Left as a Social Movement', in R. Archer (ed.), *Out of Apathy*, pp. 122–6.
72 Thompson, 'The Peculiarities of the English' (1965), 'An Open Letter to Leszek Kolakowski' (1973) and 'The Poverty of Theory: or an Orrery of Errors' (1978), in E. P. Thompson, *The Poverty of Theory* (London: Merlin Press, 1978); Thompson, 'The Politics of Theory', in Samuel, *People's History*.
73 M. Newman, *Ralph Miliband and the Politics of the New Left* (London: Merlin Press, 2002), pp. 115–20.
74 R. Williams (ed.), *May Day Manifesto 1968* (Harmondsworth: Penguin, 1968), an expanded edition of the version published by the May Day Manifesto Committee, London 1967.
75 Thompson, 'Peculiarities of the English', pp. 87–8.
76 Anderson, 'Socialism and Pseudo-Empiricism'.
77 W. Matthews, 'The Poverty of Strategy: E. P. Thompson, Perry Anderson, and the Transition to Socialism', *Labour/Le Travail*, 50 (2002), www.historycooperative.org/journals/llt/50/matthews.html (accessed 24 April 2012).
78 Thompson, 'Socialist Humanism', p. 140.
79 S. Hall, 'The "First" New Left: Life and Times', in Archer, *Out of Apathy*, pp. 15–18.
80 *Ibid.*, p. 23.
81 Thompson, *Arguments within English Marxism*, p. 147.
82 F. Fanon, Les Damnés de la Terre (Paris: François Maspero, 1961), translated as *The Wretched of the Earth* (London: MacGibbon & Kee, 1965). Thompson criticised the *New Left Review*'s attitudes to this kind of thinking in 'Where are we Now?' (unpublished memorandum), John Saville papers U DJS/109 (Hull University Archives).
83 J. Saville, 'The Welfare State', *New Reasoner*, 3 (Winter 1957–58); D. Thompson, 'The Welfare State', *New Reasoner*, 4 (Spring 1958).
84 Letter from E. P. Thompson to R. Miliband, undated January 1961 (Miliband papers).
85 E. P. Thompson, *The Heavy Dancers* (London: Merlin Press, 1985), p. 263.
86 Letter from E. P. Thompson to R. Miliband, 13 April 1960 (Miliband papers).
87 Letter from R. Miliband to E. P. Thompson, 1 April 1960 (Miliband papers).

9

Thompson and the peace movement: from CND in the 1950s and 1960s to END in the 1980s

Richard Taylor

Introduction

Throughout his adult life Edward Thompson campaigned for peace. Unlike the absolute pacifists, however, Thompson always believed that the attainment of peace was necessarily and integrally connected to radical political objectives. Similarly, in contrast to most orthodox Marxists – and certainly to the Marxist–Leninist ideologues of the Communist Party – Thompson did not believe that 'campaigning for peace' should be subordinate to class conflict and the attainment of socialism: they were rather both necessarily part of the same struggle to create a truly democratic and just society.

Thompson, too, always distrusted both orthodox political parties and even more the State. In his memoir of the tragic death of his brother Frank in Bulgaria in the Second World War, for example, he wrote of the 'total mendacity of states: the manipulation and cancellation of the motives of individuals within the amoral interests of collectivities.'[1] And, as Madeleine Davis has remarked, Thompson (in contrast to both John Saville and Ralph Miliband, to say nothing of Eric Hobsbawm) became after 1956 'increasingly suspicious of party organization' and had a 'growing distrust for traditional forms of political organization.'[2]

From the outset he was a Popular-Front, social-movement man, a perspective in harmony with the eloquent 'human agency' argument which permeates his historical as well as his political writing.[3] This chapter therefore traces these perspectives through the lens of Thompson's peace campaigning from the late 1940s until his death in 1993. Attention is focused upon three periods of particular activism:

his work in the context of the CPGB (hereafter shortened to CP) from the immediate post-war years until 1956, when, together with many others, he resigned from the CP following Khrushchev's revelations at the Twentieth Congress of the Communist Party of the Soviet Union and the subsequent suppression of the Hungarian uprising;[4] his role in the early New Left from 1956 until the early 1960s and his close involvement with CND; and his internationally recognised, high-profile role in END from late 1979 onwards.

Peace campaigning in the Communist Party

Remembering his early days as a university extramural lecturer in West Yorkshire (see chapter 2), Thompson recalled, in 1976, that he had at that time been

> very active in political work ... I was primarily responsible in my political work for work in the peace movement, above all against the Korean War. We developed a very good movement in West Yorkshire. It was a genuine alliance of Labour Party people, who often were expelled from the Labour Party, traditional left pacifists, and Communists and trade unionists. I ran a journal (Yorkshire Voice of Peace). I was on the Yorkshire district Committee of the Communist Party. This probably occupied half my time and professional teaching the other half.[5]

The *Yorkshire Voice of Peace* campaigned vigorously and consistently against the Korean War. In the Spring 1953 edition, for example, the editorial welcomed the Chinese peace initiative and was strongly critical of what was referred to as 'the Fifth Column of Death in the War', which included Chiang Kai Chek, Syngman Rhee, the arms manufacturers and the 'hawks' in the American government, most notably John Foster Dulles. Peace would only come, it stated, when 'people impose it by world-wide pressure'.[6] The CP perspective is pervasive: all the fault lies with the USA and its allies and their supporters in the media; and the Soviet Union and China are presented as reasonable and 'peace-loving' governments. But the paper also struck a resolutely Popular Front note. As well as recording support from trades councils, Labour Party bodies, and so on, there were frequent and prominent pieces from churchmen. For example, the Revd Alan Ecclestone, chairman of the Sheffield Peace Council, wrote in the Summer 1953 edition of the role of the peace movement as 'world democracy begins to take shape ... (and) the immense importance of bringing together the ordinary citizens of the world, and enabling them to discover each other as friends and as allies in a common task'. And in his 'Editor's Notebook' in the same issue, Thompson was impatient with the ' resolution mongering' through the Labour Party and urged instead that 'every honest man who knows the truth must tell this truth, openly, publicly, and ceaselessly, and tell it to the people'.[7]

The *Yorkshire Voice of Peace* continued publication, somewhat intermittently, until the autumn of 1956, when a 'Middle East Crisis' edition was published, strongly opposing the notorious Suez escapade and the 'last-gasp' imperialism of the British government.[8] This issue contained a range of opinion, national and international, opposing the war, including contributions from clergymen, peace campaigners, Labour Party MPs and councillors, and a prominent report on the views of Krishna Menon, representing the Indian government, reflecting probably Thompson's longstanding interest in India (see chapter 1).

Throughout these years, Thompson was also pursuing such Popular Front peace campaigns at a local level, through the Halifax Peace Committee and in the CP's organisational structure, through the Yorkshire District Committee of which he was a member. (Although, as John Saville was to note in his memoir of those days, Thompson frequently 'expressed disagreements with the full-time officials of the Yorkshire District'.[9])

All this political activity was, however, plunged into crisis and his whole politics changed forever, by the cataclysmic events in the communist world in 1956.

The New Left and CND[10]

The full story of the early New Left has been told elsewhere.[11] The concentration here is upon Thompson's involvement, and in particular his perspective on the peace movement and the New Left's intimate connections with CND. From the outset Thompson, more than any other leading New Left figure, saw a congruence in the cultures and approaches of the New Left and CND: neither had formal membership, nor constitutions (though later CND spent much time and effort developing a constitution, standing orders, and so on); there was no official party programme (and no aspiration to develop into a 'vanguard party'). Both represented a generalised ethos, an attitude.

Thompson, who continued to regard himself as a 'dissident Communist' at least until the early 1960s, emphasised that the new generation of CND supporters (the 'Aldermaston generation')

> never looked upon the Soviet Union as a weak but heroic Workers' State; but, rather, as the nation of the Great Purges and of Stalingrad ... their enthusiasm is not for the (Labour) party, or the movement, or the established political leaders ... they prefer the amateur organization ... of the CND.[12]

This was a generation, Thompson went on to argue, that was not alienated from politics, but which was disenchanted with both capitalism and communism.[13] Thompson saw the key to success for the new politics as the symbiosis between the experienced, non-aligned and radical politics of the New Left, and the spontaneous, radical mass movement of the idealistic younger generation, articulated through CND. As he put it, in a passionate article in the *NR*, 'The "bureaucracy" will hold the machine; but the New Left will hold the passes between it and the younger generation.'[14]

The key political demands of the New Left, as far as Thompson was concerned, were also intimately related to the CND campaign. But unilateral nuclear disarmament was not, on its own, enough. To have a real effect upon the dangerous escalation of the Cold War, the New Left urged withdrawal from NATO and the adoption of an active, positive neutralist policy. As he argued, in an article in 1958, there needed to be 'political fluidity on both sides ... nations in the West as well as in the East must break through the taboos by which the Cold War is sustained'.[15] Thompson envisaged 'not a Third Camp, nor a third force independent of both camps, but a group of European powers exercising a mediating influence between the two main contestants, parallel to the influence of India in the Far East'.[16]

Like many others in CND, Thompson also saw Britain as in a unique position to take the initiative. 'Advance in Western Europe, and further democratisation in the East, may wait upon us.'

Or, again, 'Every pointer indicates Britain as the nation best placed to take the initiative which might just succeed in bringing down the whole power-crazy system.'[17] (There are many other similar examples in Thompson's writing at this time.)

Such sentiments are reminiscent of the 'Britain must take a moral lead' argument of J. B. Priestley's article in the *New Statesman* in November 1957, which was the immediate stimulus for the birth of

CND itself.[18] Thompson had a perhaps unwarrantably romantic and Anglocentric view. However, it has to be remembered that, in the aftermath of the Second World War and the subsequent role of Churchill, Keynes and others on the world stage, there was a widespread perception that Britain had a position of major importance internationally. With hindsight, it can be argued that this was more perceived than actual; but the argument that Britain, as one of only three nuclear powers, had the potential for leadership by example was widely held in CND and was not without substance.[19]

For Thompson, the New Left and CND gave voice to the spirit of moral revolt in which the struggle for democracy and social justice, and the campaign for peace and disarmament, were intertwined. This could and should lead, in Thompson's view, to the fusion of these concerns in a new radical force in Britain and, by extension, internationally. The New Left therefore championed 'a new internationalism which is not that of the triumph of one camp over another, but the dissolution of the camps and the triumph of the common people.'[20]

Such optimism was relatively short-lived, however. Through 1958, 1959 and 1960 the movement – both the New Left and CND – grew and prospered. Public support for unilateral nuclear disarmament was reflected in the public opinion polls, in media attention, in the mounting scale and frequency of demonstrations, and most notably in the decision by the Labour Party's Annual Conference in 1960 to adopt resolutions clearly advocating a policy of unilateral nuclear disarmament (despite the fierce opposition of the Party's leader, Hugh Gaitskell). This is not the place to enter into the detailed historical record of this turbulent period.[21] The point, rather, is to discuss Thompson's and the New Left's response to the more adverse circumstances that prevailed in 1961 and beyond. Much of the energy and contention within the wider peace movement was taken up in 1960–61 with the mass direct action and civil disobedience undertaken by the Committee of 100 from late 1960, and debates over theory, strategy and tactics involving the heady mix of Ghandian positive action, anarchist and libertarian Marxist politics, and the populist insurrectionism of various elements in the radical section of the movement.

Although some in the New Left, notably Alan Lovell and George Clark, had considerable empathy and contact with the Committee of 100, most, including Thompson, did not identify with this sort of radical politics.

New Left activists turned their attention instead to more main-stream left-wing activism. Stuart Hall, a leading intellectual in the *ULR*, and later in the *NLR*, became a key figure in the formulation of detailed CND policies advocating Britain's withdrawal from NATO and drafted the contentious CND policy document 'Steps Towards Peace' in 1962. This was widely denounced in CND as revisionist as it appeared to water down the Campaign's commitment to unilateral nuclear disarmament.[22] Thompson, following the reversal of the unilateralist decision at the Labour Party Annual Conference in 1961 (after intensive lobbying by the Campaign for Democratic Socialism (CDS), led among others by the future Social Democratic Party right-winger, Bill Rodgers), advocated putting up independent peace candidates at parliamentary by-elections. This, Thompson claimed, was the 'right, the only response' in 1961 to the Berlin crisis, the Blackpool rejection of unilateralism in the Labour Party and the massive Trafalgar Square demonstrations.[23] However, there was considerable, and predictable, opposition from the Labour Left (in particular, Michael Foot), and thus from the senior ranks of CND. At the other end of the spectrum of the peace movement, the libertarians and Direct Actionists opposed the idea, on ideological grounds, as an irrelevance.

By the time the initiative – the Independent Nuclear Disarmament Election Committee (INDEC) – got off the ground in 1963, it was virtually stillborn.[24] The INDEC initiative was thus 'not very successful';[25] for the New Left it was 'the crowning failure in the efforts of New Left figures to achieve a viable fusion of old and new radical politics that would enable the New Left to act simultaneously within and apart from traditional Labour movement and socialist channels'.[26]

At the same time, Thompson was also embroiled in bitter disputes within the New Left (see chapter 8). By late 1963, he could reflect that the New Left 'has now ... dispersed itself both organizationally and (to some extent) intellectually. We failed to implement our original purposes, or even to sustain what cultural apparatus we had.'[27]

There is much truth in Sedgwick's and Young's judgements that the New Left, for all its theoretical sophistication, had a hopelessly ambivalent attitude to the Labour movement, the Labour Party and indeed to labourism. Moreover, as Sedgwick also pointed out, '(T)he only section of young people among whom the movement made any progress was its own further-educated juniors ... among the thousands of youngsters who marched with CND the New Left never established an independent socialist presence.[28] Eventually, the New Left opted for pressurising the Labour Party into pursuing socialist policies. As Sedgwick put it, 'pursuing a tactic of total theoretical entry, all its eggheads have marched into the single basket of Left reformism.'[29] At the same time, radical, broadly libertarian forces in the peace movement became more dominant. Thus, by late 1963–early 1964 there was a wide gulf politically between the New Left and the peace movement.

But, by this stage, Thompson had distanced himself from the New Left in all its manifestations. He was never interested in labour-movement tactical manoeuvring, nor in the wilder fringes of Left politics. Despite its relatively short life the New Left did produce a new orientation on the Left in Britain, bringing together the new politics of non-aligned socialism and the movement for peace. This position was rearticulated, in significantly revised form to take into account a very different context, in the 'END' years, from late 1979 through to the mid- to late 1980s.

European Nuclear Disarmament (END)

The eruption of peace protests across Western Europe in the early 1980s was as sudden and spontaneous as had been the ferment in 1958–59 in Britain which brought into being CND and the birth of mass, active opposition to nuclear weapons *per se*. The 1980s movement was, however, far larger, far more widespread and trans-national, and far less tied to the orthodox political parties of the Left, whether social democratic or communist. It was also, as I shall argue, in some respects a different movement both in its objectives and ideology, and in its culture.

Thompson's role in END and related movements in the 1980s was not merely important, as his role had been in CND in the 1950s and 1960s: it was absolutely central from the outset. His pamphlet *Protest and Survive*,[30] a riposte to a letter in *The Times* from Michael Howard, Chichele Professor of the History of War at the University of Oxford, caught the public imagination. As a result END was born. Indeed, for a time, Thompson became arguably one of the best-known public intellectuals in Britain. According to Bryan Palmer, an informal poll in *The Times* found him to be the second most influential British intellectual in the post-1945 period, A. J. P. Taylor being the first.[31] Thompson wrote frequently and at length in the serious newspapers, especially the *Guardian*, and in various left-of-centre journals, such as the *New Statesman* and *New Society*. He was even awarded that accolade of recognition by 'middle England', an appearance on BBC Radio 4's 'Desert Island Discs' (on 3 November 1991).

However, the idea for such a movement had had a long gestation. From the mid-1970s, Thompson and Ken Coates, of the Bertrand Russell Peace Foundation (BRPF) in Nottingham, had been discussing a peace initiative to try to counter the dangerous escalation of the Cold War, and in particular the marked increase in tension between the two nuclear superpowers in Europe. In February 1975, for example, Thompson wrote to Coates suggesting 'an appeal which would be endorsed by the NEC' (Labour's National Executive Committee) and also by the TUC (Trades Union Congress), recognising communist Eastern Europe's poor record on human rights, and appealing to all European trade-union and socialist organisations 'to restrain with all their power the actions of their own military or imperialist circles'.[32] These and similar suggestions came to nothing at the time: Coates was quite correct in judging that, sadly, these suggestions were impractical: or 'really dodgy', as he put it in his reply to Thompson in this particular instance.[33]

There was certainly a need for such an initiative. The Cold War intensified considerably in the 1970s. Following defeat in Vietnam, the US political establishment was worried about an upsurge of Third World revolutions, about the threat to its economic pre-eminence posed by the rise of Japan (and to an extent, Western Europe), and above all by the perceived ambitions of the Soviet Union to achieve nuclear parity. The Soviet invasion of Afghanistan considerably exacerbated the tensions.[34]

Thompson's *Protest and Survive* followed hard on the heels of the announcement by NATO in December 1979 in Brussels of the ratification of the decision to deploy cruise missiles in Europe in Britain and elsewhere in Western Europe in 1983.

These new weapons would of course remain under US control. As Thompson argued, the clear result of this development would be not only a dangerous escalation of the nuclear arms race, but it would also effectively 'localise' nuclear war, potentially, to the European 'theatre'. Moreover, the whole issue had been so obscured in the quasi-secret, jargonised discourse of the 'war establishment' (with the collusion of the press and the broadcasting media) that public, democratic debate had been almost wholly absent in Britain. Thus, right from the outset of END, Thompson linked peace campaigning directly with the assertion that free, informed public debate and human rights were being seriously curtailed. The two issues were inextricably connected.

The time was ripe for Thompson's devastating attack on the reactive, somewhat bland call by Howard for 'civil defence on a scale sufficient to give protection to a substantial number of the population in the event of such a "limited" nuclear strike'.[35] Thompson rejected this position with vehemence. On the contrary, he argued, we needed to break out of the destructive logic of the Cold War:

> 'Deterrence' is not a stationary state, it is a degenerative state. Deterrence has repressed the export of violence towards the opposing bloc, but in doing so the repressed power of the state has turned its back upon its own author ... (It) has worked its way back into the economy, the polity, the ideology and culture of the opposing power. This is the deep structure of the Cold War.[36]

Here again is the emphasis upon the indivisibility of the causes of peace and democracy and human rights. (Ironically, considering Thompson's antipathy to Orwell, there are clear overtones here of Orwell's dystopia, *Nineteen Eighty-Four*.[37]) 'Protest', Thompson argued, 'is the only realistic form of civil defence.'[38] *Protest and Survive* caught the public imagination: 50,000 copies were sold in less than a year and a little later a Penguin special, centring on *Protest and Survive*, sold 36,000 copies. Thompson's inimitable combination of moral passion, scathing polemic and a 'feel' for the popular mood of concern over the mounting nuclear and political threat acted as the catalyst for a new mass, international movement.

The upsurge of support for the new campaigning organisation, END, was remarkable. In the autumn of 1981, for example, an estimated five million people demonstrated across Europe against cruise missiles. The initial idea for END and the issuing of the END Appeal (*A Nuclear Free Europe*[39]) arose jointly from Thompson and Ken Coates of the BRPF (as is indicated by their correspondence from the mid-1970s, as noted above). According to Mary Kaldor, Thompson gave credit to Coates for the original notion of the Appeal, but clearly the new movement was in reality a joint creation. Coates was happy to acknowledge, despite later profound differences between the two men, discussed below, that at the outset it was Thompson who undertook the main drafting of the END Appeal and who had been the inspiration for so many of the people who flocked to the END cause through 1980 and 1981.

The END Appeal, which was launched at a Press Conference at the British House of Commons on 28 April 1980, and more or less simultaneously in four other European capitals, had all the hallmarks of Thompson's arresting political prose style. 'We are entering the most dangerous decade in human history. A third world war is not merely possible, but increasingly likely.' The Appeal clearly put Europe at centre stage in the forthcoming peace campaign; and Thompson insisted that both of the superpowers were responsible for the crisis: 'Guilt lies squarely upon both parties.' As Mary Kaldor has rightly observed, Thompson saw the failures of CND in the 1950s and 1960s as being due to 'its being seen as the Kremlin's fifth column'. So, in one sense, END's explicit opposition to the Communist Official Peace Committees 'began as a strategic disposition to counteract this characteristic: but quickly END became genuinely concerned and involved with human rights issues'.[40] Many in the subsequent END movement, including the Dutch Inter-Church Peace Council, Petra Kelly and the German Greens, and pre-eminently Thompson, 'put the emphasis on opposition to the Cold War and not just nuclear weapons. END called for a transcontinental movement of citizens and made an explicit link between peace and democracy or human rights.'[41]

The emphasis in the Appeal, and for Thompson, throughout the END campaign, was thus upon popular protest and action rather than working through formal parties and bureaucracies.

'We must commence to act as if a united, neutral and pacific Europe already exists. We must learn to be loyal, not to "East" or "West", but to each other, and we must disregard the prohibitions and limitations imposed by any national state.' He went on to argue that, varied though strategies would be from country to country, the objective must be the 'expulsion of nuclear weapons and bases from European soil and territorial waters … this must be part of a trans-continental movement in which every kind of exchange takes place'.[42]

The perspective of the BRPF was somewhat different. For Ken Coates, the main objective was to build a European movement, through the political parties of the Left, and related bodies such as trade unions, to force Western nations to refuse cruise and Pershing on their territory in order to create a nuclear-free zone. Coates and the BRPF saw this process as centred on successive Conventions, held in various European cities throughout the 1980s (Brussels, Berlin, Perugia, Amsterdam, Paris, Lund, and so on). Coates was certainly not sympathetic to the communist parties of Eastern Europe. He had, after all, a long history on the far left of the Labour Party, with political sympathies that were more Trotskyist or quasi-Trotskyist than they were orthodox communist. (He was referred to on occasion by some of those in END who disagreed with his position as 'the Renegade Coatesky'.)

For Coates, the END movement was essentially about bringing together those in the Western European countries sympathetic to the Appeal to develop through their political parties and industrial organisations a campaign to create a nuclear-free Europe. Coates was dismissive of the potential for involving those from Eastern Europe. 'I didn't see our task as being to concentrate on European disarmament for the East; I brought all the people who came from the East into these discussions, but they were a handful.'[43] For Coates and his colleagues at the BRPF, the Conventions were, as noted, the major focus for this campaign; and for Coates, the second Convention, in Berlin, was 'amazing ... It was the first time we had all the Social Democratic parties, and all the Communist parties except one, the Greens en masse ... plus all the peace movements. There were about 4000 people at this conference ... I think it was our finest hour.'[44]

According to Coates, Thompson 'didn't want to be in a movement which had all the Social Democrats and all the Communists kicking into the same goal. I did want to be in that.'[45]

Thompson saw things differently, and in a much broader and more innovative context. END was a social movement, working with other analogous movements across Eastern and Western Europe, to move beyond the Cold War, to undermine the orthodoxies of both East and West. As he wrote in 1982, it 'is not a question of refusing to talk with them – these quasi-official bodies can be useful for exchanging messages. But they should not be confused with *peace movements*, and it is very wrong to talk with them only.'[46] Earlier, in March 1981, he had written a typically lengthy letter-cum-paper to Ken Coates, expressing his concerns about concentrating upon organising big Conventions. They are 'very costly, time-taking and full of problems'. Although the BRPF had an excellent record in organising large and successful events of this sort, Thompson argued that 'we are *not* now involved in a one-off event. We are involved in a protracted running European campaign, in a fluid political situation. Large movements have arisen in Europe which wish to enter into direct relations with each other.'[47]

Relations between Ken Coates and his colleagues at the BRPF, and Thompson and the END Committee in London, deteriorated severely through 1981 and 1982. Thompson, for example, wrote to Michael

Barratt Brown in December 1982 'in despair, because none of us in END can understand what is up with Ken Coates'. He asks Barratt Brown ' to lay a restraining hand on Ken's shoulder and ask him to cool down for a month nor two, and to put factional activities aside'.[48]

As is all too common in such situations, there were numerous disputes about finance, organisational matters and, more seriously, political control of the movement. Such irritations absorbed much time, energy and the writing of 'position papers', as is common on the Left. There is considerable correspondence in the files indicating that frustrations spread across the movement,[49] with even that most diplomatic and sensible of peace-movement figures, Bruce Kent, giving vent to some irritation.[50]

Underlying all these difficulties which, at least in this context, do not merit detailed analysis, were more fundamental ideological differences. Ken Coates and the BRPF believed in the Realpolitik of working through the organisations of the Left, in the long struggle in committees, in the formal political arena and in the orthodox political framework. For Coates, political change, when it came in radical form with the rise of Gorbachev in the USSR and the series of Eastern European 'revolutions', came through the formal political system.

By the late 1980s Coates had become a member of the European Parliament (MEP) and was in the process of arranging for a joint meeting with the Supreme Soviet when Gorbachev fell from power in Russia and Yeltsin took over. As far as Coates was concerned, that was the point at which 'I think END stopped'. As an indefatigable political 'old pro', he then moved on to other political campaigns, recalling: 'The next thing I did was to run an offensive to get the European churches on board for full employment'.[51]

For Thompson, in contrast, END was at its core a movement which aimed at a more fundamental change in the political culture of Europe, and by extension internationally. The removal of nuclear weapons from the whole of Europe (East as well as West) was, of course, a central, initial campaigning demand. But from the outset, as noted, Thompson saw the causes of peace, and civil freedoms and human rights, as indivisible. It was a movement of the people, uniting those of very different cultures and beliefs in a fluid, popular and intensive campaign for a new way of politics: an 'anti-politics', as George Konrad termed it. This anti-politics was 'the ethos of civil society and civil society is the antithesis of military society ... military society is the reality, civil society is the utopia'.[52]

At one level, therefore, the two men were representative of two different sorts of politics. Coates, a former miner, adult education student and tutor, was a highly intelligent, politically committed socialist steeped in left Labour politics. He was pragmatic, determined, energetic and very much at home in the world of party organisations, committees, bureaucracies and factional infighting. He was, in short, an able exponent of 'old (left) Labour'. He was, too, a good debater, not intimidated by intellectuals, and he had a substantial reputation on that section of the far Left that was particularly engaged in industrial and economic matters. He was the moving force, for example, behind the Institute for Workers' Control (IWC), and had longstanding friendships with, amongst others, Michael Barratt Brown and Stuart Holland. He believed passionately in the cause of a nuclear-free Europe: on that, he and Thompson were at one. But he saw the main, indeed in effect the only, way to achieve this as being through the orthodox political machine and tactics: hence the centrality, for Coates and the BRPF, of the Convention process. He also had a somewhat controlling personal style, and naturally enough perhaps, was rather prickly about what he saw as the BRPF's position as the lead body in Britain in the international movement for the creation of a nuclear-free Europe. Coates and Thompson had of course much in common politically, as is evident from their frequent and comradely correspondence in the 1970s, and in the earliest END period. It is also interesting, and may be instructive, that Coates, in common of course with Thompson, had great respect and admiration for William Blake.[53]

However, their political differences were greater, as argued above. Thompson was a first-class, original intellectual from an upper-middle-class, academic and politically radical background (see chapter 1). His erudition across a range of academic disciplines and intellectual and political areas was remarkable by any standards. He was a Romantic and a believer in 'the common people' and in the power of human agency. He had, as noted, a deep distrust of state bureaucracies and orthodox political parties. There are, as David Goodway has argued, strongly libertarian elements in Thompson's politics and personality (although he was never fully an anarchist, as Goodway notes).[54] He was, too, a splendid polemicist and an excellent writer in general (see chapter 5, Spencer; appendix). He was not, however, given to brevity; nor was he a good committee man: he was often prickly and did not take criticism well. He had a tendency to 'sulk in his tent' on occasion. He was, all in all, a somewhat difficult person to work with. And he also was certainly a 'prima donna', as were many of the leading left-wing intellectuals of this period (see, for example, Michael Newman's analysis in chapter 8 of this book). Thompson had a long record of falling out with colleagues and comrades on the Left, from Perry Anderson to the cultural theorists of the later New Left.[55] It was thus not surprising that, in these difficult circumstances, there were personality clashes in the END years.

Thompson as theorist of the European peace movement

Thompson, in his path-breaking article on 'Exterminism', and in his alternative Dimbleby Lecture, *Beyond the Cold War*, was both the instigator and the theorist for this new politics.[56] He argued that there was a 'deep structure' to the Cold War, a mutually re-enforcing and relentless drive to an outcome of exterminism. As Wright Mills remarked in 1958, 'the immediate cause of World War III is the preparation for it'. The USA and the USSR, Thompson argued, 'do not *have* military-industrial complexes: they *are* such complexes.'[57] He thus posited not a determinism,[58] but an 'inertial thrust and (a) reciprocal logic of the opposed weapons systems'.[59] 'The ruling interests on both sides have become ideologically addicted.'[60] Moreover, the dominant exterminist ideology of both superpowers legitimated arms manufacturers, massive 'defence' expenditure and, crucially, the ever-more stringent policing of dissent and the consequent restrictions on human rights. Anti-communism has been the means of ideological control in the West; 'Stalinism' in the East. Parallel to this, there was a mutual hostility to any genuine non-alignment (*vide* the fate of Dubček and Allende). As Thompson reminded us, 'bonding-by-exclusion is intrinsic to human socialisation …War has been a constant recourse throughout history.'[61]

Thompson concludes *Beyond the Cold War* with a reiteration of his consistent advocacy over the years of Popular Front activism:

> Only an alliance which takes in churches, Eurocommunists, Labour-ists, East European dissidents … Soviet citizens unmediated by Party structures, trade unionists, ecologists – only this can possibly muster the force and internationalist elan to throw the Cruise missiles and the SS-20s back.[62]

(It is significant that, despite the prominence of feminist peace activism, especially at the Greenham Common missile base, Thompson does not include feminism amongst his constituencies for the Popular Front he was advocating.)

Thompson was arguing that the movement needed to go further than the campaign against the missiles. 'We must go behind the missiles to the Cold War itself. We must begin to put Europe back into one piece.'[63] With the rise of dissident movements in the East, and protest movements in the West, Thompson argued that détente between nation-states had been superseded by 'a détente of peoples', working both to undermine state structures and to link, independently of the blocs, kindred spirits across the divide.[64]

As is implicit in the foregoing discussion, through the early 1980s Thompson became increasingly concerned with linking the broader social movements for human rights and political change in Eastern Europe with progressive forces in the West. The contribution of END, in Mary Kaldor's view, was to make the intellectual as well as the political case for ensuring that the campaigns for peace and for human rights were seen as indivisible. Thompson 'provided the language for the END idea'. This took the level of debate, the whole discourse, beyond the old paradigms of political parties and nation-states.

It was here, Kaldor argues persuasively, that Thompson's stance in the 1980s was significantly different from his advocacy of active, positive neutralism in the 1950s and early 1960s. Whereas the latter was 'about building a non-aligned bloc of nation states, END was about getting rid of alliances, building a bottom-up movement of European citizens. It was détente from below, or, in Edward's phrase, "citizens' détente".'[65]

Looking back from the early twenty-first century, and assessing the importance of END, Kaldor argued that the revolutions of 1989 and beyond in the USSR and subsequently across the whole of Eastern Europe owed much to the coming together of the peace and human rights campaigns in the earlier 1980s. The people and the movements that made the 1989 revolutions were generally, she has argued, the political activists of those earlier movements. These were 'people's revolutions', above and beyond the orthodox, official party organisations of the Left.[66]

Intellectual thought on the progressive Left in the 1950s and 1960s had been within the context of a reformed, more humanistic Marxism (Lukács and Kolakowski, for example). After 1968, dissent was concentrated largely outside communist parties and focused as much upon libertarian, civil-society issues as upon collectivist politics. The parallel movements in the West, in addition to peace campaigning, emphasised the need to radicalise democracy, and to work through civil society and social movements rather than political parties. This 'new politics' was articulated through the peace and feminist movements.

The major shifts in politics in the late 1980s and early 1990s thus had their origins in part in this 'new politics'. Of course, the fundamental economic and political problems of the USSR and its satellite states in Eastern Europe, and the consequent rise of Gorbachev *et al.*, were very important. However, it is equally important to recognise that the activists from this period were a significant element in the movements that made the revolutions of 1989; and the ideology inspiring this politics derived from this fusion in the earlier 1980s between the movements for peace and for civil freedoms. As Mary Kaldor recalled Thompson saying, 'history is made by the people but it is never subsequently told that way'.[67] In this process, of both inspiring and providing a theorisation for the new movements, Thompson clearly played a central role.

Conclusion

It remains to make some concluding observations on Thompson's overall peace campaigning over the forty years or so of the turbulent second half of the twentieth century, and its impact upon the politics of the Left.

As noted in chapter 1, the influence on Thompson of his father and brother and their moral radicalism should never be underestimated. Throughout his life, Thompson retained this moral core to his politics. He also believed strongly in the necessary connection between political theory and political action:

> The immobilism sometimes found on the Marxist Left is founded on a great error: that theoretical rigour, or throwing oneself into a 'revolutionary' posture, is the end of politics ... The end of politics is to act, and to act *with effect*.[68]

Throughout his adult life, Thompson placed emphasis upon *political* action. He was consistent, too, in his persisting belief in the human agency of the common people.

Thompson had seemingly endless energy and commitment for the cause of peace, linked explicitly, especially latterly, to the popular movements for human rights. He was, by common consent, both one of the most charismatic public speakers and pre-eminent as a polemicist, theorist and above all writer on peace issues. He was engaged, prescient and passionate and had a huge influence for the good in his own time. His politics and example remain as relevant today as they were in his lifetime: and peace campaigners, amongst others, will return to his writing and his political perspectives for the foreseeable future. In his obituary notice, Christopher Hill cited Thompson:

> One must, to survive as an unassimilated socialist in this infinitely assimilative culture, put oneself into a school of awkwardness, one must make one's sensibility all knobbly – all knees and elbows of susceptibility and refusal … .[69]

This characteristic of political and intellectual 'awkwardness' was to the fore in Thompson's peace-movement activities. He believed, as Bruce Kent has written, in attaining peace through 'disarmament, citizen power, justice and dialogue. It was a good line, and one that has stood the test of time.'[70]

Notes

1 E. P. Thompson, *Beyond the Frontier: The Politics of a Failed Mission: Bulgaria 1944* (Woodbridge, UK and Stanford, CA: Merlin Press and Stanford University Press, 1997), pp. 98–9 (published posthumously and edited with an epilogue and a note on sources by D. Thompson).

2 M. Davis, 'The *New Reasoner* and the Early New Left', in D. Howell, D. Kirby and K. Morgan (eds), *John Saville: Commitment and History: Themes from the Life and Work of a Socialist Historian* (London: Lawrence & Wishart in association with the Socialist History Society, 2011), pp. 44, 48.

3 See, e.g., E. P. Thompson, *The Making of The English Working Class* (London: Gollancz, 1963); E. P. Thompson, 'The Poverty of Theory : or an Orrery of Errors', in *The Poverty of Theory and Other Essays* (London: Merlin Press, 1978), pp. 193–397.

4 Thompson joined the Communist Party in 1942 whilst an undergraduate student at the University of Cambridge. His membership lapsed during the war but he rejoined shortly afterwards. (B. D. Palmer, *E. P. Thompson: Objections and Oppositions* [London and New York: Verso, 1994], p. 42ff.)

5 M. Merrill, 'An Interview with E. P. Thompson', in MARHO, *Visions of History* (Manchester: Manchester University Press, 1983), p. 12.

6 *Yorkshire Voice of Peace* (Spring 1953), Editorial, 1. (I am indebted to my colleague David Goodway for access to his private collection of this political newspaper.)

7 Revd A. Ecclestone, 'Why I Support the Peace Movement', *Yorkshire Voice of Peace*, Summer 1953, pp. 2–3.

8 On the Suez crisis, see K. Kyle, *Suez* (London, 1991).

9 J. Saville, 'Edward Thompson, the Communist Party and 1956', in R. Miliband and L. Panitch (eds), *Socialist Register*, 1994 (London: Merlin Press, 1994), pp. 20–31.

10 This section draws on the analysis in R. Taylor, 'The British Nuclear Disarmament Movement of 1958 to 1965 and its Legacy to the Left', Ph.D. thesis, University of Leeds, 1983, pp. 454–88. A shortened version of this appeared subsequently: R. Taylor, *Against the Bomb: the British Peace Movement of 1958–1965* (Oxford: Clarendon Press, 1988). On the early New Left, see pp. 331–8.

11 For the history and politics of the first New Left in general, see M. Kenny, *The First New Left* (London: Lawrence & Wishart,1995); Lin Chun, *The British New Left* (Edinburgh: Edinburgh University Press, 1993); M. Davis, 'The Origins of the British New Left', in M. Klinke and J. Scherlock (eds), *1968 in Europe* (Basingstoke: Palgrave Macmillan, 2008); Davis, 'The New Reasoner and the Early New Left'; D. R. Holden, 'The First New Left in Britain', Ph.D. thesis, University of Wisconsin-Madison, USA, 1976.

12 *New Reasoner* (Spring 1958).

13 As Frank Parkin demonstrated in his study of CND, supporters were not at all alienated from society. On the contrary, it was precisely because they were so integrated that they were prepared to take such a major part in social and political protest on a moral issue. F. Parkin, *Middle Class Radicalism: The Social Bases of the British Campaign for Nuclear Disarmament* (Manchester: Manchester University Press, 1968).

14 E. P. Thompson, 'The New Left', *New Reasoner*, 9 (Summer 1959), pp. 16–17.

15 E. P. Thompson, 'NATO, Neutralism and Survival', *Universities and Left Review*, 4 (1958), 50.

16 *Ibid.*

17 E. P. Thompson, 'Revolution', in E. P. Thompson (ed.), *Out of Apathy* (London: Stevens & Sons/New Left Books, 1960), p. 308: and Thompson, 'NATO, Neutralism and Survival', p. 51.

18 J. B. Priestley, 'Britain and the Nuclear Bombs', *New Statesman*, 2 November 1957.

19 For a full discussion of the origins and early years of CND, see Taylor, 'The British Nuclear Disarmament Movement of 1958 to 1965' chs 2, 3.

20 *New Reasoner*, Editorial (Summer 1959). However, it is worth noting the *New Reasoner*'s strong caveats on condemning the Communist societies of Eastern Europe: 'We (do not) believe that advanced industrialism itself has given rise to a "mass society" in which the antagonism between the power elite, or state bureaucracy, and the alienated individual has superseded, in

importance, class antagonisms. The water-shed of the October Revolution cannot be argued away; and we believe that in an atmosphere of relaxed international tension, the Soviet Union and Eastern Europe will prove to be the area of expanding liberty and human fulfilment, whereas the West, unless transformed by a strong democratic and revolutionary movement, will prove to be the area of encroaching authoritarianism.'

21 For a detailed analysis and discussion, see Taylor, 'The British Nuclear Disarmament Movement of 1958 to 1965', esp. chs 3, 4, 6; and for the Direct Action and Committee of 100 movements, see chs 7, 8.

22 See *ibid.*, chs 5, 6.

23 N. Young, *An Infantile Disorder? The Crisis and Decline of the New Left* (London: Routledge & Kegan Paul, 1977), p. 74.

24 See *ibid.* and Taylor, 'The British Nuclear Disarmament Movement of 1958 to 1965', ch. 3, pp. 175–85.

25 P. Duff, *Left, Left, Left* (London: Allison & Busby, 1971) p. 196.

26 Holden, 'The First New Left in Britain', p. 323.

27 E. P. Thompson, Review of Wright Mills in *Peace News*, 29 November 1963, cited in Peter Sedgwick, 'The Two New Lefts', in D. Widgery (ed.), *The Left in Britain 1956–1968* (Harmondsworth: Penguin, 1976), p. 131.

28 Sedgwick, 'The Two New Lefts', pp. 144–53; Young, 'An Infantile Disorder', pp. 144–53; and, on the youth issue, Sedgwick, 'The Two New Lefts', pp. 140–1.

29 Sedgwick, 'The Two New Lefts', p. 151.

30 E. P. Thompson, *Protest and Survive*, Spokesman Pamphlet 71 (CND and BRPF, 1980).

31 Palmer, *E. P Thompson*, p. 132.

32 BRPF END Archive. Letter, E. P. Thompson to K. Coates, 3 February 1975.

33 BRPF END Archive. Letter, K. Coates to E. P. Thompson, 6 February 1975.

34 J. Hinton, *Protests and Visions: Peace Politics in Twentieth Century Britain* (London: Hutchinson, 1989).

35 M. Howard, letter, *The Times*, 30 January 1980.

36 Thompson, *Protest and Survive*, p. 28.

37 G. Orwell, *Nineteen Eighty-Four* (London: Secker & Warburg, 1949; numerous Penguin edns since 1954). See E. P. Thompson's attack on Orwell, 'Outside the Whale', in Thompson, *Out of Apathy*, reprinted in Thompson, *The Poverty of Theory*, pp. 1–33.

38 Thompson, *Protest and Survive*, p. 30.

39 END Appeal, *A Nuclear-Free Europe*.

40 M. Kaldor, in conversation with R. Taylor, 24 May 2012.

41 M. Kaldor, *Global Civil Society: An Answer to War* (Cambridge: Polity Press, 2003), p. 60.

42 END Appeal, *A Nuclear Free Europe*.

43 K. Coates, 'A Political Life', interview with G. Lambie, *The Spokesman: Resist Much, Obey Little*, 116 (2012), BRPF Nottingham, 38.

44 *Ibid.*, pp. 39–40.

45 *Ibid.*

46 E. P. Thompson, 'Healing the Wound', *END Journal*, 1 (December 1982/January 1983), 10–11.

47 BRPF END Archive. Letter, E. P. Thompson to K. Coates, 3 March 1981.

48 BRPF END Archive. Letter, E. P. Thompson to M. Barratt Brown, 8 December 1982. (The letter is peppered with pejorative phrases: 'incomprehensible behaviour'; 'quite petty'; 'his factional zeal has become quite manic'; is he 'unbalanced?' etc.)

49 BRPF END Archive. E.g. letters from R. Fieldhouse, on behalf of West Yorkshire END, 20 December 1982; J. Field, Northern College, 31 July 1983.

50 BRPF END Archive. B. Kent, letter to K. Fleet of BRPF, 1 October 1982.

51 Coates, 'A Political Life'.

52 G. Konrad, *Anti-Politics: An Essay* (New York and London: Harcourt Brace Jovanovich, translated into English 1984), p. 92, cited in Kaldor, *Global Civil Society*, pp. 57–8.

53 See T. Simpson, Editorial, *Spokesman*, 116 (2012), 4: 'We have turned to William Blake, whose work Ken Coates loved, to help illustrate this collection.' And Thompson's last major book was his biography of Blake: *Witness Against the Beast: William Blake and the Moral Law* (Cambridge: Cambridge University Press, 1994).

54 In his survey of left libertarian thought in Britain in the twentieth century, David Goodway includes a chapter on E. P. Thompson. See D. Goodway, 'Nuclear Disarmament, the New Left – and the Case of E. P. Thompson', in D. Goodway, *Anarchist Seeds Beneath the Snow, Left-Libertarian Thought and British Writers from William Morris to Colin Ward* (Liverpool: Liverpool University Press, 2006) , pp. 260–87.

55 See, e.g., a long, frustrated and angry letter from D. Smith to E. P. Thompson, 10 August 1982, in which Thompson is accused of 'insult and abuse', and urged that in future he should learn to be critical, where he thought it was necessary, but not to be personally abusive. 'I don't know if you understand how destructive it is to anybody who gets on the wrong side of you.' END Papers. M. Kaldor's Archive.

56 E. P. Thompson, 'Notes on Exterminism, the Last Stage of Civilisation', *New Left Review*, 121 (May–June 1980); reprinted in E. P. Thompson, *Zero Option* (London: Merlin Press, 1982), pp. 41–80; and E. P. Thompson, printed version of a lecture given on 26 November 1981, *Beyond The Cold War* (London: END, 1982).

57 Thompson, 'Notes on Exterminism', p. 64, citing C. Wright Mills, *The Causes of World War III* (New York: Simon & Schuster, 1958), p. 47.

58 As he was at pains to point out in his essay 'Exterminism Reviewed', in *Exterminism and Cold War* (London: Verso and New Left Books 1982);

reprinted in E. P. Thompson, *The Heavy Dancers* (New York: Pantheon Books 1985), pp. 135–52.

59 Thompson, *The Heavy Dancers*, p. 136.
60 Thompson, *Beyond the Cold War*, p. 19.
61 Thompson, 'Notes on Exterminism', p. 76.
62 Thompson, *Beyond the Cold War*, pp. 18–19.
63 *Ibid.*, p. 25.
64 *Ibid.*, p. 29.
65 Both quotations are from M. Kaldor, in conversation, 2012.
66 See Kaldor, *The Global Civil Society*, esp. ch. 3.
67 Kaldor, in conversation, 2012.
68 E. P. Thompson, 'The State of the Nation', in E. P. Thompson, *Writing By Candlelight* (London: Merlin Press, 1980), pp. 254–6.
69 C. Hill, Obituary, 'From the Awkward School', *Guardian*, 30 August 1993.
70 B. Kent, Obituary, *CND Today* (Winter 1993), 8.

Part III

E. P. Thompson:
an overview

10

Paradox and the Thompson 'School of Awkwardness'

Bryan D. Palmer

E. P. Thompson offered to all who would listen many words on the complications crucial to understanding the past. He put this with the flourish of metaphorical simplicity in his *The Poverty of Theory*, proclaiming 'History knows no regular verbs.' By this he meant that

> In investigating history we are not flicking through a series of 'stills', each of which shows us a moment of social time transfixed into a single eternal pose: for each one of these 'stills' is not only a moment of being but also a moment of becoming: and even within each seemingly-static section there will be found contradictions and liaisons, dominant and subordinate elements, declining or ascending energies. Any historical moment is both a result of prior process and an index towards the direction of its future flow.

'Oh, but one must be a dialectician to understand how this world goes!' he wrote in his open letter to Leszek Kolakowski.[1]

In what follows I do not so much address Thompson's positions on a wide variety of topics, over a significant number of decades of change. Such assessments appear in the chapters above, where a range of commentators offer judgements on Thompson's views and whether they have stood the test of time. I am looking, in this overview, for something rather different, an explication that is, at the same time, a plea for caution. Moreover, while I allude to most of Thompson's major writings, I rely less on these canonical texts – most of which are of course discussed by the contributors to this volume – than on writings more likely to be unfamiliar, including a body of spirited reviews. I try to approach Thompson through a discussion of his general approach, which I maintain was characterised by a coherence that nonetheless defies easy categorisation precisely because it was often paradoxical. This was the awkward school in which Thompson insisted on placing himself. Its instruction has an urgency that, through time, remains relevant to all of those who refuse to adapt complacently to power's many incursions on freedom, and its infinite capacity to define lives subject to its governance in disfiguring restraints.

Like William Blake, whom Thompson so admired, Thompson articulated a way 'of breaking out from received wisdom and moralism, and entering upon new possibilities'. This was done through 'attack' and, as in Blake, the ways that Thompson did this grew out of 'thought and feeling' that were 'unique'. Thompson's concluding assessment of Blake was in some ways an apt self-portrait. Blake had his own way of keeping 'the divine vision in time of trouble', wrote Thompson, and he took characteristic and received positions of dissent 'into more esoteric ways'. In this there was 'obscurity and perhaps even some oddity' as 'incompatible traditions' met. The resulting intellectual system was a creative historical hybrid. Past systems of thought blurred into present concerns and in the process 'tried to marry – argued as contraries – were held in polarized tension'. This was Blake's awkwardness, according to Thompson, but it was also his own. And as Thompson stressed, within Blake, in spite of this friction of contentions, there was a foundation of continuity: 'there is never ... sign of submission to "Satan's Kingdom". Never, on any page of Blake, is there the least complicity with the kingdom of the Beast.'[2]

Dialectics and argument/sensibility and tone

All learning 'worthy of the name involves a relationship of mutuality, a dialectic', Thompson once declared. He envisioned extending democracy through adult education. But this lofty ideal would only be realised by introducing into the lesson plan 'the abrasion of different worlds of experience, in which ideas are brought to the test of life'. Empirical evidence and abstract theorisation had to be made to converse with one another. Out of the clash of seeming opposites and contradictory difference, Thompson fashioned fresh ways of utilising a tired language with which to address the needs and aspirations of men and women situated among particular kinds of tension-ridden social relations, erecting a new interpretive edifice within which such relations could be analytically housed. As Thompson once said of the ways in which Christopher Caudwell enriched and illuminated Marxism's varied understandings, 'What then is communicated is not just a new "idea" (or an old idea freshly communicated) but a new

way of seeing. ... a rupture with a whole received view of the world.'
All of this, for Thompson, was a 'dialectics of historical knowledge'.[3]

Its movement was *argument.* Thompson self-deprecatingly likened
himself to an earth-bound bustard, who might yet give high-flying
intellectual eagles 'a peck or two about their gizzards'. An opposi-
tionist, Thompson refused to be silenced by criticism and pressures
to conform.[4] Indeed, what might be called Thompsonian analytic
sensibilities invested a great deal of significance in the form in which
intellectual and political stands were taken. When Perry Anderson
was writing in the *London Review of Books* on Michael Oakeshott,
whom he appraised as an 'outstanding European theorist of the
intransigent right', Thompson let it be known that he disapproved, not
of the subject, but of the *ways* in which he was being written about.
'Oakeshott was a scoundrel', Thompson said with feeling, advising
Anderson to 'stiffen his tone'.[5] Often devastatingly brutal, Thompson's
remarkable rhetoric of reconsideration was also strikingly effective,
charged as it was with charisma *and* commitment. Most often associated with *The Making of the English Working Class*, which one trans-
atlantic commentator would later describe as sending 'a quenching
shower of spring rain across a parched landscape', this fertile prose
passion was evident in almost all of Thompson's writing.[6] In finding
fault with histories in which '[t]he blind alleys, the lost causes, and the
losers themselves are forgotten', Thompson exposed the centrality of
contingency in historical process, reminding us that the imbalances of
power relations must be appreciated as influencing outcomes which
were themselves contested. History's seeming ends were seldom if
ever inevitable; reversals were potentially always in the making. What
Thompson thus taught was that the everyday lives of people struggling to survive within, and sometimes to transform, their social
order, should never be suppressed in an unreflective privileging of
'subsequent preoccupations'.[7]

Reviews and critique

Commenting on two 1970s books on family history, Lawrence Stone's
The Family, Sex, and Marriage in England, 1500–1800 and Edward
Shorter's *The Making of the Modern Family*, Thompson's dissatisfac-
tions with skewed presentations of the past were made clear:

> I am persuaded that we are different, as parents or as lovers, from those
> in the past; but I am not persuaded that we are so much better, more

companionate, more caring, than our forefathers and mothers. It may depend, somewhat, upon class and occupation, then and now ... It annoys me that both Professor Stone and Professor Shorter leave their readers to feel so complacent about their own modernity. It annoys me even more that both should indict the poor, on so little evidence, of indifference to their children and of callous complicity in their high rate of mortality.

Where Stone saw liberal affective individualism moving, osmosis-like, in a creep of modernisation's beneficence, from the elite downwards to the plebeian masses, Shorter imagined liberated sexuality coming about as the 'lads and lasses set free by the industrial revolution' charted new territories of libidinal adventure, not unlike contemporary fashion trends working their way out of the ghetto and into club scenes frequented by teenage celebrities and jet-setting 'trust funders'. One view was paternalist; another populist. No matter, Thompson concluded, 'neither ... is supported by any relevant evidence'. Each, in its own way, was ordered by 'culture-bound assumption, an expectation learned within our own immature but sexually overstimulated time'. Presenting this as historical interpretation made Thompson 'cross'.[8]

Equally vexing were literary productions like D. N. Furbank's 1985 *The Unholy Pleasure: The Idea of Social Class*. Thompson thought the book a good example of a kind of 'English intellectual amateurism', in which stimulating digressions and sardonic witticisms were used to deflate the pretensions of professional academics. So far, so good, but Furbank could not quite bring himself to believe that 'the historical events of class' even existed, or that the object of enquiring into them was valid. Thompson likened the enterprise to a voyeuristic exercise in which Furbank and a few friends crash a 'banqueting hall' of 'historians, sociologists, critics and some (but not all) novelists', carrying on a 'garrulous and boring discourse about class'. They observe the proceedings, 'making wry faces and ridiculing the gaudy feast'. Thompson thought the result a 'complacent pharisaism', the chit-chat's trajectory one of boring declension. 'Mr Furbank has talked himself out,' Thompson concluded, 'hiccupping scraps of Joyce and Proust, sprawled on the table where he and his readers fall asleep.'[9]

Someone regarded as an 'old colleague and mentor' might find himself exposed in embarrassing vulnerabilities by Thompson's cutting considerations. George Rudé, hounded from academic positions in England during the Cold War, was driven into exile in Australia and

Canada: researches beckoned into the lot of those nineteenth-century 'industrial and political felons' sent by the state to Van Diemen's Land. The resulting book, *Protest and Punishment*, angered Thompson. He thought Rudé insufficiently attentive to the extant historical evidence, prone to lapse into 'criminological generalization' based on inadequate statistics. Enticed into a convenient evidentiary lair, Rudé relied on reports of what the transported *said* they had been exiled for upon their obligatory arrival interrogation in the penal colony. Thompson was incredulous that Rudé proved so willing to accept statements that riots had been motivated solely by demands for '*an increase in wages*'. Failing to understand that these were words the prison officers might want to hear, Rudé seemed unable to fathom that such depositions would rarely voice more defiant aspirations, such as 'any high-flying bourgeois democratic false consciousness', including 'staying on strike until the Charter was the law of the land'. Shed the condescension of posterity, rid oneself of the notion that working-class people are pure and simple response mechanisms to the wage relation, however important that relation may be, and a more rounded understanding of proletarian life as something other than 'brutish, instrumental, casual or almost unstructured' emerged. 'The only adequate critic' for many of Rudé's pages, Thompson snorted, 'would be a pair of scissors.'[10]

This sensibility (and this irreverent tone) was the genius of *The Making of the English Working Class*, which rejected the conventional chronicle of class formation as a static equation, in which 'steam power plus the factory system equals the working class'.[11] Central to Thompson's success was his admonition to *listen* to voices seldom admitted to the High Table of university-generated research. This was elevated to an injunction that informed all questions of method and interpretation. Beginning with his encounter with Wordsworth in his adult education teaching, Thompson took inspiration from the Romantic poet's compassion and capacity to hear 'From mouths of lowly men and of obscure / A tale of honour'. This was turned by Thompson into a necessity charged with political and intellectual import:

> When I began to inquire,
> To watch and question those I met, and held
> Familiar talk with them, the lonely roads
> Were schools to me in which I daily read
> With most delight the passions of mankind
> There saw into the depths of human souls,
> Souls that appear to have no depth at all

To vulgar eyes. And now convinced at heart
How little that to which alone we give
The name of education hath to do
With real feeling and just sense[12]

Nowhere, perhaps, was this revealed more tellingly than in a lengthy, seldom-cited review of a sociological work on religion at the coalface: Robert Moore's *Pit-Men, Preachers and Politics: The Effects of Methodism in a Durham Mining Community*. Thompson was adamant that Moore had missed an important part of how miners negotiated lives of oppression and exploitation. 'The weapons of the weak' included rude, ribald or risqué mockery. Laughter, in this context, might serve as 'a kind of criticism, a kind of self-defence'; the social balloon of hegemony's expectation of deference could be pricked in ways that destabilised the self-confidence of the powerful. 'Dr. Moore's book altogether lacks the control of this laughter', Thompson concluded, and as a result the sociologist was blind to all manner of other behaviours and class responses that modified the impact of nonconformist religious dominance: backsliding, agnosticism, boredom, humour, irreverence, sarcasm, even the gritty earthiness of blasphemy. 'People are more paradoxical in their behaviour than typologies allow', Thompson concluded. When he saw too little of these dialectics of abrasion in Moore's account, Thompson grew exasperated.[13]

A close reading of Thompson's texts reveals that if his designated opponents have been many and varied, his indignation at a superficial gloss on subjects deserving a more sustained, perhaps empathetic, engagement, produced prose passages that bristled with insight. In his many refusals, be they of the optimistic school that excused the tragedy and alienating imperatives of England's Industrial Revolution with a satisfied calculation of increased caloric intake over the course of the 1840s, or of the constitutionalist quarter of the emerging labour movement that justified its reform-minded concessions to capitalist triumphalism with a smug, social democratic dismissal of night marauders and machine breakers, Thompson reconstructed his sense of the working-class past with unrivalled brio. Who can forget Thompson's account of the 'average' working man's share in the 'benefits of economic progress', nurtured in the shadows of the 'dark Satanic mills' of early capitalism: 'more potatoes, a few articles of cotton clothing for his family, soap and candles, some tea and sugar, and a great many articles in the *Economic History Review*'. Or, alternatively, his rebuttal to those conservative economic historians like R. M. Hartwell, whose judgement on child labour and early industrialism was deformed by a misplaced relativism. Hartwell, writing in 1959, insisted that modern readers, 'well disciplined by familiarity with concentration camps', were 'comparatively unmoved' by unduly sentimental tales of the ways in which children were harnessed to the machine age of the early 1800s. Thompson's rejoinder was a gruff refusal: 'We may be allowed to reaffirm a more traditional view: that the exploitation of little children, on this scale and with this intensity, was one of the most shameful events in our history'.[14]

Refusing assimilation: in a school of awkwardness

Thompson had no truck with what he once referred to as the 'conservative bias of the orthodox academic tradition'.[15] It was given the political equivalent of a rough musicking in his contribution to a critique of the business university, *Warwick University Ltd.* An account of student protest at a 'new university' located in the industrial West Midlands, where Thompson taught in the late 1960s, this edited collection was produced in the aftermath of the youth radicalism that exploded across campuses in England, Europe, North America and elsewhere. Thompson was not necessarily impressed with a great deal of what passed for political agitation in this era. Nonetheless, he found the pomposity, instinctual caution and inclination to retreat from argument and controversy of many university-based colleagues even more difficult to stomach. Shown 'the last ditch for the defence of liberty', Thompson railed, and these sorts would 'walk backwards into the sea, complaining that the ditch is very ill dug, that they cannot possibly be asked to defend it alongside such a ragged and seditious-looking set of fellows, and, in any case, it would surely be better to write out a tactful remonstrance and present it on inscribed vellum, to the enemy'. Living in 'Awe of Propriety', *academici superciliosi* encouraged 'an atmosphere of institutional loyalty' which defrauded students 'of some of the essential intellectual dialectic from which their own orientations should be worked out'.[16]

A committed contrarian, Thompson believed deeply that it was absolutely necessary to guard relentlessly against the myriad of forces that drew one into 'the infinitely assimilative culture'.[17] When Conor Cruise O'Brien penned a 1979 rant in the *Observer*, denouncing Labour Party Marxists for ostensibly luring striking lorry workers into their 'hateful' lair, leading society 'towards the abyss', Thompson's response was a sharp and scathing indictment. He defended labouring people's legitimate right to strike, suggesting that in spite of the inconvenience to the public and rare instances of real suffering, the picketing workers were exercising an understandable withdrawal of services with 'surprising good humour and self-control'. Thompson chastised O'Brien's imploding irrationality, warning of the dangers that could come of unbridled bigotry and political narrow-mindedness. He thus rejected the social construction of class crisis concocted in O'Brien's great fear of a 'Nauseous Marxist–Methodist Cocktail'.[18]

Thompson could thus not forgo stressing how imperative it was to strain 'at every turn in one's thought and to resist the assumption that what one observes and what one is is the very course of nature'.[19] In the opening line of his 1960 essay, 'Revolution', Thompson declared, 'At every point the way out of apathy leads us outside the conventions within which life is confined.' This principled separation from all manner of compromise made it mandatory, in Thompson's view, to place oneself, repeatedly and routinely, 'into a school of awkwardness'. Thompson's peace activism, which highlighted the necessity to step outside one's received education in any national culture, demanded a critical interrogation of the official, proselytising state curriculum, replete with its socio-political primers.[20] 'One must make one's sensibility all knobbly – all knees and elbows of susceptibility and refusal – if one is not to be pressed through the grid into the universal mishmash of the received assumptions of the intellectual culture', he concluded.[21]

The personal assessment: not quite political enough

So what? Can not all of this be 'explained' with acknowledgement that Thompson was just 'difficult'? The accounts of Thompson and the fissiparous years of the rise and fall of the British New Left are replete with reference to Thompson as, however inspirational and creative, a movement 'problem'. He was given to 'venting his personal anger' (Chun); a 'persistent behind-the-scenes critic' who besieged co-workers like Stuart Hall with 'highly critical and sometimes angry letters', a barrage of 'ceaseless pressure, and worse' (Dworkin); 'volatile, suspicious and disinclined to compromise', a 'prima donna' who tended to hit out 'in anger without expecting the victim not to take it too seriously' (Newman).[22] In published polemics that took aim at a younger cohort of New Leftists associated with Hall and those around him in the dissident journal, *Universities and Left Review* (*ULR*), and later, in a brilliant, but decisively critical, reaction to Raymond Williams's *The Long Revolution*, Thompson raised predictable objections.[23] Madeleine Davis has recently characterised Thompson's response to the *ULR* discussion of 'classlessness' as a 'furious outburst' that 'had the effect of closing down rather than opening up debate within the New Left about the critical issue of class', but it must be noted that she provides no evidence for this interpretive assertion. Williams implied that Thompson's review caused tensions between two senior figures associated with the early New Left, etching lines in the sand of dissent that separated others into specific camps, but he accepted much of the critique and would soon collaborate with Thompson on the 1967 May Day Manifesto Committee.[24]

My own small cache of Thompson letters from three different decades, which I have spilled out onto my desk in writing this paragraph, will confirm, if read piecemeal, a sense of Thompson as combative, hasty in his condemnations, and capable of brusque dismissals and wounding caricature.[25] Thompson *was* difficult, *very difficult.*[26] Yet being difficult, incomprehensible though this may be to most academics, is a part of what building movements of resistance entails, however regrettable. Individuals in positions of leadership and responsibility find themselves in conflict over tactics, strategies, and even such a basic issue as what an oppositional mobilisation is about. Exchanges among such people are on occasion private for a reason: they were never intended to be 'open' to the public.[27] Historians benefit from seeing such correspondence. Few advocate ignoring or suppressing material of this kind. But this internal documentary record needs to be assessed with care, harsh sentences set against recognition of the kinds of behaviour and failures of responsibility that might well have prompted lashing language. Thompson had the commitment of the old communist to the discipline of the organisation, and he valued those who could be counted on to carry out their assignments responsibly. He imposed on himself the same expectations he had of others.[28]

Moreover, there were often political issues extending well beyond Thompson's personal style, centrally important in disputes within particular mobilisations and movements. Consider, for instance, Thompson's devastating 1963 document of departure from the *New Left Review*. Thompson's objections and oppositions to the *Review's* drift into certain stands on internationalism and a kind of abdication before the 'Third Worldist' glorification of violence evident in Jean-Paul Sartre's preface to Frantz Fanon's *Les Damnés de la Terre* were posed seriously and with some insight. He was demanding of the *Review* something more than a First World political tailism. Thompson wondered aloud (and his words seem eerily prophetic in 2013, however abstract and hypothetical) about casting the New Left's lot with an 'ardent Moslem militarist, of feudal stock, who at the same time' as he was righteously opposing imperialist occupation and colonial subordination, was also more than willing to lock up 'trade unionists and peasant agitators' and suppress 'birth control propaganda'. Knowing well the sorry denouement of Stalinism, Thompson declared, 'The clothes of revolution only too easily become the habit of pious scoundrels.' He thus argued again the awkward nature of political responsibility:

> We have a task which is difficult, easily misrepresented, and quite probably one that will not quickly be understood in the Third World itself. We have at one and the same time to see (and interpret) the great liberating impulses of the Soviet and Chinese revolutions, and of the emergent nationalisms of Asia and Africa; and to adopt a critical and at times uncompromising stand as to certain socialist principles and humanist values. It is the critical standpoint which is truly that of internationalism. The execution of Communist trade unionists in Iraq and of intellectuals (again, often Communist) in China is no prettier because these events happen in a third world: they happen also in our world, and the victims have the right to expect from us the duties of solidarity. Because one's heart has leapt at the Cuban revolution, and because one pukes at the libels upon Ghana in the *Daily Express*, this does not mean that one can pass over in silence offensive ideological or authoritarian tendencies in these countries. If the 'third world consciousness' appears to us to be compounded of truth and of illusion, we do poor service, to them and to ourselves, if we propagate the illusion as well as the truth.

Thompson also tried to pull his younger comrades back into recognition of what remained available in Britain:

> Attention, internationalists and intellectual workers! The old mole, revolution, may still be at work in Battersea and Fife, in Tyneside and Ebbw Vale. It may manifest itself in conflicts far removed from your scheme ... Perhaps something 'real' could happen ... even in Britain? Perhaps, if we turn away from our own people, this might be the worst way in which we could also betray the First, the Second, and the Third World?

214

'Internationalism', Thompson stressed, 'should imply, not a translating agency working one way, but a discourse in which we participate.' One route into such exchange was argument.[29]

Beyond reductionism

Thompson found himself in his perennial school of awkwardness, this time standing in the corner, pondering how he was to be sent home for his bad behaviour in the New Left class. What meaning, beyond a personal proclivity to be difficult, can we draw out of this sensibility?

Little is to be gained by classifying Thompson according to a variety of social constructivist projects firmly embedded in the polemics of a particular period, be they associated with the mid-1960s, when Perry Anderson situated Thompson in an 'impressionist, inspirational tradition' that harboured 'brilliant, imaginative' histories as well as 'a vacuous political analysis';[30] the late 1970s 'culturalist' critique of Richard Johnson and his allies in Cultural Studies at Birmingham,[31] which precipitated Thompson into the 'gladiatorial combat' of the infamous History Workshop debate at Oxford;[32] or the recent reading of Scott Hamilton, which sees in this anti-Althusserian moment a divide fragmenting Thompson's political life-course.[33] Thompson responded to such classifying criticism repeatedly, insisting that he had been engaged in a project quite different than these schematic orderings suggested. He was struggling to rehabilitate 'lost categories and a lost vocabulary in the Marxist tradition', attempting to fill a void in Marx's own undertaking, bringing back to life the 'unarticulated assumptions and unrealized mediations' of the plebeian and labouring people. 'I am examining the dialectic of interaction, the dialectic between "economics" and "values"', Thompson explained in 1976, adding, 'This preoccupation has run through all my work, historical and political.'[34]

Thompsonian provincialism: metaphorical geographies of awkwardness

Arguably the most impressive and stimulating of recent attempts to fix Thompson's meaning in a particular analytics is Wade Matthews's refusal of the standard claims, also figuring in this collection, that Thompson was, in the phrasing of W. L. Webb's obituary, 'a thoroughly English dissident'.[35] At its most scapegoating, this classification, origi-

nating in the Anderson–Nairn critique of the mid-1960s, impaled
Thompson on a tradition of 'messianic nationalism', altogether too
English in its aversion to theory; quick to reduce the difficulties of
socialist initiative to a populist faith in 'the British people's' capacity to
realise its transformative destiny; and prone to inflate 'living English
traditions' into self-delusional and moralising claims of dissenting
possibilities that bore no relationship to reality.[36] Hobsbawm offered
a benevolent, refining version: Thompson's persona was that of 'the
traditional English (not British) country gentleman of the radical left'.
'Big cities', Hobsbawm remarked of Thompson's tastes, 'were places
to visit, not for living.'[37] A man of the provinces, with an aversion to
what he once called 'intellectual metropolitomania', Thompson was
convinced that much of what was of value in the history of dissenting
opposition had come out of an 'indistinct nether region', places like
the Yorkshire that had nurtured a 'forgotten "provincial"' of English
socialism, Tom Maguire.[38]

As Matthews shows, however, Thompson could hardly be confined
to any kind of English provincialism, however positive a reading one
might offer of such a space, both physical and intellectual. Thompson's provincialism was, paradoxically, profoundly internationalist.
Nowhere does this appear more forcefully than in Thompson's appreciation of two American dissidents, neither of whom fit comfortably
in easily constructed containers: the larger-than-life sociological
stargazer and gadfly, C. Wright Mills,[39] whom Thompson recognised
as inconsistent, impatient and incorruptible in his commitments,
and the North Dakotan outlaw poet, Tom McGrath. Of McGrath's
oeuvre, Thompson wrote: 'It is true that McGrath's *politics* are given
a very distinct American location; they are not the extrapolation of
some theorized cosmopolitan prescription. But these are interpreted
through his poetic grid of reference which, if not universal, is as
universal as his selection of poetic values allows it to be.' Thompson's
provinces were places where men and women laboured, the ground
on which love and loss occur, through which relationships to nature
are forged in thwarted aspirations for 'communitas', where oppression, exploitation and resistance are ever-present forces. Such places
have proven, historically, to be geographies of a 'common imbrication
in the capitalist nexus'.[40] Matthews provides a brilliant travelogue of
how Thompson's thinking was formed in 'provinces' like his father's
India, his brother's Yugoslavia and the woollen district of the West
Riding. The birthplace of much that Thompson valued was in just

such shadowy metaphorical peripheries and, as Matthews notes, the 'tracer beams' of his polemics, the rich texture of his argued histories, and much of the immediacy of his political interventions came out of such places. 'Socialist internationalism, the "spirit of Europe", the tradition of the "freeborn Englishman" – each makes some sense of Thompson', concludes Matthews. 'But only if it is remembered that he approached all three awkwardly.'[41]

Awkwardness and the dialectic of paradox

It is this awkwardness that is crucial in understanding Thompson, and that produces what is undeniably the dialectic of paradox that defeats any simplified attempt to locate him within a singular sighting. For even as Thompson was indeed an internationalist he was also, as this volume suggests, a characteristic English radical. Matthews perhaps too easily sidesteps the tension always pulling at Thompson's polemics and politics, perhaps even his histories, in which internationalism and Englishness (with its allusions to 'our people' and its ostensibly identifiable empirical idiom) are engaged in a tug-of-war of allegiance.[42]

In 'Where Are We Now' this paradox of internationalism and Englishness jostled awkwardly on every page:

> What is surely required – and here I burn my last boat – is that social-
> ists of our kind should now be somewhat more plain-spoken and less
> clever: more willing to break our demands down into programmes:
> more willing to defend our positions, and less willing to drop them at
> the first hint that they ain't respectable, or that something *far* cleverer
> has been published in Paris or said in Balliol ... to put our boots into
> the British scene and walk around among British people; listen to them
> a bit more; have a touch of humility before their experience, without
> a precious fear that the least contact with programmes or slogans will
> soil our intellectual integrity ... we can surely see the British people
> bumping up against facts: and we should surely be in there with them,
> helping to draw conclusions? Because if in our muddled way we were
> able to break or grow through to a new kind of socialist society, this
> would be an event of comparable importance for Europe with 1789 ...
> There will be no way out of the Cold War, except through the consum-
> mation of fire, unless somewhere in the advanced capitalist world, one
> nation can move. From the very perversity of historical development,
> that nation might be our own. If we fail to enlarge what slender possi-
> bilities there are, we fail ourselves *and* we fail the world ... we are not
> finished ... the world is tied in a contradiction, one of whose knots lies

across London, Paris and Rome. And English Socialists! Insular, moralistic, empirical, affluent, compromised – nevertheless, three worlds
might be waiting for us.[43]

Such a perspective congealed the solidarities of internationalism and
the particularities of Englishness.

Paradoxes of other kinds also cut through Thompson's presence in
intellectual and political circles. His nature as a polymath, like the
Caudwell he so admired,[44] meant that he approached knowledge,
politics and the productions of the writing desk from a variety of
vantage points, none of which could be comfortably slotted into the
conventional boxes of contemporary critical theory, orthodoxies or
movements of the Left, or 'university standards'. Thompson's romanticism, with its critique of the cash nexus,[45] reached from William
Blake and the 1790s into William Morris and the late nineteenth-
century socialist movement. It also infused his writing with passions
that seemed perpetually out of step with many dissenting traditions.
More tellingly, all of this meant that Thompson wrote history in ways
that were not unrelated to his intense desire to change its course, to
actually *make* history. This imperative often left Thompson awkwardly
situated, appreciative of radical history's necessity, but aware of the
ways in which it could be 'hemmed in' by 'playing safe', constrained
by failures of originality and vitality. In a 1985 New York lecture,
Thompson discussed all of this, stressing the need to always bring
to bear on academic scholarship some consideration of the relations
of such work and 'active experience' that promotes 'distrust of easy
assimilation by the [h]ost society', whose institutional and ideological
determinations are not only weighty, but 'founded upon unreason, or
on the reasons of power and the reasons of money'.[46]

In the realm of theory Thompson's paradoxical nature was patently
obvious, and might be quite heretical. He was a theorist quick to
offer denials of his contributions and capacities. This was often done
tongue-in-cheek, as in his 'Notes on Exterminism', where he declares,
'I cannot, as is well known, understand economics'.[47] Nonetheless,
whatever Thompson's vulnerabilities and jaundiced appraisals of his
theoretical acumen, he had a particular sense of theory that enriched
not only historical writing but other scholarly realms as well. At times
Thompson abandoned his self-denigration and back-pedalling, and
became quite insistent that he was addressing theoretical questions
with rigour and sophistication. 'I have presented myself to you as a

more muddled and Anglo-Saxon character than is quite true', he told an interviewer in New York in 1976, answering a question about why he had not written about the culture industry of advanced capitalism and its impact on the radicalism of the nineteenth century. 'I have always written about this,' Thompson replied, 'but I have written about it mainly at the level of theory.'[48] The Reasoners of 1956 and the social historians of the 1970s/1980s attending to class and customary cultures were always orientated by Thompson to consider their subject, be it a political movement or an historical research endeavour, as emanating, in part, from theoretical concerns, indeed out of theoretical necessity.[49] His political commitment to socialist humanism, for instance, entailed not only a repudiation of Stalinism, but a thoroughgoing questioning and rejection of the base-super-structure metaphor.[50] Thompson thus entered endlessly into theoretical debate, far more so than most conventional historians, often taking on the heaviest of philosophical thinkers, whom he engaged on *their* terms, not his.

This relationship to theory was, again, awkward, because Thompson saw theory not so much as being self-generating and free-standing, but as being relational, extended and developed in critique/polemic. Argument was theory's engine, driving understanding to new realisations, quickening the pace of conceptualisation and its refinement. And precisely because of Thompson's resolute insistence that theory mattered *because* it could contribute to changing the world, there were times when theory took a back seat to popular mobilisations, when the theoreticians had to either move in light of social circumstances or be left very much behind. Thompson felt that the disarmament mobilisations of the 1980s were just such a radical moment of re-education.[51] As a polymath, moreover, Thompson had come to think, as early as the 1970s, that not only was theory provisional, dependent always on establishing its claims through argument and counter-argument, but that the very notion of being guided by any 'all-embracing theory' was itself wrong-headed.[52] This was not the standard stance of theorists.

The awkward school in which Thompson found it necessary to place himself produced paradox and, driven by argument, difference. This did not mean that there were no continuities and no fundamental overall unifying features in Thompson's political and intellectual activity. There was such continuity and unity, but they persevered through decades of different political and intellectual circumstance. Thompson inevitably reacted to such developments and in the process changed, albeit not so strikingly that we can actually locate ruptures of meaning. The most obvious area in which Thompson shifted his perspective relates to the politics of Marxism, within which he underwent a series of reconstructions associated with the 1950s, 1960s, 1970s and 1980s.[53] Yet the causes in which he invested political energies in the 1970s and 1980s, defending democratic institutions and practices in the face of state encroachments and erosions[54] and then lending his public persona, on a full-time basis, to an internationalist discourse on peace, disarmament, and the nature of freedoms in the East and the West, as well as India of the Emergency (1975–77),[55] represented no break with Thompson's past commitments. Rather, they proved an extension of them into new historical periods and challenges. They took an English radical to a score of countries. There Thompson addressed hundreds of meetings and attended countless committees, some of them, in situations of authoritarian repression, clandestine gatherings of the underground.

In his homeland, Thompson became a public figure who could poll a popularity surpassed only by the Queen, the Queen Mother and Margaret Thatcher. Hobsbawm notes that Thompson's death, in 1993, was 'probably received with more personal grief than that of any other British historian of his time'.[56] Hundreds of thousands had grown accustomed to Thompson's theatrical presentations before the mass rallies of the 1980s peace movement, aware that as he bounded on to the stage, his white hair flying, his lanky body leaning into an historical allusion to William Blake, his passion exploding, no longer on the page, but across a sea of listeners, they were being treated to refusals and arguments and oppositions to the consolidating 'doomsday consensus'. It all harkened back to the best oratorical traditions of the English working class in the early nineteenth century. If Paine had changed the world with a pamphlet, Thompson's *Protest and Survive*, with its sales in the hundreds of thousands, failed to have the same impact, but it came as close as any comparable modern publication.

Thompson as historical happening

Thompson's negotiation of the related processes of making and writing history, of living complex acts of refusal and translating them into both art and a form of dissenting, combative truth, has few modern precedents. He was, in many ways, *sui generis*, and to complicate matters his uniqueness was often paradoxical. Thompson managed to translate his awkwardness into a kind of genius, his being difficult into appreciations and reverence. It was an alchemy no other figure of his generation managed in quite the same way, or with the same intensity. How is all of this to be understood? We can perhaps appreciate Thompson and his meaning by turning to his own understandings of class. 'The finest-meshed sociological net cannot give us a pure specimen of class, any more than it can give us one of deference or of love',[57] Thompson wrote, and no classification, category or analytic label can, similarly, capture the totality of Thompson's being. Always situated inside historical developments, Thompson could engage only by active interventions that brought him *into* argument, opposition and resolution. Thompson's substance, like that of class, is therefore inseparable from *historically* constituted relations: with individuals and their ideas, as well as Thompson's sense of their responsibilities and duties; with movements and mobilisations, and Thompson's contributions to these collectivities and his expectations of them; and with research, and its dialogue of evidence and theory, a dance of the dialectic in which past, present, and future are brought into mutual consideration.

Made inside history, but always refusing to be made *only* by it, Thompson reminds us of one of his favoured passages in William Morris's *A Dream of John Ball*: 'men fight and lose the battle, and the thing they fought for comes about in spite of their defeat, and when it comes turns out to be not what they meant, and other men had to fight for what they meant under another name'.[58] Thompson's meaning, then, can never be titled, except in rather clumsy ways. It 'owes as much to agency as to conditioning' and unifies 'disparate and seemingly unconnected' aspects of 'experience and consciousness'. Thompson, like class, had a 'fluency which evades analysis if we attempt to stop it dead at any given moment and atomise its structure'.[59] We might do no better, then, in understanding Thompson, than see him as he often saw his subject, as an immensely creative *historical happening*.

Notes

1 E. P. Thompson, 'The Poverty of Theory: or an Orrery of Errors' and 'An Open Letter to Leszek Kolakowski', in E. P. Thompson, *The Poverty of Theory and Other Essays* (London: Merlin Press, 1978), pp. 238–9, p. 183.

2 E. P. Thompson, *Witness Against the Beast: William Blake and the Moral Law* (New York: New Press, 1993), pp. 20–1, 228–9.

3 E. P. Thompson, *Education and Experience: Fifth Mansbridge Memorial Lecture* (Leeds: University of Leeds, 1968), pp. 1, 22–3; Thompson, 'The Poverty of Theory' and 'Letter to Kolakowski', pp. 235, 112; E. P. Thompson, *The Making of the English Working Class* (New York: Vintage, 1963), esp. pp. 10–12. Thompson's rich but difficult essay, 'Caudwell', first appeared in J. Saville and R. Miliband (eds), *Socialist Register, 1977* (London: Merlin Press, 1977), pp. 228–76, reprinted in E. P. Thompson, *Persons and Polemics: Historical Essays* (London: Merlin Press, 1994), pp. 78–140, at pp. 89, 125.

4 Thompson, 'Letter to Kolakowski', p. 110; E. P. Thompson, 'My Study' and 'The Place Called Choice', in E. P. Thompson, *Collected Poems* (Newcastle-upon-Tyne: Bloodaxe, 1999), pp. 59, 80–1.

5 P. Anderson, 'Diary', *London Review of Books*, 21 October 1993, pp. 24–5.

6 A. Dawley, 'E. P. Thompson and the Peculiarities of the Americans', *Radical History Review*, 19 (Winter 1978–79), 39. See also E. J. Hobsbawm, 'Edward Palmer Thompson, 1924–1993', *Proceedings of the British Academy*, 90 (1996), 521–39; B. Palmer, *E. P. Thompson: Objections and Oppositions* (London and New York: Verso, 1994), pp. 1–5.

7 Thompson, *The Making of the English Working Class*, pp. 12–13.

8 E. P. Thompson, 'Happy Families', *New Society* (8 September 1977), reprinted in Thompson, *Persons and Polemics*, pp. 301–11. See also E. P. Thompson, 'The Grid of Inheritance: A Comment', in J. Goody, J. Thirsk and E. P. Thompson (eds), *Family and Inheritance: Rural Society in Western Europe, 1200–1800* (London and New York: Cambridge University Press, 1976), pp. 328–60; E. P. Thompson, *Customs in Common: Studies in Traditional Popular Culture* (New York: New Press, 1993).

9 E. P. Thompson, 'Table Talk About Class', *The Listener*, 6 June 1985.

10 Thompson, *The Making of the English Working Class*, p. 12; E. P. Thompson, 'Sold Like a Sheep for a Pound', *New Society* (14 December 1978), reprinted in Thompson, *Persons and Polemics*, pp. 193–200, a review of G. Rudé, *Protest and Punishment: The Study of the Social and Political Protesters Transported to Australia, 1788–1868* (Oxford: Clarendon Press, 1978).

11 H. Abelove *et al.* (eds), *Visions of History* (New York: Pantheon, 1983), pp. 6–7.

12 E. P. Thompson, quoting Wordsworth, *Education and Experience*, pp. 6, 8. Note also Thompson's discussion of Wordsworth in 'Disenchantment or Default: A Lay Sermon', in C. C. O'Brien and W. D. Vanech (eds), *Power*

and *Consciousness: The Schweitzer Lectures* (New York: New York University Press, 1969), pp. 149–82; E. P. Thompson, 'Wordsworth's Crisis', *London Review of Books*, 10 (8 December 1988), 3–6; E. P. Thompson (ed. D. Thompson), *The Romantics: England in a Revolutionary Age* (New York: New Press, 1997), pp. 107–55.

13 E. P. Thompson, 'On History, Sociology and Historical Relevance', *British Journal of Sociology*, 27 (September 1976), 387–402. See also J. C. Scott, *Weapons of the Weak: Everyday Forms of Peasant Resistance* (New Haven, CT: Yale University Press, 1985).

14 Thompson, *The Making of the English Working Class*, pp. 318, 349.

15 *Ibid.*, p. 592.

16 E. P. Thompson (ed.), *Warwick University Ltd* (Harmondsworth: Penguin, 1970), pp. 153–4. For a more lengthy extract from this caustic polemic, see the Appendix to this book.

17 Thompson, 'Letter to Kolakowski', p. 183; E. P. Thompson, 'The Segregation of Dissent', *The New University*, 6 (6 May 1961), 13–17.

18 E. P. Thompson, 'The Acceptable Faces of Marxism', *Observer* (4 February 1979), republished as 'The Great Fear of Marxism', in E. P. Thompson, *Writing by Candlelight* (London: Merlin Press, 1980), pp. 181–6.

19 Thompson, 'Letter to Kolakowski', pp. 183–4. This is central to other discussions relating to disenchantment, on the one hand, and apostasy, on the other. See E. P. Thompson, 'Disenchantment or Default?', in O'Brien and Vanech (eds), *Power and Consciousness*, pp. 149–82, reprinted in Thompson, *The Romantics*, pp. 107–55, which also contains Thompson's reflections on Coleridge. In contrast to Thelwall, Coleridge was a sadder case of apostasy: 'the impotence of his own self-isolation' was 'an excuse for a reconciliation with the status quo' (p. 131). See E. P. Thompson, 'Hunting the Jacobin Fox', *Past and Present*, 142 (February 1994), 94–140, reprinted in Thompson, *The Romantics*, pp. 156–217. For the 1930s, see E. P. Thompson, 'Outside the Whale', in Thompson, *The Poverty of Theory and Other Essays*, pp. 211–44, which is discussed at length in S. Hamilton, *The Crisis of Theory: E. P. Thompson, the New Left, and Post-War British Politics* (Manchester: Manchester University Press, 2011), pp. 49–92.

20 The classic statement is E. P. Thompson, 'Notes on Exterminism: The Last Stage of Civilization', *New Left Review*, 121 (May–June 1980), 3–31, reprinted, along with other statements of importance, in Thompson's 1980s peace campaigning in E. P. Thompson, *Beyond the Cold War: A New Approach to the Arms Race and Nuclear Annihilation* (New York: Pantheon, 1982). See also the widely influential E. P. Thompson and D. Smith (eds), *Protest and Survive* (Harmondsworth: Penguin, 1980).

21 Thompson, 'Letter to Kolawkowski', pp. 183–4. See also C. Hill, 'From the Awkward School', *Guardian* (30 August 1993); E. P. Thompson,

'Revolution', in E. P. Thompson (ed.), *Out of Apathy* (London: Stevens & Sons/New Left Books, 1960), p. 287.

22 Lin Chun, *The British New Left* (Edinburgh: Edinburgh University Press, 1993), p. 64; D. Dworkin, *Cultural Marxism in Postwar Britain: History, the New Left, and the Origins of Cultural Studies* (Durham, NC and London: Duke University Press, 1997), p. 68; M. Newman, *Ralph Miliband and the Politics of the New Left* (London: Merlin Press, 2002), pp. 68-9.

23 E. P. Thompson, 'Commitment and Politics', *Universities and Left Review*, 6 (Spring 1959), 50-5; 'The Long Revolution 1', *New Left Review*, 9 (May–June 1961), 24-33; 'The Long Revolution 2', *New Left Review*, 10 (July–August 1961), 34-9.

24 M. Davis, 'Arguing Affluence: New Left Contributions to the Socialist Debate, 1957–1963', *Twentieth Century British History* (2011), doi:10.1093/tcbh/hwr033, 25-6; R. Williams, *Politics and Letters: Interviews with New Left Review* (London: New Left Books, 1979), pp. 135-6; R. Williams (ed.), *May Day Manifesto, 1968* (Harmondsworth: Penguin, 1968).

25 There is allusion to this in A. M. Givertz and M. Klee, 'Historicizing Thompson: An Interview with Bryan D. Palmer', *Left History*, 1 (Fall 1993), 112-13.

26 I am indebted to Wade Matthews, who has shared with me his researches into Thompson, including important material in the John Saville Papers, Hull University Archives, U DJS/109, especially Thompson's extraordinarily pointed attack on the direction of the *New Left Review*, a wide-ranging, detailed and lengthy document entitled 'Where Are We Now?' (n.d., but *c.*March–April 1963) and a detailed letter (Thompson to Saville, 12 May 1963?) outlining his reasons for resignation from the editorial board.

27 Thompson commented on the issue of private/public correspondence, writing of how the minefield of 'personal' letters available to those studying William Godwin and Mary Wollstonecraft was 'fortunate ... for biographers'. But as Thompson noted, 'We have scarcely begun to establish the facts before we begin to mix them up with our own moralising additives: scandalised, or apologetic, or admiring or condescending ... I doubt how far any of us would wish to be judged – or judged in a public sense – on evidence of this casual, and essentially unconsidered kind.' See E. P. Thompson, 'Mary Wollstonecraft', in Thompson, *Persons and Polemics*, pp. 2-4.

28 Note Eric Hobsbawm's jocular account of the organisationally dishevelled mode of work of one New Left figure of this period, Raphael Samuel, in *Interesting Times: A Twentieth-Century Life* (London: Allen Lane, 2002), pp. 210-14. One Thompson critique of the conduct and style of work of Hall and others from the *Universities and Left Review* is in Thompson's letter to Saville, 12 May 1963 (see n. 26 above).

29 The above paragraphs draw on Thompson, 'Where Are We Now', esp. pp. 2, 5–7, 15–16. Thompson took exception to K. Buchanan, 'The Third World – Its Emergence and Contours', *New Left Review*, 18 (January–February 1963), 5–23.

30 P. Anderson, 'Socialism and Pseudo-Empiricism', *New Left Review*, 35 (January–February 1965), p. 39, a harsh judgement tempered years later in P. Anderson, *Arguments Within English Marxism* (London: Verso, 1980), which nonetheless concluded on terms which yet again accented a gulf in Thompson between the inspirational and the programmatic (pp. 204, 206). Bernard Crick was, in contrast, describing the Thompson of this period as 'the best political essayist today in the tradition of Swift, Hazlitt, Cobbett, and Orwell': B. Crick, 'Thompson and Liberty!', *Manchester Guardian Weekly*, 11 May 1980.

31 R. Johnson, 'Edward Thompson, Eugene Genovese, and Socialist-Humanist History', *History Workshop*, 6 (Autumn 1978), 79–100; J. Clarke, C. Critcher and R. Johnson (eds), *Working Class Culture: Studies in History and Theory* (London: Hutchinson, 1979).

32 Succinct overviews appear in Dworkin, *Cultural Marxism in Postwar Britain*, pp. 232–45, which is not particularly sympathetic to Thompson, and R. Samuel (ed.), *People's History and Socialist Theory* (London: Routledge & Kegan Paul, 1981), pp. 375–408.

33 Hamilton, *The Crisis of Theory*, esp. pp. 268–78, containing many contentious claims.

34 M. Merrill, 'Interview with E. P. Thompson', in Abelove *et al.* (eds), *Visions of History* (New York: Pantheon, 1983), pp. 14–15, 21.

35 W. L. Webb, 'A Thoroughly English Dissident', *Guardian*, 30 August 1993.

36 Anderson, 'Socialism and Pseudo-Empiricism', pp. 35–6; T. Nairn, *The Break-Up of Britain: Crisis and Neo-Nationalism* (London: New Left Books, 1977), pp. 303–4.

37 E. J. Hobsbawm, 'Obituary: E. P. Thompson'; E. J. Hobsbawm, 'Edward Palmer Thompson', pp. 521–39.

38 E. P. Thompson, 'The Peculiarities of the English', in R. Miliband and J. Saville (eds), *The Socialist Register, 1965* (London: Merlin Press, 1965), pp. 330, 332; E. P. Thompson, 'Homage to Tom Maguire', in A. Briggs and J. Saville (eds), *Essays in Labour History: In Memory of G. D. H. Cole, 25 September 1889–14 January 1959* (London: Macmillan, 1960), p. 315.

39 E. P. Thompson, 'C. Wright Mills: The Responsible Craftsman', *Radical History Review*, 13 (July–August 1979), 61–73, esp. p. 63.

40 E. P. Thompson, 'Homage to Thomas McGrath', in R. Gibbons and T. Des Pres (eds), 'Thomas McGrath: Life and Poem', *TriQuarterly*, 70 (Fall 1987), 158–92, esp. pp. 133–4.

41 See Wade Matthews, 'E. P. Thompson in the Provinces', Ch. 3 of a forthcoming study in the Historical Materialism Series, *International of the*

Imagination: The New Left, National Identity, and the Break-Up of Britain (Leiden: Brill, 2013). There are useful comments in J. Ree, 'E. P. Thompson and the Drama of Authority', *History Workshop Journal*, 47 (Spring 1999), 211-21.

42 Thompson's brother Frank was executed by fascists as he marched with Bulgarian partisans in May 1944. His internationalism is commemorated in the edited collection of letters and poems extolling the anti-fascist spirit that was arising throughout war-torn Europe: T. J. and E. P. Thompson, *There Is a Spirit in Europe: A Memoir of Frank Thompson* (London: Victor Gollancz, 1947) and later in E. P. Thompson, *Beyond the Frontier: The Politics of a Failed Mission – Bulgaria, 1944* (Stanford, CA: Stanford University Press, 1977). But Frank had written to Edward (1941?): 'To Palmer. Looking forward to the time when we shall be back among our own people, doing the job that we were cut out to do.' (Inscription in Ilya Ehrenburgh, *The Fall of Paris* [London: Hutchinson, n.d.], front endpaper, in possession of the author.)

43 Thompson, 'Where Are We Now?', p. 20; Thompson, 'Peculiarities of the English'.

44 Thompson, 'Caudwell', pp. 78-142.

45 An entreé into this aspect of Thompson is the close analysis of Blake's poem *London* in Thompson, *Witness Against the Beast*, pp. 174-94.

46 Thompson, 'Agenda for Radical History', in Thompson, *Persons and Polemics*, pp. 360-6.

47 Thompson, 'Notes on Exterminism', p. 19. See also Thompson, 'Poverty of Theory', p. 197.

48 Merrill, 'Interview with E. P. Thompson', p. 15.

49 See, e.g., E. P. Thompson, 'History and Anthropology', in *Persons and Polemics*, pp. 201-27; Thompson, 'Agenda for Radical History'; Merrill, 'Interview with E. P. Thompson', pp. 15-22.

50 E. P. Thompson, 'Socialist Humanism: An Epistle to the Philistines', *New Reasoner*, 1 (Summer 1957), 105-43; E. P. Thompson, 'Agency and Choice: A Reply to Criticism', *New Reasoner*, 5 (Summer 1958), 89-106; E. P. Thompson, 'A Psessay in Ephology', *New Reasoner*, 10 (Autumn 1959), 1-8, a theoretical discussion that he developed in 'The Poverty of Theory'.

51 Thompson, 'Notes on Exterminism', p. 31.

52 Merrill, 'Interview with E. P. Thompson', pp. 18-19.

53 One of Thompson's last abbreviated statements on his shifting relationship to Marxism is 'Agenda for Radical History'.

54 See Thompson, *Writing by Candlelight*.

55 Much could be cited on this development, but of particular note are E. P. Thompson, 'Détente and Dissent', in K. Coates (ed.), *Détente and Socialist Democracy: A Discussion with Roy Medvedev* (New York: Monad Press, 1976), pp. 119-38; E. P. Thompson, *Double Exposure* (London: Merlin

Press, 1985); and the unpublished (for the safety of Indian dissidents) E. P. Thompson, 'Strictly Confidential: Six Weeks in India' (n.d., 1977?), Saville Papers, Hull University Archives.

56 Hobsbawm, 'Obituary: E. P. Thompson'; Hobsbawm, 'Edward Palmer Thompson'.

57 Thompson, *The Making of the English Working Class*, p. 9.

58 William Morris, *A Dream of John Ball*, pp. 19–20, quoted in E. P. Thompson, *William Morris: Romantic to Revolutionary* (New York: Pantheon, 1977), p. 722; Thompson, 'Agency and Choice', *New Reasoner*, 4 (Summer 1958), 106.

59 Thompson, *The Making of the English Working Class*, p. 9.

Afterword

Roger Fieldhouse and Richard Taylor

At the beginning of this book we said we would attempt to review the many and varied facets of Thompson's work as a unified whole. We hope that the analyses in the foregoing chapters have illustrated both Thompson's remarkable range of interests and achievements, and the coherence of his moral passion and intellectual purpose.

In his youth Thompson was drawn to Marxism, but for Thompson it was always a humanistic, voluntaristic and libertarian perspective: he was never attracted to deterministic, structuralist interpretations of Marxism. In his years in the Communist Party, Thompson accepted as necessary evils the dogma and party discipline because he saw the Party as the only political force and agency that might halt the march of fascism – and later, the imperialism of the USA and the Cold War from the late 1940s. It was this continuing belief in the ideals of equality, liberty and fairness which underpinned all his work throughout his life.

In his professional work the same ideals prevailed. He resisted the somewhat elitist model of university adult education that character-ised the University of Leeds's Extramural Department, and encour-aged his adult students to use and apply their experience in order to participate fully in their learning. At the same time, this philosophy greatly influenced the writing of *The Making of the English Working Class*, and enabled him to forge a new and distinctively radical way of looking at history. But his was not simply a vision of a fair society: rather it was one in which the poor, downtrodden common people would themselves *make* it fair. They were the agents of their own destiny, not beneficiaries of liberal benevolence, still less of predeter-mined, mechanistic 'forces of history'.

It was this emphasis on *human agency* that also characterised his political writing and activity, in the early New Left in the late 1950s and early 1960s; in his passionate polemics against Marxist structuralism; and in his peace-movement campaigning in the 1980s. Similarly, his writings on the bases of social class formation, struggle, identity and consciousness emphasise the relations between real people in specific historical circumstances. In all these varying political contexts and campaigns Thompson centred his arguments on clear moral precepts and developed a passionate, yet coherent, philosophy of 'socialist humanism'.

Thompson's work was also permeated by his deep interest in, and knowledge of, poetry and literature. His works on Morris and Blake, for example, and his poetry, were not 'add-ons' but were an integral part of his political and moral sensibility.

Thompson was thus a man of many parts. His influence and his example were profound. The English radical tradition which he did so much to delineate, and to which he contributed so greatly, remains an inspirational alternative to contemporary neoliberal negativity, and a challenge to politically disabling deterministic arguments and fatalistic political quietism. As Sheila Rowbotham has observed, Thompson 'with all his might ... struggled to keep open the common footpaths of radical inquiry'.[1] The need for a revitalised radicalism is as great now as it was in Thompson's time: and his work and his example have a contemporary resonance, as we have argued throughout this book.

Note

1 S. Rowbotham, 'E. P. Thompson: A Life of Radical Dissent', *New Statesman and Society* (3 September 1993), pp. 14–15.

Appendix:
Three examples of Thompson's writing style

1 Extracts from the Preface to
The Making of the English Working Class (1963)[1]

This book has a clumsy title, but it is one which meets its purpose. *Making*, because it is a study in an active process, which owes as much to agency as to conditioning. The working class did not rise like the sun at an appointed time. It was present at its own making. *Class*, rather than classes, for reasons which it is one purpose of this book to examine. There is, of course, a difference. 'Working classes' is a descriptive term, which evades as much as it defines. It ties loosely together a bundle of discrete phenomena. There were tailors here and weavers there, and together they make up the working classes.

By class I understand a historical phenomenon, unifying a number of disparate and seemingly unconnected events, both in the raw material of experience and in consciousness. I emphasize that it is a *historical* phenomenon. I do not see class as a 'structure', nor even as a 'category', but as something which in fact happens (and can be shown to have happened) in human relationships.

More than this, the notion of class entails the notion of historical relationship. Like any other relationship, it is a fluency which evades analysis if we attempt to stop it dead at any given moment and anatomize its structure. The finest-meshed sociological net cannot give us a pure specimen of class, any more than it can give us one of deference or of love. The relationship must always be embodied in real people and in a real context. Moreover, we cannot have two distinct classes, each with an independent being, and then bring them *into* relationship with each other. We cannot have love without lovers, nor deference without squires and labourers. And class happens when some men, as a result of common experiences (inherited or shared), feel and articulate the identity of their interests as between themselves, and as against other men whose interests are different from (and usually opposed to) theirs. The class experience is largely determined by the productive relations into which men are born – or enter involuntarily. Class-consciousness is the way in which these experiences are handled in cultural terms: embodied in traditions, value-systems, ideas, and institutional forms. If the experience appears as determined, class-consciousness does not. We can see a *logic* in the responses of similar occupational groups undergoing similar experiences, but we cannot predicate any *law*. Consciousness of class arises in the same way in different times and places, but never in just the same way.

There is today an ever-present temptation to suppose that class is a thing. This was not Marx's meaning, in his own historical writing, yet the error vitiates much latter-day 'Marxist' writing. 'It', the working class, is assumed to have a real existence, which can be defined almost mathematically – so many men who stand in a certain relation to the means of production. Once this is assumed it becomes possible to deduce the class-consciousness which 'it' ought to have (but seldom does have) if 'it' was properly aware of its own position and real interests. There is a cultural superstructure, through which this recognition dawns in inefficient ways. These cultural 'lags' and distortions are a nuisance, so that it is easy to pass from this to some theory of substitution: the party, sect, or theorist, who disclose class-consciousness, not as it is, but as it ought to be.

But a similar error is committed daily on the other side of the ideological divide. In one form, this is a plain negative. Since the crude notion of class attributed to Marx can be faulted without difficulty, it is assumed that any notion of class is a pejorative theoretical construct, imposed upon the evidence. It is denied that class has happened at all. In another form, and by a curious inversion, it is possible to pass from a dynamic to a static view of class. 'It' – the working class – exists, and can be defined with some accuracy as a component of the social structure. Class-consciousness, however, is a bad thing, invented by displaced intellectuals, since everything which disturbs the harmonious coexistence of groups performing different 'social roles' (and which thereby retards economic growth) is to be deplored as an 'unjustified disturbance-symptom'. The problem is to determine how best 'it' can be conditioned to accept its social role, and how its grievances may best be 'handled and channelled'.

If we remember that class is a relationship, and not a thing, we cannot think in this way. 'It' does not exist, either to have an ideal interest or consciousness, or to lie as a patient on the Adjustor's table. ...

The question, of course, is how the individual got to be in the 'social role', and how the particular social organization (with its property-rights and structure of authority) got to be there. And these are historical questions. If we stop history at a given point, then there are no classes but simply a multitude of individuals and a multitude of experiences. But if we watch these men over an adequate period of social change, we observe patterns in their relationships, their ideas, and their institutions. Class is defined by men as they live their own history, and, in the end, this is its only definition.

If I have shown insufficient understanding of the methodological preoccupations of certain sociologists, nevertheless I hope this book will be seen as a contribution to the understanding of class. For I am convinced that we cannot understand class unless we see it as a social and cultural formation, arising from processes which can only be studied as they work themselves out over a considerable historical period. In the years between 1780 and 1832 most English working people came to feel an identity of interests as between themselves, and as against their rulers and employers. This ruling class was itself much divided, and in fact only gained in cohesion over the same years because certain antagonisms were resolved (or faded into relative insignificance) in the face of an insurgent working class. Thus the working-class presence was, in 1832, the most significant factor in British political life. ...

I am seeking to rescue the poor stockinger, the Luddite cropper, the 'obsolete' hand-loom weaver, the 'utopian' artisan, and even the deluded follower of Joanna Southcott, from the enormous condescension of posterity. Their crafts and traditions may have been dying. Their hostility to the new industrialism may have been backward-looking. Their communitarian ideals may have been fantasies. Their insurrectionary conspiracies may have been foolhardy. But they lived through these times of acute social disturbance, and we did not. Their aspirations were valid in terms of their own experience; and, if they were casualties of history, they remain, condemned in their own lives, as casualties.

Our only criterion of judgement should not be whether or not a man's actions are justified in the light of subsequent evolution. After all, we are not at the end of social evolution ourselves. In some of the lost causes of the people of the Industrial Revolution we may discover insights into social evils which we have yet to cure. Moreover, the greater part of the world today is still undergoing problems of industrialization, and of the formation of democratic institutions, analogous to our own experience during the Industrial Revolution. Causes which were lost in England might, in Asia or Africa, yet be won.

2 Extract from 'The Peculiarities of the English, I' (1965)[2]

Early in 1962, when the affairs of *New Left Review* were in some confusion, the New Left Board invited an able contributor, Perry Anderson, to take over the editorship. We found (as we had hoped) in Comrade Anderson the decision and the intellectual coherence necessary to ensure the review's continuance. More than that, we discovered that we had appointed a veritable Dr. Beeching of the socialist intelligentsia. All the uneconomic branch-lines and socio-cultural sidings of the New Left which were, in any case, carrying less and less traffic, were abruptly closed down. The main lines of the review underwent an equally ruthless modernisation. Old Left steam-engines were swept off the tracks; wayside halts ("Commitment," "What Next for C.N.D.?", "Women in Love") were boarded up; and the lines were electrified for the speedy traffic from the marxistentialist Left Bank. In less than a year the founders of the review discovered, to their chagrin, that the Board lived on a branch-line which, after rigorous intellectual costing, had been found uneconomic. Finding ourselves redundant we submitted to dissolution.

Three years have elapsed since the new direction was taken, and it now seems possible to examine the general tendency of the "new" New Left. For simplicity this may be located in three major areas: analysis of the "Third World": definitions (mainly oblique) of Marxist theory: and the ambitious work of analysis of British history and social structure commenced in a series of articles by Anderson and Tom Nairn. The first area – the Third World – lies beyond the scope of this article. It is undoubtedly the area in which some of the most original and well-informed work of the two new editors has been carried out. I shall confine myself here to the other two.

These articles, taken together, represent a sustained attempt to develop a coherent historical account of British society. Undoubtedly the seminal article is Anderson's *Origins of the Present Crisis*. But, if Nairn's work is less inspired, nevertheless both writers clearly inhabit the same mental universe. Both feel themselves to be exiles from an 'English ideology' which 'in its drooling old age ... gives rise to a kind of twilight, where "empiricism" has become myopia and "liberalism" a sort of blinking uncertainty.' Nairn extends the indictment:

English separateness and provincialism; English backwardness and traditionalism; English religiosity and moralistic vapouring, paltry English 'empiricism', or instinctive distrust of reason ...

There is 'the nullity of native intellectual traditions,' the 'secular, insular stultification' of British culture, 'the impenetrable blanket of complacency' of British social life, 'the stony recesses of British trade union conservatism,' and 'the centuries of stale constipation and sedimentary ancestor-worship' of British society. The English ideology has

Embraced a dilettante literary culture descended from the aristocracy and the crudest of lumpen-bourgeois utilitarian philosophies, and held them together in a bizarre Jekyll-and-Hyde union of attraction and repulsion.

'The very urban world' of England 'is the image of this archaic, bastard conservatism – an urban world which has nothing to do with urban *civilization*, as this is conceived in other countries with an old and unified bourgeois culture.' These judgements are resumed in Anderson's *Origins*:

The two great chemical elements of this blanketing English fog are 'traditionalism' and 'empiricism': in it, visibility – of any social or historical reality – is always zero ... A comprehensive, coagulated conservatism is the result, covering the whole of of society with a thick pall of simultaneous philistinism (towards ideas) and mystagogy (towards institutions), for which England has justly won an international reputation.

And the essence of both authors' analysis of Labourism may be found in Anderson's phrase – 'in England, a supine bourgeoisie produced a subordinate proletariat.' No doubt in particular contexts certain of these judgements might be sustained. But what is evident, wherever such judgements protrude, is the loosening of emotional control and the displacement of analysis by commination. There is, about them, the air of an inverted Podsnappery. 'We Englishmen are Very Proud of our Constitution, Sir,' Mr. Podsnap explained with a sense of meritorious proprietorship:

'It was Bestowed Upon Us By Providence. No Other Country is so
Favoured as This Country ...'
'And *other* countries,' said the foreign gentleman. 'They do how?'
'They do, Sir,' returned Mr. Podsnap, gravely shaking his head; 'they
do – I am sorry to be obliged to say it – *as* they do.'

But now the roles are reversed. Mr Podsnap (who has swelled to
engross all British culture over the past 400 years) is being arraigned
in his turn.

'And *other* countries,' said Mr. Podsnap remorsefully, 'They do how?'
'They do,' returned Messrs. Anderson and Nairn severely: 'They do
– we are sorry to be obliged to say it – in Every Respect Better. Their
Bourgeois Revolutions have been Mature. Their class Struggles have
been Sanguinary and Unequivocal. Their Intelligentsia has been Autonomous and Integrated Vertically. Their Morphology has been Typologi-
cally Concrete. Their Proletariat has been Hegemonic.'

There is, indeed, throughout their analysis an undisclosed model of
Other Countries, whose typological symmetry offers a reproach to
British exceptionalism. Set against this model, the English working
class is 'one of the enigmas of modern history,' the historical experi-
ence of the English bourgeoisie has been 'fragmented and incomplete,'
English intellectuals have not constituted 'a true intelligentsia.'

Every historical experience is of course in a certain sense unique.
Too much protestation about this calls into question, not the experience (which remains there to be explained) but the relevance of the
model against which it is judged. (We may leave aside the point that
Other Countries, if we survey advanced industrial nations over the
past fifty years, have not always and in every respect done better
that the British, despite their vertical intelligentsia and their hegemonic proletariat.) The Anderson–Nairn model clearly approximates
most closely to the French experience, or to a particular interpretation of that experience; and in this they follow the major, pre-1917
Marxist tradition. When set beside this, English experience fails in
three important respects: (1) in the premature, unfulfilled character
of the seventeenth-century revolution. In the ensuing compromises of
1688 and 1832, the industrial bourgeoisie failed to attain to an undis-
puted hegemony, and to remake the ruling institutions of society
in its own image. Rather a 'deliberate, systematized symbiosis' took
place between the landed aristocracy and the industrial bourgeoisie,
in which, however, the aristocracy remained as senior partners;

(2) Because the seventeenth-century revolution was 'impure', and the struggle was conducted in religious terms, the bourgeoisie never developed any coherent world-view or self-knowledge, and made do with an 'ideology' of 'empiricism' which has apparently characterized English intellectual culture until the present day:

> ... the ideological legacy of the Revolution was almost nil ... Because of its 'primitive', pre-Enlightenment character, the ideology of the Revolution founded no significant tradition, and left no major after-effects ...

(3) A premature bourgeois revolution gave rise to a premature working-class movement, whose heroic struggles during the Industrial Revolution were nullified by the absence of any commensurate theoretical growth: 'its maximum ardour and insurgency coincided with the minimum availability of socialism as a structured ideology.' When this movement fell apart after Chartism (through 'exhaustion') there followed a 'profound caesura in English working-class history', and the 'most insurgent working class in Europe became the most numbed and docile.' 'Marxism came too late', whereas in Other Countries 'Marxism swept the working class.' Thereafter, the post-1880 Labour movement has nullified its entire existence by expressing only corporative (and not hegemonic) virtues, and by becoming subject (with Fabianism) to an ideology which mimics, with impoverished equipment, the banal empiricism of the bourgeoisie.

Our authors bring to this analysis the zest of explorers. They set out on their circumnavigation by discarding, with derision, the old speculative charts. Anderson notes 'the complete lack of any serious global history of British society', and 'nervelessness of our historiography', 'no attempt has ever been made at even the outline of a "totalizing" history of modern British society.' Nairn finds that there is not even a 'rudimentary historical debate regarding the total development of British society.' But our explorers are heroic and missionary. We hold our breath in suspense as the first Marxist landfall is made upon the unchartered Northland. Amidst the tundra and sphagnum moss of English empiricism they are willing to build true conventicles to convert the poor trade unionist aborigines from their corporative myths to the hegemonic light:

> Enmeshed in the dense web of archaic superstructure grafted on to British capitalism ... the working class could not distance itself aggressively from society and constitute its own autonomous movement towards social hegemony. The cutting instrument needed for this task

237

was lacking. That is, an intellectual stratum torn adrift from the social consensus with sufficient force and capable of functioning as catalyst to the new force striving for expression against consensus.

The problem is 'to create theory in an environment rendered impervious to rationality as such,' to create 'the intense rational consciousness and activity' which are 'the necessary pre-requisites of revolution in this society of totemized and emasculated consciousness.' Pulling their snowcaps over their ears, they disembark and struggle onwards to bring the intense rational consciousness of their cutting instruments to the 'traditional intelligentsia once buried entirely in the tribal rites of Oxford or literary London'. There is a sense of rising suspense as they – the First White Marxists – approach the astonished aborigines.

3 Extract from *Warwick University Ltd.* (1970)[3]

Coming to Warwick from seventeen years of extra-mural teaching, I have never ceased to be astounded when observing the preening and mating habits of fully grown specimens of the species *Academicus Superciliosus.*

The behaviour patterns of one of the true members of the species are unmistakable. He is inflated with self-esteem and perpetually self-congratulatory as to the high vocation of the university teacher; but he knows almost nothing about any other vocation, and he will lie down and let himself be walked over if anyone enters from the outer world who has money or power or even a tough line in realist talk. He is a consummate politician in university committees and can scull over every inch of his own duckpond; but – apart from one or two distant landmarks, such as the UGC or the SSRC, which stand like windmills on the horizon – he knows next to nothing of the world outside his own farmyard. (*Academicus Superciliosus* are never able to see beyond their next meeting, and are continually overcome with amazement and indignation when uninvited intruders – public opinion, the Press, local political movements – interpolate themselves upon the agenda.) *Superciliosus* is the most divisible and rulable creature in the country, being so intent upon crafty calculations of short-term advantages – this favour for his department, that chance of promotion – or upon rolling the log of a colleague who, next week at the next committee, has promised to roll a log for *him*, that he has never even tried to imagine the wood out of which all the timber rolls. He can scurry furiously and self-importantly around in his committees, like a white mouse running in a wheel, while his master is carrying him, cage and all, to be sold at the local pet-shop. These people annoy me a good deal more than the red moles. Academic freedom is for ever on their lips, and is forever disregarded in their actions. They are the last people to whom it can be safely entrusted, since the present moment is never the opportune moment to stand and fight. Show them the last ditch for the defence of liberty, and they will walk backwards into the sea, complaining that the ditch is very ill dug, that they cannot possibly be asked to defend it alongside such a ragged and seditious-looking set of fellows, and, in any case, it would surely be better to write out a tactful remonstrance and present it, on inscribed vellum, to the enemy?

The one unmistakable means of identification of *Academicus Superciliosus* is that he over-reacts to *any* sign of student self-activity. Even a polite deputation or a petition throws him into a tizzy. His life is lived in a kind of Awe of Propriety. Whatever the students or the younger staff do is wrong, since it is always embarrassing him in some delicate tactical manoeuvre on a higher committee. If he disagrees with student demands he will not go and argue it out with them, face to face, in a rational way, but he will thumb through old Senate minutes and utter a low disciplinary hiss. He encourages an atmosphere of institutional loyalty, which would have astonished the undergraduates of fourteenth-century Oxford or eighteenth-century Cambridge, in which it appears as somehow sensational and 'disloyal' for any member of staff to voice publicly at a student meeting criticisms of the university's policies – or, even, sharply expressed intellectual disagreements. Hence the students are defrauded of some of the essential intellectual dialectic from which their own orientations should be worked out. Above all, any serious episode of student 'unrest' – a sit-in, a rough music, or a heckling – is received with lowered voices, as if it were some aboriginal calamity.

We may leave him there, walking backwards into the sea to his final academically reputable 'glug glug glug' as the waves cover his liberal brow.

Notes

1 First published by Victor Gollancz, 1963; rev. edns Penguin, 1968, 1980.
2 Published in R. Miliband and J. Saville (eds), *The Socialist Register 1965* (London: Merlin, 1965), reprinted in E. P. Thompson, *The Poverty of Theory and Other Essays* (London: Merlin, 1978), pp. 35–8.
3 E. P. Thompson (ed.), *Warwick University Ltd* (Harmondsworth: Penguin, 1970), pp. 153–4.

Select bibliography

Primary sources

Note: Thompson's private papers have not been available in the writing of this book because they are deposited in the Bodleian Library, Oxford as a closed collection.

Bertrand Russell Peace Foundation (BRPF), Nottingham: END Archive (mainly Ken Coates's papers).
Bradford University, Special Collections: END Papers (Ted Edwards).
Hull University Archive, John Saville Papers.
Leeds University Archive (LUA). The relevant Leeds Extramural Department records consist of three related collections: Departmental Records (DEP/076) Adult Education; Adult Education and Extramural Studies, Papers of S. G. Raybould; and Adult Education Supplementary Papers. [Note on Class Reports in the Departmental Records and Supplementary Papers: tutors were required to write fairly detailed reports on their classes at the end of each teaching year. The original reports for Thompson's first seven years (1948/9 – 1954/5) survive in the Departmental Records, Box 47, but the later ones appear to be lost. A virtually complete set of photocopied reports is in the Supplementary Papers.]
University of Leeds Library, Special Collections: Miliband papers.
University of Warwick, Modern Records Centre: James Hinton Papers (CND and END).

Correspondence and interviews

Caldwell, Tom, letters, 10 August 2010, 4 March 2012; interview, 12 September 2010.
Hodgkin, Thomas, interview, 16–17 November 1979.
Jennings, Bernard, letter, 10 August 2010.
Kaldor, Mary, interview, 24 May 2012.

Select bibliography

E. P. Thompson's published work

This is a select list of Thompson's publications quoted in or consulted for this book. More comprehensive lists can be found in H. J. Kaye and K. McClelland (eds), *E. P. Thompson: Critical Perspectives*, Cambridge: Polity Press, 1990, and J. Rule and R. Malcolmson (eds), *Protest and Survival*, London: Merlin Press, 1993.

1947 (with T. J. Thompson), *There is a Spirit in Europe: A Memoir of Frank Thompson*, London: Victor Gollancz.

1948, *The Railway: An Adventure in Construction*, London: The British-Yugoslav Association.

1950, 'Against "University" Standards', *University of Leeds Department of Extramural Studies Adult Education Papers*, 1:4 (July).

1951, 'The Murder of William Morris', *Arena*, April/May.

1951, 'William Morris and the Moral Issues To-Day', *The American Threat to British Culture*, *Arena* special issue.

1955, *William Morris: Romantic to Revolutionary*, London: Lawrence & Wishart.

1956, 'Through the Smoke of Budapest', *The Reasoner*, 3.

1957, 'Socialism and the intellectuals', *Universities and Left Review*, 1.

1957, 'Socialist Humanism: An Epistle to the Philistines', *The New Reasoner*, 1.

1958, 'Agency and Choice', *The New Reasoner*, 5.

1958, 'NATO, Neutralism and Survival', *Universities and Left Review*, 4.

1959, 'Commitment in Politics', *Universities and Left Review*, 6.

1959, 'The New Left', *The New Reasoner*, 9.

1959, 'A Psessay in Ephology', *The New Reasoner*, 10.

1960, 'Homage to Tom Maguire', in A. Briggs and J. Saville (eds), *Essays in Labour History: In memory of G. D. H. Cole, 25 September 1889–14 January 1959*, London: Macmillan.

1960 (ed.), *Out of Apathy*, London: Stevens & Sons/New Left Books.

1960, 'The Point of Production', *New Left Review*, 1:1.

1960, 'Revolution', *New Left Review*, 1:3.

1960, 'Revolution Again! Or Shut your Ears and Run', *New Left Review*, 1:6.

1961, 'The Long Revolution' (Part 1), *New Left Review* 1:9.

1961, 'The Long Revolution' (Part 2), *New Left Review* 1:10.

1961, 'The Segregation of Dissent', *The New University*, 6.

1962, 'Tom Mann and His Times, 1890–92', *Our History*, 26–7.

1963, *The Making of the English Working Class*, London and New York: Victor Gollancz and Vintage.

1965, 'The Peculiarities of the English', in R. Miliband and J. Saville (eds), *The Socialist Register*, 1965, London: Merlin Press.

1967, 'Time, Work Discipline and Industrial Capitalism', *Past and Present*, 38.

1968, *Education and Experience*, Leeds: Leeds University Press.

1968, 'Introduction to the Fourth Edition', in Frank Peel, *The Risings of the Luddites, Chartists and Plug-Drawers*, London: Frank Cass.

1968, *The Making of the English Working Class*, rev. edn, Harmondsworth: Pelican.

1968 (with R. Williams and S. Hall), *The May Day Manifesto*, rev. edn, ed. R. Williams, Harmondsworth: Pelican.

1969, 'Disenchantment or Default: A Lay Sermon', in C. C. O'Brien and W. D. Vanech (eds), *Power and Consciousness: The Schweitzer Lectures*, New York: New York University Press.

1970 (ed.), *Warwick University Ltd*, Harmondsworth: Penguin.

1974, 'Patrician Society, Plebeian Culture', *Journal of Social History*, 7:4.

1975 (ed. with D. Hay *et al.*), *Albion's Fatal Tree: Crime and Society in Eighteenth-Century England*, London and New York: Allen Lane and Pantheon.

1975, *Whigs and Hunters: The Origins of the Black Acts*, London and New York: Allen Lane and Pantheon.

1976, 'Détente and Dissent', in K. Coates (ed.), *Détente and Socialist Democracy: A Discussion with Roy Medvedev*, New York: Monad Press.

1976 (ed. with J. Goody and J. Thirsk), *Family and Inheritance: Rural society in Western Europe, 1200–1800*, Cambridge: Cambridge University Press.

1976, 'On History, Sociology and Historical Relevance', *British Journal of Sociology*, 27

1976, *William Morris: Romantic to Revolutionary*, rev. edn, London: Merlin Press.

1977, 'Caudwell', in J. Saville and R. Miliband (eds), *The Socialist Register*, London: Merlin Press, reprinted in E. P. Thompson, *Persons and Polemics: Historical Essays*, London: Merlin Press, 1994.

1977, 'Happy Families', *New Society* (8 September), reprinted in Thompson, *Persons and Polemics*.

1977, *Whigs and Hunters: The Origins of the Black Acts*, rev. edn with new postscript, Harmondsworth: Penguin.

1978, 'Eighteenth-Century English Society: Class Struggle without Class', *Social History*, 3:2.

1978, *The Poverty of Theory and Other Essays*, London: Merlin Press.

1978, 'Sold Like a Sheep for a Pound', *New Society* (14 December), reprinted in Thompson, *Persons and Polemics*.

1979, 'The Acceptable Faces of Marxism', *Observer* (4 February), republished as 'The Great Fear of Marxism', in E. P. Thompson, *Writing by Candlelight*, London: Merlin Press.

1979, 'C. Wright Mills: The Responsible Craftsman', *Radical History Review*, 13.

1980, *The Making of the English Working Class*, 3rd edn, Harmondsworth: Penguin.

1980, 'Notes on Exterminism, the Last Stage of Civilisation', *New Left Review*, 121.

1980, *Protest and Survive*, Spokesman Pamphlet 71, CND and BRPF.

1980, *Writing by Candlelight*, London: Merlin Press.

1981, 'The Politics of Theory', in R. Samuel (ed.), *People's History and Socialist Theory*, London: Routledge & Kegan Paul.

Select bibliography

1982, *Beyond The Cold War*, London and New York: END and Pantheon.
1982, *Exterminism and Cold War*, London: Verso and New Left Books.
1982, *Zero Option*, London: Merlin Press.
1982–83, 'Healing the Wound', *END Journal*, 1.
1985, *Double Exposure*, London: Merlin Press.
1985, *The Heavy Dancers*, London: Merlin Press.
1985 (ed.), *Star Wars*, Harmondsworth: Penguin.
1985, 'Table Talk About Class' ,*The Listener*, 6 June.
1987, 'Homage to Thomas McGrath', in R. Gibbons and T. D. Pres (eds), 'Thomas McGrath: Life and Poem', *TriQuarterly*, 70.
1987 (ed. with D. Smith), *Prospects for a Habitable Planet*, Harmondsworth: Penguin.
1988, *The Sykaos Papers*, London: Bloomsbury.
1988, 'Wordsworth's Crisis', *London Review of Books*, 8 December.
1989, 'Protest and Revise', *END Journal*, 37.
1991, *Customs in Common*, London and New York: Merlin Press and New Press.
1993, *Witness Against the Beast: William Blake and the Moral Law*, Cambridge: Cambridge University Press.
1994, 'Edward Thompson, 1924–1993: Scholar and Activist', edited transcript of BBC Radio Three interview, 20 May 1993, *Socialist History*, 6.
1994, *Persons and Polemics*, London: Merlin Press.
1997, *Beyond the Frontier: The Politics of a Failed Mission*, London and Stanford, CA: Merlin Press and Stanford University Press.
1999, *Collected Poems*, Newcastle-upon-Tyne: Bloodaxe.

Other works

Abelove, H. *et al.* (eds), 1983, *Visions of History*, New York: Pantheon; Manchester: Manchester University Press, 1984.
Althusser, L., 1969, *For Marx*, Harmondsworth: Penguin.
Anderson. P., 1964, 'Origins of the Present Crisis', *New Left Review*, 23, reprinted in P. Anderson and R. Blackburn (eds), *Towards Socialism*, London: Fontana, 1965.
—, 1966, 'Socialism and Pseudo-Empiricism', *New Left Review*, 1:35, January–February.
—, 1980, *Arguments Within English Marxism*, London: New Left Books and Verso.
—, 1992, *English Questions*, London: Verso.
—, 1993, 'Diary', *London Review of Books*, 21 October, reprinted in P. Anderson, *Spectrum*, London: Verso, 2005.
—, 2005, *Spectrum*, London: Verso.
Archard, D., 1984, *Consciousness and the Unconscious*, London: Hutchinson.
Bahro, R., 1978, *Socialism and Survival*, London: Heretic.
Bax, E. B., 1967 [1918], *Reminiscences and Reflexions of a Mid and Late Victorian*, New York: Augustus M. Kelley.

Select bibliography

Beckett, F., 1995, *Enemy Within: the Rise and Fall of the British Communist Party*, London: John Murray.

Bess, M., 1993, *Realism, Utopia and the Mushroom Cloud: Four Activist Intellectuals and Their Strategies for Peace, 1945–1989*, Chicago: University of Chicago Press.

Bevir, M., 1993, 'Ernest Belfort Bax: Marxist, Idealist, and Positivist', *Journal of the History of Ideas*, 54.

Bromley, S., and J. Rosenberg, 1988, 'After Exterminism', *New Left Review*, 168.

Calhoun, C., 1982, *The Question of Class Struggle: Social Foundations of Popular Radicalism during the Industrial Revolution*, Chicago: University of Chicago Press.

Centre for Contemporary Cultural Studies, 1982, 'E. P. Thompson and the Discipline of Historical Context', in *Making Histories: Studies in History-Writing and Politics*, London: Hutchinson.

Chakrabarty, D., 1989, *Rethinking Working Class History: Bengal, 1890–1940*, Princeton, NJ: Princeton University Press.

Chun, L., 1993, *The British New Left*, Edinburgh: Edinburgh University Press.

Clark, A., 1995, *The Struggle for the Breeches: Gender and the Making of the British Working Class*, Berkeley: University of California Press.

Clarke, J., C. Critcher and R. Johnson (eds), 1979, *Working Class Culture: Studies in History and Theory*, London: Hutchinson.

Coates, K. (ed.), 1975, *Détente and Socialist Democracy*, Nottingham: Spokesman Books.

—, 1984, *The Most Dangerous Decade*, Nottingham: Spokesman Books.

—, 1987, *Listening for Peace*, Nottingham: Spokesman Books.

—, 2012, 'A Political Life', interview with George Lambie, *The Spokesman: Resist Much, Obey Little*, 116, Nottingham: BRPF.

Cohen, G. A., 1980, *Karl Marx's Theory of History: A Defence*, Princeton, NJ: Princeton University Press.

Colley, L., 1992, *Britons: Forging the Nation*, New Haven, CT: Yale University Press.

Conradi, P. J., 2012, *A Very English Hero: The Making of Frank Thompson*, London: Bloomsbury.

Cornforth, M. (ed.), 1978, *Rebels and Their Causes: Essays in Honour of A. L. Morton*, London: Lawrence & Wishart.

Cowan, B., 2005, *The Social Life of Coffee: The Emergence of the British Coffeehouse*, New Haven, CT: Yale University Press.

Crafts, N. F. R., 1985, *British Economic Growth during the Industrial Revolution*, Oxford: Oxford University Press.

Crick, B., 1980, 'Thompson and Liberty!', *Manchester Guardian Weekly*, 11 May.

Croft, A., 1995, 'Walthamstow, Little Gidding and Middlesbrough: Edward Thompson, Adult Education and Literature', *Socialist History*, 8.

—, 1996, 'Walthamstow, Little Gidding and Middlesbrough: Edward Thompson the Literature Tutor', in R. Taylor (ed.), *Beyond the Walls*, Leeds: University of Leeds.

Crosland, C. A. R., 1956, *The Future of Socialism*, London: Cape.

Davis, M., 2008, 'The Origins of the British New Left', in M. Klinke and J. Scherlock (eds), *1968 in Europe*, Basingstoke: Palgrave Macmillan.

—, 2011, 'Arguing Affluence: New Left Contributions to the Socialist Debate 1957–63', *Twentieth Century British History*, first published online 2 September.

— (ed.), 2011, *Class and Gender in British Labour History*, London: Merlin Press.

—, 2011,'The *New Reasoner* and the early New Left', in D. Howell, D. Kirby and K. Morgan (eds), *John Saville: Commitment and History. Themes from the Life and Work of a Socialist Historian*, London: Lawrence & Wishart in association with the Socialist History Society.

Dawley, A., 1978–79, 'E.P. Thompson and the Peculiarities of the Americans', *Radical History Review*, 19.

Drasdo, H., 1963, 'Alex Comfort's Art and Scope', *Anarchy*, 33.

Duff, P., 1971, *Left, Left, Left*, London: Allison & Busby.

Dworkin, D., 1997, *Cultural Marxism: History, the New Left and the Origins of Cultural Studies*, Durham, NC and London: Duke University Press.

Earle, P., 1989, *The Making of the English Middle Class: Business, Society and Family Life in London, 1660–1730*, Berkeley: University of California Press.

Ecclestone, A., 1953, 'Why I Support the Peace Movement', *Yorkshire Voice of Peace*, Summer.

Fanon, F., 1961, *Les Damnés de la Terre*, Paris: François Maspero. Translated into English as *The Wretched of the Earth*, London: McGibbon & Kee, 1965.

Fieldhouse, R., 1985, *Adult Education and the Cold War*, Leeds: University of Leeds.

—, 1985, 'The Problem of Objectivity, Social Purpose and Ideological Commitment in English University Adult Education', in R. Taylor, K. Rockhill and R. Fieldhouse, *University Adult Education in England and the USA*, London: Croom Helm.

—, 1996, *A History of Modern British Adult Education*, Leicester: National Institute of Adult Continuing Education (NIACE).

—, 1996, 'Sidney Raybould, Fred Sedgwick and the early Department', in R. Taylor (ed.), *Beyond the Walls*, Leeds: University of Leeds.

—, 1998, 'A Collective Political Biography of Four Influential British Adult Educators', in M. Friedenthal-Hasse (ed.), *Personality and Biography in the History of Adult Education*, vol. 2, Frankfurt: Peter Lang.

Fischer, M., 1983, 'The Literary Importance of E. P. Thompson's Marxism', *English Literary History*, 50:4 Winter.

Fromm, E. (ed.), 1965, *Socialist Humanism*, London: Allen Lane.

Givertz, A. M., 1993, 'Interview with Bryan Palmer', *Left History*, 1:2.

Goode, J., 1990, 'E. P. Thompson and "the Significance of Literature"', in H. J. Kaye and K. McClelland (eds), *E .P. Thompson: Critical Perspectives*, Cambridge: Polity Press.

Goodway, D., 1996, 'E. P. Thompson and the Making of *The Making of the*

English Working Class', in R. Taylor (ed.), *Beyond the Walls*, Leeds: University of Leeds.

—, 2002, 'Dorothy Greenald', *Guardian*, 15 April.

—, 2006, *Anarchist Seeds Beneath the Snow: Left-Libertarian Thought and British Writers from William Morris to Colin Ward*, Liverpool: Liverpool University Press.

Gramsci, A., 1971, *Selections from the Prison Notebooks*, ed. and trans. Q. Hoare and G. Nowell-Smith, New York: International.

Hall, C., 1990, 'The Tale of Samuel and Jemima: Gender and Working-class Culture in Nineteenth-Century England', in H. J. Kaye and K. McClelland (eds), *E. P. Thompson: Critical Perspectives*, Cambridge: Polity Press.

Hall, S., 1958, 'A Sense of Classnessness', *Universities and Left Review*, 5 Autumn.

—, 1989, 'The "First" New Left: Life and Times', in R. Archer (ed.), *Out of Apathy: Voices of the New Left Thirty Years On*, London and New York: Verso.

Hamilton, S., 2011, *The Crisis of Theory: E. P. Thompson, the New Left and Post-war British Politics*, Manchester: Manchester University Press.

Hammond, J. L. and Hammond, B., 1911, *The Village Labourer*, London: Longman.

Harrison, J. F. C., 1961, *Learning and Living 1790–1960*, London: Routledge & Kegan Paul.

—, 1969, *The Quest for a New Moral World: Robert Owen and the Owenites in Britain and America*, New York: Scribners.

Hayles, N. K., 1999, *How We Became Posthuman: Virtual Bodies in Cybernetics, Literature and Informatics*, Chicago: Chicago University Press.

Hill, C., 1993, 'From the Awkward School', *Guardian*, 30 August.

Hinton, J., 1989, *Protests and Visions: Peace Politics in Twentieth Century Britain*, London: Hutchinson.

Hobsbawm, E. J., 1993, Obituary of E. P. Thompson, *Independent*, 30 August, reprinted in *Radical History Review*, 58 Winter 1994.

—, 1996, 'Edward Palmer Thompson, 1924–1993', *Proceedings of the British Academy*, 90.

— and G. Rudé, 1969, *Captain Swing*, London: Lawrence & Wishart.

Hoggart, R., 1957, *The Uses of Literacy: Aspects of Working Class Life*, London: Chatto & Windus.

Holden, D. R., 'The First New Left in Britain', Ph.D. thesis, University of Wisconsin-Madison, 1976.

Holston, J., 2002, *Ehud's Dagger: Class Struggle in the English Revolution*, London: Verso.

Hughes, G., 1975, *Millstone Grit*, London: Victor Gollancz.

—, 1993, 'Withering Heights', *Observer Magazine*, 30 May.

Hunt, M. R., 1996, *The Middling Sort: Commerce, Gender and Family in England: 1680–1780*, Berkeley: University of California Press.

Johnson, R., 1978, 'Edward Thompson, Eugene Genovese, and Socialist-Humanist History', *History Workshop*, 6.

Kaldor, M., 2003, *Global Civil Society: An Answer to War*, Cambridge: Polity Press.

Kaye, H. J., 1984, *The British Marxist Historians*, Cambridge: Polity Press.

—, 1995, 'Towards a Biography of E. P. Thompson', *Socialist History*, 8.

— and McClelland, K. (eds), 1990, *E. P. Thompson: Critical Perspectives*, Cambridge: Polity Press.

Kenny, M., 1995, *The First New Left: British Intellectuals after Stalin*, London: Lawrence & Wishart.

Kinna, R., 2000, *William Morris: The Art of Socialism*, Cardiff: University of Wales Press.

Koditschek, T., 1996, 'Marxism and the Historiography of Modern Britain: From Engels to Thompson to Deconstruction and Beyond', in T. Brotherstone and G. Pilling (eds), *History, Economic History and the Future of Marxism*, London: Porcupine.

Konrad, G., 1984, *Anti-Politics: An Essay*, New York and London: Harcourt Brace Jovanovich.

Kreidte, P., H. Medick and J. Schlumbohm, 1981, *Industrialization Before Industrialization: Rural Industry in the Genesis of Capitalism*, Cambridge: Cambridge University Press.

Lago, M., 2001, *India's Prisoner: A Biography of Edward John Thompson 1886–1946*, Columbia: University of Missouri Press.

Langbein, J., 1983, 'Albion's Fatal Flaws', *Past and Present*, 98:1.

Lee, C. H., 1986, *The British Economy since 1700; A Macroeconomic Perspective*, Cambridge: Cambridge University Press.

Linebaugh, P., 1993, 'From the Upper West Side to Wick Episcopi', *New Left Review*, 201.

— and Rediker, M., 2000, *The Many-Headed Hydra: Sailors, Slaves, Commoners and the Hidden History of the Revolutionary Atlantic*, Boston: Beacon.

MacIntyre, A., 1958, 'Notes from the Moral Wilderness, 1, *The New Reasoner*, 7 Winter.

Mandler, P., 1993, 'Written by Candlelight', *Dissent*, Spring.

Marcuse, H., 1964, *One Dimensional Man*, London: Routledge & Kegan Paul.

Matthews, W., 'Intellectuals and the Labour Movement: the Letters of E. P. Thompson 1956–1960', unpublished paper, n.d.

—, 2002, 'The Poverty of Strategy: E. P. Thompson, Perry Anderson, and the Transition to Socialism', *Labour/ Travail*, 50.

—, 2013, *The New Left, National Identity and the Break-up of Britain*, Leiden and Boston: Brill.

McKendrick, N., J. Brewer and J. H. Plumb, 1982, *The Birth of A Consumer Society: The Commercialization of Eighteenth Century England*, Bloomington: Indiana University Press.

Mendels, F., 1972, 'Proto-Industrialization: The First Phase of the Industrialization Process', *Journal of Economic History*, 32:1.

Merrill, M., 1984, 'An Interview with E. P. Thompson', in MARHO, *Visions of History*, Manchester: Manchester University Press (see also Abelove, H. *et al.*, *Visions of History.*

Nairn, T., 1977, *The Break-Up of Britain: Crisis and Neo-Nationalism*, London: New Left Books.

Newman, M., 2002, *Ralph Miliband and the Politics of the New Left*, London: Merlin Press.

Orwell, G., 1949 (Penguin edns since 1954), *Nineteen Eighty-Four*, London: Secker & Warburg.

Palmer, B., 1981, *The Making of E. P. Thompson: Marxism, Humanism and History*, Toronto: New Hogtown Press.

—, 1994, *E. P. Thompson: Objections and Oppositions*, London: Verso.

Parkin, F., 1968, *Middle Class Radicalism: The Social Bases of the British Campaign for Nuclear Disarmament*, Manchester: Manchester University Press.

Paulin, P., 1998, *The Day-Star of Liberty: William Hazlitt's Radical Style*, London: Faber & Faber.

Peers, R., 1958, *Adult Education: A Comparative Study*, London: Routledge & Kegan Paul.

Priestley, J. B., 1957, 'Britain and the Nuclear Bombs', *New Statesman*, 2 November.

Rattenbury, A., 1997, 'Convenient Death of a Hero', *London Review of Books*, 8 May.

Raybould, S. G., 1950, 'Research in Adult Education', *Adult Education*, 23.

—, 1951, *The English Universities and Adult Education*, London: Workers' Educational Association (WEA).

—, 1952, 'Leeds University Department of Adult Education and Extra-Mural Studies', *Tutors' Bulletin of Adult Education*, 85, January.

Ree, J., 1999, 'E. P. Thompson and the Drama of Authority', *History Workshop Journal*, 47 Spring.

Rose, J., 2011, 'What More Could We Want of Ourselves?', *London Review of Books*, 16 June.

Rose, S., 1992, *Limited Livelihoods: Class and Gender in Nineteenth-Century England*, Berkeley: University of California Press.

Rowbotham, S., 1993, 'E. P. Thompson: A Life of Radical Dissent', *New Statesman and Society*, 3 September.

— 1993, 'The Personal and the Political', *New Left Review*, 200 July/August.

Rule, J. and R. Malcolmson (eds), 1993, *Protest and Survival: Essays for E. P. Thompson*, London: Merlin Press.

Rustin, M., 1989, 'The New Left as a Social Movement', in R. Archer (ed.), *Out of Apathy: Voices of the New Left Thirty Years On*, London and New York: Verso.

Samuel, R. (ed.), 1981, *People's History and Socialist Theory*, London: Routledge & Kegan Paul.

—, 2002, *Interesting Times: A Twentieth-Century Life*, London: Allen Lane.

Sartre, J-P., 1963 [1960], *Search for a Method* (trans. H. E. Barnes), London and New York: Methuen and Vintage Books.

—, 1974, *Between Marxism and Existentialism* (trans. J. Mathews), London: New Left Books.

—, 1981 [1971], *The Family Idiot: Gustave Flaubert 1821–1857* (trans. C. Cosman), Chicago: University of Chicago Press.

Saville, J., 1957–8, 'The Welfare State', *The New Reasoner*, 3 Winter.

—, 1976, 'The Twentieth Congress and the British Communist Party', in R. Miliband and J. Saville (eds), *The Socialist Register*, 1976, London: Merlin Press.

—, 1994, 'Edward Thompson, the Communist Party and 1956', in R. Miliband and L. Panitch (eds), *The Socialist Register*, 30, London: Merlin Press.

—, 2003, *Memoirs from the Left,* London: Merlin Press.

Schwartz, B., 1982, '"The People" in History: The Communist Party Historians' Group, 1946–56', in Centre for Contemporary Cultural Studies, *Making Histories: Studies in History-Writing and Politics*, London: Hutchinson.

Scott, J. C., 1976, *The Moral Economy of the Peasant: Rebellion and Subsistence in Southeast Asia*, New Haven, CT: Yale University Press.

Scott, J. W., 1988, *Gender and the Politics of History*, New York: Columbia University Press.

Searby, P., 1993, 'Edward Thompson as a Teacher', in J. Rule and R. Malcolmson (eds), *Protest and Survival*, London: Merlin Press.

Sedgwick, P., 1976, 'The Two New Lefts', in D. Widgery (ed.), *The New Left in Britain 1956–1968*, Harmondsworth: Penguin.

Shaw, R., 1996, 'Recalling Raybould's Department', in R. Taylor (ed.), *Beyond the Walls*, Leeds: University of Leeds.

Smail, J., 1994, *The Origins of Middle-Class Culture: Halifax, Yorkshire, 1660–1780*, Ithaca, NY: Cornell University Press.

Soper, K., 1990, 'Socialist Humanism', in H. J. Kaye and K. McClelland (eds), *E. P. Thompson: Critical Perspectives*, Cambridge: Polity Press.

—, 2000, 'Liberalism, Feminism, Enlightenment', in M. Evans (ed.), *The Edinburgh Companion to Contemporary Liberalism*, Edinburgh: Edinburgh University Press.

—, Ryle, M. and Thomas, L. (eds), 2009, *The Politics and Pleasures of Consuming Differently*, London: Palgrave.

Steele, T., 1997, *The Emergence of Cultural Studies 1945–1965: Cultural Politics, Adult Education and the English Question*, London: Lawrence & Wishart, Ch. 7.

Strachey, J., 1956, *Contemporary Capitalism*, London: Victor Gollancz.

Tairov, T., 1988, Interview, *END Journal*, 36 Autumn.

Taylor, B., 1983, *Eve and the New Jerusalem, Socialism and Feminism in the Nineteenth Century*, New York: Pantheon.

Taylor, C., 1957, 'Marxism and Humanism', *The New Reasoner*, 2 Spring.

Taylor, R., 1983, 'The British Nuclear Disarmament Movement of 1958 to 1965 and its Legacy to the Left', Ph.D. thesis, University of Leeds.

— 1988, *Against the Bomb: The British Peace Movement, 1958–1965*, Oxford: Clarendon Press.

— (ed.), 1996, *Beyond the Walls*, Leeds: University of Leeds.
—, K. Rockhill and R. Fieldhouse, 1985, *University Adult Education in England and the USA*, London: Croom Helm.
—. and T. Steele, 2011, *British Labour and Higher Education 1945-2000*. London: Continuum.
Thompson, D., 1958, 'The Welfare State', *The New Reasoner*, 4 Spring.
—, 1971, *The Early Chartists*, London: Macmillan.
—, 1984, *The Chartists: Popular Politics in the Industrial Revolution*, New York: Pantheon.
—, 1993, *Outsiders: Class, Gender, Nation*, London: Verso.
—, 1997, *The Romantics: England in a Revolutionary Age*, Suffolk: Merlin Press.
— (ed.), 2001, *The Essential E. P. Thompson*, New York: New Press.
— 2007, *Pessimism of the Intellect? A History of New Left Review*, London: Merlin Press.
Torr, D., 1956, *Tom Mann and His Times: Volume One (1856-1890)*, London: Lawrence & Wishart.
Weatherill, L., 1996, *Consumer Behaviour and Material Culture in Britain: 1660-1760*, 2nd edn, London: Routledge.
Webb, W. L, 1993, 'A Thoroughly English Dissident', *Guardian*, 30 August.
Widgery, D. (ed.), 1976, *The Left in Britain 1956-1968*, Harmondsworth: Penguin.
Willett, J. (trans.), 1978, *Brecht on Theatre*, London: Eyre Methuen.
Williams, G., 1960, 'The Concept of "Egemonia" in the Thought of Antonio Gramsci', *Journal of the History of Ideas*, 21.
Williams, R., 1950, 'The British New Left', *Partisan Review*, 27 Spring.
—, 1961, *Culture and Society, 1780-1950*, Harmondsworth: Penguin.
— (ed.), 1968, *The May Day Manifesto*, rev. edn Harmondsworth: Penguin.
—, 1975, 'You're a Marxist, Aren't You?', in B. Parekh (ed.), *The Concept of Socialism*, London: Croom Helm.
—, 1976, *Keywords: A Vocabulary of Culture and Society*, Glasgow: Collins Fontana.
—, 1979, *Politics and Letters*, London: New Left Books.
Wolfe, C., 2009, *What is Posthumanism?*, Minneapolis: University of Minnesota Press.
Wood, E. M., 1995, *Democracy Against Capitalism: Renewing Historical Materialism*, Cambridge: Cambridge University Press.
Wood, N., 1959, *Communism and British Intellectuals*, London: Victor Gollancz.
Young, N., 1977, *An Infantile Disorder? The Crisis and Decline of the New Left*, London: Routledge & Kegan Paul.

Index

Books and articles written by Thompson and referred to in the text appear in the index in italics in alphabetical order of titles. Books and other texts by other authors are only listed (under the author's name) if central to the subject.

Index

Index

Index

Index

Lightning Source UK Ltd.
Milton Keynes UK
UKOW05f0249030615

252797UK00008B/103/P